Mercedes Lynch Maloney, mother of five, is a continuing education instructor at Mount Mary College in Wisconsin.

Anne Maloney, her daughter, is a lecturer at Marquette University in Wisconsin.

THE HAND THAT ROCKS THE CRADLE

MOTHERS, SONS & LEADERSHIP

Mercedes Lynch Maloney
and Anne Maloney

Prentice-Hall, Inc.,
Englewood Cliffs, New Jersey 07632

Library of Congress Cataloging-in-Publication Data

Maloney, Mercedes Lynch.
 The hand that rocks the cradle

 Bibliography: p.
 Includes index.
 1. Mothers and sons—Case studies. 2. Leadership—
Case studies. 3. Motherhood-Psychological aspects—
Case studies. I. Maloney, Anne. II. Title.
HQ759.M33 1985   306.8'743   85-16895
ISBN 0-13-372418-2

This book is dedicated with love and gratitude to the memory of Mayme Durkin Lynch.

10 9 8 7 6 5 4 3 2 1

Printed in the United States of America

Editorial/production supervision
by Eric Newman and Rhonda K. Mirabella
Book design by Maria Carella
Jacket design copyright © 1985 by Robert Anthony, Inc.
Manufacturing buyer: Carol Bystrom

This book is available at a special discount when ordered in
bulk quantities. Contact Prentice-Hall, Inc., General
Publishing Division, Special Sales, Englewood Cliffs, N.J. 07632.

CONTENTS

PREFACE

Where were the women? All those men and women who love to sit down at night with the tales of long-past adventures, wars, and political campaigns, must ask themselves that question. We all read of kings and congresses, wars and inventions, explorations and retreats, and we wonder. Where were the women?

In the past one hundred years, more people than ever before have tried to find the answer to that question. They have pointed to women who have wielded power in a male-dominated power structure: Catherine the Great, Queen Victoria, Elizabeth I, Marie Curie, and Eleanor Roosevelt, to name only a few. Colleges and universities offer courses on Women in History, Women in Fiction, Women in Science.

Such efforts are valuable, and they are long overdue. But they are not enough. Yes, there are women who have entered the arenas traditionally reserved for men and have succeeded in those arenas. But there are vast numbers of women in the far reaches of history who have been ignored and are still being ignored—women who exercised power on their own terms, women who were kept from influencing history directly, yet who influenced history irrevocably. Those women were mothers.

Everyone has a mother. Everyone has some idea of the power, for better or for worse, that a mother can wield. The men who, in great part, shaped the world we live in today were no different. They had mothers. And their mothers were powerful women.

Where were the women? To find them, we must not limit ourselves to the obvious, to the women who have actually broken through the barriers of prejudice to compete in the political world. Those who have done so are pioneers, and they have made it possible for more women to have a direct influence on human history. But to see and applaud such women is to fail to give a complete answer to the guiding question of this book.

Where were the women? They were here—guiding, cajoling, pushing, indulging, and loving. We cannot know history without knowing the tales of the people who shaped it. Most of those historymakers are men. But we cannot know those men without first learning the stories of their mothers.

No work of love is ever accomplished in isolation. This book is no exception. With thanks to Mount Mary College, Marquette University, Mary Kennan, Laura Likely, Eric Newman, Stephen Heaney, all the women who answered our letters, and our family, especially Jack F. Maloney, John F. Maloney, Marbeth Foley, and Jamie Maloney, who started it all in 1971.

INTRODUCTION

Almost everyone has heard the line "The hand that rocks the cradle is the hand that rules the world." It is said at times humorously, at other times philosophically, even derisively. The line itself is from a poem by William Ross Wallace, "The Hand That Rocks the Cradle Is the Hand That Rules the World."

> *Blessings on the hand of women!*
> *Angels guard its strength and grace,*
> *In the palace, cottage, hovel,*
> *Oh, no matter where the place;*
> *Would that never storms assailed it,*
> *Rainbows ever gently curled;*
> *For the hand that rocks the cradle*
> *Is the hand that rules the world.*[1]

Wallace's literary defects are compensated for by his sheer sentimentality, but the artistic quality of this stanza is not as pertinent here as the world view it expresses. *Does* the hand that rocks the cradle *really* "rule the world"? Or is Wallace's poem echoing a popular and mistaken assumption about mothers and motherhood?

The aim of this book is to answer that question. It is a journey of discovery, a long backward glance at various influential and notorious figures in history, with an eye cast specifically at their mothers. Our goal in writing this book was to see what, if anything, history can teach us about mothers specifically and about women in general.

A quick glance at the table of contents reveals a telling fact: The only women in this study are mothers of great men or men who were part of great events. There are no female history makers included. Anyone can point to Marie Curie, Queen Victoria, or Golda Meir as evidence of women's *non*maternal roles. Such women are omitted for good reason. First, they are as rare as silver half-dollars on the beach. History has been virtually a male forum; a few brilliant women have broken through, but they belong more properly to another study. In writing this book, we had to face an unpleasant truth: For the most part, women have been allowed neither to make nor to write history. We see indications of change in the late twentieth century and are gratified. But this is a book about national and world events and political history, and until very recently, *history has been a male bastion.*

For roughly 2,000 years, Western women have been expected to find contentment and meaning in the traditional role of wife and mother. Their influence on world events has been limited to their influence on the men who shaped those events. The Wallace poem is a perfect example of this attitude. Women in the twentieth century, however, have begun to question such thinking. This book aims to help in that questioning process by studying how much influence mothers actually have on their children—in this case, their sons. In so doing, it arrives at certain conclusions, not just about certain historical figures, but about the importance of motherhood itself. Perhaps those who read this book will experience the same emotions we did in studying these women: empathy, frustration, awe, pride, and not a little love.

We do hope that each reader will be able to use the fears and triumphs of these women to come to a deeper understanding of the institution of motherhood.

The lines from Wallace's poem embrace the theme of this book, but it is not the only well-known saying about motherhood. Most people have also heard such lines as "Who holds the souls of children holds the nation"; "Give me four years to teach the children, and the seed I have sown will never be uprooted"; "The child is father to the man"; "He who would understand himself needs first to understand his mother."

Society's attitude toward motherhood is ambivalent and complex; mothers are viewed with deference, even reverence, at the same time that they are ignored or dismissed. Lines such as the ones cited in the previous paragraph point to an attitude of respect and even awe, but many present-day mothers actually experience a far different reaction from society. It is not unusual to hear a woman say, "Oh, I'm just a housewife." One woman who taught classics and studied for her Ph.D. in theology before marriage lamented recently that she had been at a dinner party at which no one had paid any attention to her because she was introduced as "Julie, who has three children." Susan was a practicing attorney until she had her first son and elected to stay at home with him. To her dismay, she noticed that her brother, also an attorney, simply ceased talking to her after the birth of her son, assuming that they no longer knew or cared about the same things.

It is hard, given such experiences, to hold onto the attitude expressed by one mother, Rose Kennedy:

> *I looked on child rearing not only as a work of love and duty but as a profession that was fully as interesting and challenging as any honorable profession in the world and one that demanded the best I could bring to it.*[2]

The modern era has been a revolutionary time for women. They have fewer limitations and more options than ever before. Marriage is no longer considered the only road to fulfillment; terms such as *old maid* and *spinster* have gone the way of five-cent candy bars. Given the rising number of women practicing birth control, motherhood itself has become optional. Women today act more by conscious choice than by the dictates of society or biology.

The revolution in women's lives has had its effects on the role motherhood plays in those lives. It is often viewed as one facet of a woman's life, rather than the central focus. The responsibility of mothering is shared today in more ways than ever before, as women rely on day-care centers, pre–nursery schools, professional "mothers" who are paid to care for neighborhood children, and even grandma, assuming she is not busy with a life of her own. This is the era of "quality time" versus "quantity time"—motherhood as part of a woman's life but not the whole of it.

Such a shift from the aproned mom happily greeting her children at the door with homemade cookies and milk is perhaps the natural consequence of the changes in the Western world. With the communications revolution, two world wars (in which women stayed behind and kept their countries running), the vast improvements in birth-control methods, the rise of psycho-analysis, and the wane of traditional religions, women became better informed, more sexually liberated, more independent, more politically involved, and more interested in defining their identity apart from men and children.

Women have a long way to go before they achieve economic and social parity with men, but they have taken some giant steps toward that goal. Women now have opportunities once undreamed of in education, in economics, in their overall life choices, and in their relationships. How have these revolutionary changes in women's lives altered the institution of motherhood? Have they hurt it or strengthened it?

As motherhood has become more of an option and less of a fate, as it has become only one aspect of multifaceted lives, has its cultural significance diminished? Will tomorrow's men and women still look to their mothers in order to understand themselves?

It is not possible to answer these questions from our limited perspective, but few people today will disagree with Sigmund Freud that infancy and childhood are the most crucial years in the formation of human beings. The first relationship an infant has is almost always with its mother; in fact, it is now believed that in the early part of infancy, a baby does not even realize that it is a being separate from its mother. Thus, despite all the changes and upheavals in women's roles over the past century, one truth has remained constant: For better or for worse, mothers are one of the most important influences on all of us, on those who have made history and on those who have read it.

After digesting the stories of the mothers included in these pages, each reader will probably reach his or her own conclusions about these women. After having researched the lives of more than one hundred mothers, we too reached some conclusions. Any work—whether historical, philosophical, or literary, even scientific—entails taking a perspective, and that is true of this work. Although it does present a fair amount of factual information, it does not pretend to be scientific; although essentially historical in focus, it does not shy from philosophy. It is not, and could not be, a laboratory experiment with certain conclusions. It is, rather, a careful rumination of the women who gave birth to men who charted the course of history. As such, it is primarily, though not wholly, centered on the recent historical past and on the American perspective. A universally neutral study of all mothers throughout time would neither be possible nor especially desirable, and it is certainly not the goal of this book.

Having acknowledged the taking of a perspective, let us now state that perspective. The conclusion to which the women we have studied in the last three years have led us is simply this: No one, poet and historian alike, has yet fully appreciated the significance of the mother's role in the life of her child. This truth was felt, if not openly stated, by many of the women in these pages. A child's first experiences of life and of love are usually at his or her mother's knee. A child's world view is influenced, if not determined, by that of his or her mother. Mother is often the chief source of a child's ability to achieve, to form relationships, to take on responsibility. Sometimes this influence is acknowledged; more often it is not.

Despite the very real experience of women such as Julie, who felt insignificant when introduced as a "mother of three," or Susan, who found her interest value waning once she left the work force, there are few roles more important or influential than that of mother. But society does not always acknowledge this truth, and history has too long ignored it.

This fact became painfully clear during the research that went into this book. Several times, one man or another whom we had originally intended to include had to be scrapped, because there was little or no information to be had on his mother. Sometimes our research was frustrated by men who seemed deliberately, almost willfully silent on the subject of their mothers. For example, Thomas Jefferson's mother is shrouded in mystery, primarily because Jefferson was so uncommunicative about her. His silence is made more perplexing by his own experience as a parent. Jefferson's wife, Martha, bore six children, but only two lived to become adults. When his wife died after ten years of marriage, Jefferson reared the two girls with dedication and enthusiasm, and he expected them to return his love and concern. At one point, he wrote to his daughter Martha:

> *No one in the world can make me so happy, or so miserable as you. To your sister and yourself I look to render the evening of my life serene and contented.* [3]

Clearly, this was a man who felt keenly the joy and fear of being a parent. Yet the same man who wrote such heartfelt words to his daughter is dry and curt on the subject of his own mother.

Why? Was Jane Randolph a ghoulish figure, a childhood nightmare better left forgotten? Certainly not. By all accounts, she was simply an aristocratic English girl, a member of Virginia's *crème de la crème* who married Peter Jefferson when he was thirty-one and she was nineteen. The Randolphs could trace their roots back to England and Scotland, but Thomas later scoffed at the merits of such a heritage. As far as Thomas was concerned, a coat of arms was no more expensive than a cloth coat, twice as useless but just as easily purchased. Jane bore a child in each of the first three years of her marriage; Thomas was her first son, but not her last. Peter and Jane had ten children altogether, including Thomas.

As a member of a leading Virginia family, Jane had been given a proper young lady's education. She had received formal schooling—unlike her husband, who had to teach himself reading and mathematics. But Peter Jefferson was a resourceful and ambitious man; by the time he married Jane, he had passed the county surveyor's test and already owned a substantial piece of land.

Thomas was far more fascinated by his father than by his mother, if his own writings are a reliable witness. He used the connections that his Randolph heritage afforded him, but he did not respect them. The true object of his admiration was the enterprising and self-reliant example of his father, who earned rather than inherited his every advantage. Jefferson's adulation of his father may have been partially caused by the fact that Peter Jefferson died when Thomas was fourteen, and a young boy's fond memory is often kinder than a living, critical eye might be. Jefferson lived with his mother for twenty-seven years; few people canonize their living companions, and Jefferson was no exception.

Yet Jefferson's silence on the subject of his mother is made even more inexplicable by the character of Jefferson himself. Thomas Jefferson's driving ambition was to be immortal. He played to the audience of history; he wanted his name and his deeds to be remembered forever. Why did a man with this burning desire for immortality, this man who preserved virtually every slip of paper for posterity, destroy his letters to and from his mother and his wife?

Jefferson was a paradox. He wanted to be remembered, and yet he could be intensely private. Such men are exasperating for historians, but their right to personal loyalties is inalienable. The meager facts that come to the surface about Jane Randolph do little to dispel the mystery. The only mention Jefferson makes of her in his memoirs is of her name and lineage. The family letters that remain intact do not mention Jane. His financial accounts show that at regular intervals he sent her corn, beef, and hogs—and charged her the going rate for them.

When Jane died at the age of fifty-six, a notation in Jefferson's pocket account book marks the occasion. "My mother died about eight o'clock this morning in the 57th year of her age of an illness not lasting more than an hour."[4] Beyond this cold statement, we know nothing of Jefferson's feelings for Jane Randolph. This man who felt so much for his own children, who esteemed his father so highly, appears to have felt very little for his mother.

Thomas Jefferson did not hate his mother; he did not even appear to think ill of her. He simply did not think of her at all. What his life with her was like, what their relationship was, will forever remain between them. Perhaps Jefferson's silence has an eloquence of its own; such silence certainly leaves historians in the misty world of speculation.

It is at such times that the few bare facts which history does yield can become a temptation to move beyond them and into conjecture. Such little information might be given, yet so much might be felt to have existed in the past, forgotten by historians and now lost. Benjamin Franklin's mother, Abiah Folger, is another example of such a temptation. When Josiah Franklin's first wife died, leaving him with five children to care for (she had had seven, but two did not survive infancy), he decided to marry again, and Abiah was the lucky women. Josiah and Abiah were wed within six months of his first wife's death, and Abiah bore him an additional ten children.

Benjamin was the youngest son of the second set of children, and Abiah's seventh child. He left home when he was seventeen. This is not surprising, considering how crowded the living conditions must have been. (Thirteen of the family's seventeen children survived until adulthood, an amazing statistic for the times.) Franklin spoke on a wide variety of topics throughout his public career, but he rarely mentioned his mother. It is tempting to assume that he barely knew her well enough to speak to her.

Only as a much older man did Benjamin Franklin mention his mother, and even then he did not have a lot to say. He mentioned feeling indebted to her, because her common sense instilled in him the good judgment and concise perception for which he became renowned. Beyond that, the records are silent on the subject of relations between Abiah and her son. When his mother died at the age of eighty-five, Franklin accepted it tranquilly, writing that Abiah had lived a long and good life and no doubt now was happy. He composed her epitaph himself, saying of his mother that she was "discreet" and "virtuous." Beyond that, we know nothing of this woman who married a widower with five children, bore him ten more, and raised thirteen of them, one of whom assumed a crucial role in forming the eighteenth century's most dramatic and successful democratic experiment. It is hard not to wish that Benjamin could have known his mother more fully and that we could have shared in that knowledge. Franklin made history. How interesting it might have been to become acquainted with the woman who helped to make Franklin.

Abiah's story, or lack of one, attests to the curious schizophrenic attitude that society has historically had toward women. Motherhood is revered as a hallowed, even sacred calling, yet the women who do actually give their lives to the rearing of children are all but forgotten. Of another "founding father," John Adams, much is known about his wife, Abigail, but little of his mother, Susanna Boyleston. We do know that she married John's father when she was twenty-six years old; descended from one of the colonies' most successful families, Susanna provided the only noteworthy connection in the Adams family up to that time. Susanna bore her husband three sons, one of whom would help to draft and sign the Declaration of Independence, serve his fledgling country for two terms as its vice-president under George Washington, and succeed Washington in the presidency. Of Susanna herself, we have reports only that she was lively and talkative and that she kept her cap immaculate. She survived her husband (he died in 1761 when Susanna was fifty years old) and remarried five years later, only to survive her second husband by seventeen years. When Susanna died at the ripe age of ninety, John mentioned in a letter to Abigail that "my mother's countenance and conversation was a source of enjoyment that is now dried up forever."[5] This sentiment is balanced by a strikingly utilitarian streak in John's relationship with his mother: As vice-president, he tried to persuade Susanna to move in with him and Abigail, because it would improve his public image. To her credit, she refused. But indications are that John valued his mother and expected to miss her presence in his life. However, his feeling for her did not motivate him sufficiently to leave her story in the pages of his letters or journals. Whatever his mother meant to him remained in his heart, and men's hearts are not the province of historians.

Men such as Franklin and Adams seem rather blithely unaware of their mothers, yet there is no indication that they felt anything lacking in their filial relationships. Susanna Adams stands as representative of many mothers who are missing from the pages of history. We are fortunate for the stories that we do possess, but mothers whose lives are well accounted for do not make us miss less the mothers whose stories will never be told.

But there are those women of whom records have been kept, stories told, and facts documented. You will meet many of them in the following chapters. These women's stories tell us today of many things: of lively moments, of tragic loss, of uncommon strength, of enduring love. They point out that motherhood is one of the most potentially powerful roles a woman can play. It is also one of the most demanding and least recognized. There are no paid vacations, no leisurely conventions, no bonuses or yearly raises. It is a unique task in that it requires both total dedication and the ability to let go. It requires that a woman be firm and in control, and yet it demands that she know when to yield and when to give up control. A mother is expected to teach and to enlighten and yet must know when to remain silent. She must help her children to develop the very wings they will use to fly away from her. Motherhood requires the most selfless and the most difficult love of all: the love that fosters not dependency but freedom. An old Chinese proverb says it all: "The mother must know when to let go the hand."

These pages include mothers who lived up to these awesome requirements. They include women of dignity, of courage, and of deep love. They also tell of women who devour their children, who treat "love" as a kind of I.O.U. rather than the gift it is. They tell of sincere but misguided women who try to protect their children from danger and adversity, refusing to realize that growth and maturation are the fruits of struggle.

In the course of researching the lives of these women, we came upon a book that was written in 1883 entitled *Mothers of Great Men*. In the preface, the author wrote about the difficulty of her task because of the lack of information on the mothers of her subjects. She went on to say that she hoped that one day someone would take up her task. Here we are, more than one hundred years later, faced with the same obstacles but guided by the same conviction: If the story of human history is to be told truthfully, it must include the stories of these women. A more diverse, variegated, unusual group would be hard to find, but all the women in this book share one trait: They were mothers. As such, they belong in the saga of human events.

CHAPTER ONE

SIGMUND FREUD: THE MAN WHO MADE MOTHER FAMOUS

A book on the mothers of famous men in history might not have been written were it not for Sigmund Freud. Before Freud's seminal impact on Western civilization, few people had looked to childhood as the source of a person's accomplishments. Few people had looked at significant human actions and sought explanation in the women who give birth to great men. Given this, it is only proper that a book on the influence of motherhood pause to reflect on the son who first recognized and credited the crucial part Mother plays in every human life.

Apart from this rather obvious reason for beginning this book with a section on Freud lie other reasons. No thinker has been more influential in the twentieth century. Freud revolutionized the way people look at the world and at themselves. Just as Darwin offered a new way of seeing humanity, just as Copernicus opened up a new perspective on the universe, just as Newton and Einstein altered traditional beliefs about nature's laws, so did Sigmund Freud unlock a corner of the human world that had previously been only a matter of conjecture.

Until the late nineteenth century, Western civilization was centered on the moral structure of the Judeo-Christian world view. Then, in 1883, Friedrich Nietzsche declared that God was dead. In so saying, he did not mean that God had once existed and no longer did. Rather, Nietzsche saw that God had ceased to be the focus of meaning in human life. When human life was centered on the Christian perspective, men and women had sought meaning in the hope for salvation. They looked at their world with the eyes of the Christian moral system and saw life far differently than they do in the twentieth century. The death of that system created a vacuum, and scepticism mushroomed about civilization's rules and morality's standards; tenets that had been accepted for centuries were thrown over, and disorder replaced them. Sigmund Freud did much to systematize that chaos, to fill that vacuum. When the human race rejected the tenets of Christianity, when they had stopped defining the world in terms of sin and grace, Freud stepped in with a new way to look at the world and its inhabitants, offering the option of defining it instead in terms of repression and therapy.

Freud's impact has been so pervasive that it has become almost undetectable. Many of his insights are such common knowledge that they are taken for granted rather than viewed as the revolutionary thoughts that they are. His teachings have permeated twentieth-century literature, art, sociology, and philosophy. Without his work in the area of dreams and the unconscious, James Joyce, T. S. Eliot, William Faulkner, and Salvador Dali would never have produced the kind of work they did. Freud's influence, whether acknowledged or not, is very real. Although he wrote *The Interpretation of Dreams* at the turn of the century, his impact did not show itself until the World War I era and took firm root by the end of World War II. In the latter half of the twentieth century his impact has become so great that he has influenced people who have never heard of him.

In contemporary culture, Freud's vocabulary has been absorbed into common speech. People who have never read a word of Freud commonly use Freudian words and phrases like *complex, repression,* and *free association.* A young man returning from a funeral comments that it was one of the nicest *weddings* he ever attended, and his girlfriend wonders if he views marriage as a kind of death. Every moment of every day, someone commits such a verbal slip and ponders the unconscious wish behind it. Freud's work on the unconscious has had still other ramifications in everyday life. A woman is rejected by yet another man and wonders what childhood forces cause her to fall in love with men who leave her. Before Freud, such a woman would be far more likely to blame her bad luck than her past. Before Freud, someone who was invariably late for every important appointment would be considered inefficient; since Freud, such a person might just as easily be presumed to be secretly hostile.

It is only after Freud unlocked the mechanism of unconscious wishes and longings that advertisers have been able to capitalize on human vulnerability. Thus do men and women in contemporary culture associate success with a certain kind of car, romance and friendship with a certain brand of beer, security with a certain variety of lemonade. Before Freud, those who broke the law were punished; it is only since Freud uncovered the importance of childhood deprivation and offered the option of analysis that many criminals are instead rehabilitated. Freud himself was not responsible for all of the fallout of his philosophy, and in fact he would no doubt have been appalled at some of it, but nevertheless it was his original insights that precipitated what followed.

Even more common than all of these examples are the people who find themselves in the midst of a crisis, a depression, or a failure and seek guidance from a self-help book or a therapist rather than turn to a priest or minister. Whereas moral failure was once the province of blame and forgiveness, in this age of Freud it is the province of insight and analysis. As Philip Rieff pointed out in *Freud: Mind of the Moralist,* people who once turned to religion in order to be saved from their misery now turn instead to psychoanalysis. As the impact of psychoanalysis has increased, the importance of public standards has diminished in favor of private feelings. It was Freud who uncovered the profound impact a person's hidden emotions can have upon his public life. Inquiries into instinct have taken over the role once played by conventional morality; before Freud, instinct was studied by zoologists rather than sociologists. Whereas sex was once considered to be an interesting adjunct to human life, since Freud it is often viewed as the undercurrent of every human relationship and the core of every human behavior.

It was Freud who first strove to find out what unconscious forces motivate conscious behavior, Freud who pointed out that a person's relationship with his or her parents is a complex mixture of love and jealousy and need and shame, Freud who convinced us that childhood shapes the adults we become, and Freud who uncovered the fact that men and women often act on instincts that are hidden from even themselves.

Without Freud, human beings in the twentieth century would not be as aware as they are of the crucial role that childhood plays in human development, of how important to one's future maturity and mental health is one's mother. It was Freud who opened the avenues of insight into human relationships that have led historians and biographers to look at a person's family relationships in order to understand that person. It is the Freudian outlook that makes possible a book such as this one. It is only appropriate, then, to begin the book with a look at Freud's own childhood and at his discovery of the overriding importance of that human symbol of love and security: the mother.

Amalie Nathonson was a twenty-year-old girl living in

Vienna when she met and married forty-year-old Jakob Freud, a gentle but stern wool merchant who was visiting the city. Freud had been married before; in fact, his eldest son was the same age as his new wife. But Jakob had been taken with the lovely Amalie from the moment of their first meeting. He was a quiet man, and Amalie seemed to charge every room she was in with her vitality and her quick wit. Slender and pretty with dark hair and dark eyes, Amalie always seemed to be moving, laughing, and talking, and Jakob felt more alive just being in her presence.

After they were married, Jakob took Amalie to Freiburg, Austria, the home of his wool business, and settled her into a modest house very close to the homes of his two grown sons. Freiburg was a quiet rural village in Moravia, mostly Roman Catholic in population. Only about 2 percent of the citizens were Jewish, as the Freuds were, so they confined their world mostly to family and a few friends. It was an ideal place to raise a family, and Amalie's pregnancy soon after her wedding did nothing to deaden her zest for life; she was excited and eager to have her new baby.

When the baby was born on May 6, 1856, Amalie named him Sigmund, which derives from a word meaning "victory." From the moment the baby was born, with a head of silky black hair and a red face, she was convinced that he would one day be a great man. Amalie had always believed in signs and omens; hers was an intuitive and sentimental nature. Sigmund had been born with a caul, a traditional omen of fame and happiness, and Amalie took the omen completely to heart.

Amalie was in love with Sigmund from the moment of his birth. Because of his dark hair, she called him "my little blackamoor," but before long she switched to "my golden Sigi." The baby's coloring was as dark as ever, but as far as Amalie was concerned, he was her gold, her treasure. Despite the fact that she continued to have children—eight in fourteen years—Sigmund was her undisputed favorite, and everyone in the family knew it. As for Sigmund, he was so close to his mother that he did not know where Amalie ended and he began. Freud later recalled that even as a baby, he loved this mother who radiated love and vitality, who fed him and tended to him and rocked him to sleep.

Sigmund's idyll was rudely shattered when other babies

began to appear regularly on the scene. As it was, his family was a labyrinth of complicated relationships; his father, Jakob, was already a grandfather when Sigmund was born, making Sigmund younger than John Freud, his nephew. In addition to this, his half-brother Emmanuel (Jakob's son) was his mother's age. To Sigmund's confused little-boy mind, the man who was his father should have been his grandfather, his half-brother should have been his father, and his nephew should have been his brother or cousin. It was while he was still trying to figure out this welter of confusing family ties that his mother began to have more babies.

Sigmund could not understand why his mother was bringing so many interlopers into the family circle. When his brother Julius was born, Sigmund even had to share his mother's breast. No doubt he wished that this rival for Amalie's affection would disappear, and in fact Julius died when he was only eight months old. But there were more rivals to come. As Sigmund matured, he kept trying to make sense of his family and his place in it. He was completely secure in his mother's love, and he reveled in it, but his mother did not love him alone. She loved Jakob, and she loved the other children that kept appearing. Sigmund, who wanted Amalie all to himself, loved his father and his siblings, too. But these people he loved made him feel jealous and angry. This he could not understand.

Sigmund's feelings for his father were further complicated by the fact that Jakob was the authority figure. Whereas Amalie was his source of comfort and acceptance, Jakob was the one who restricted him, denied him things he wanted, and commanded him to do things he did not want to do. Amalie's life was centered on the firm conviction that Sigmund would be a great man; Jakob, however, once commented in anger that he would "never amount to anything." Recalling this incident later, Sigmund remembered that he had promised himself at the time to prove his father wrong and vindicate Amalie.

The stories and portents surrounding Sigmund's birth became family lore, because Amalie repeated them thoroughly and often. Sigmund's brothers and sisters were more familiar with these tales than they were with any of their own childhood stories. There was the day when Sigmund was just a baby, and Amalie was in the bakery. An old woman approached them unbidden and exclaimed that Amalie was a lucky mother because the whole world would one day talk about her boy. At another time, when Sigmund was out to dinner with his parents, a man was entertaining the patrons (for tips) by improvising verses about whatever subject the diners chose. When Amalie and Jakob sent Sigmund over to fetch the poet, he looked once at the young boy and rattled off a verse about a bright future, asking first for neither a fee nor a subject matter. The verse predicted that Freud would become a minister—a governmental appointee—one of the most impressive positions an Austrian Jew could attain.

Sigmund never appeared to take these prophecies as seriously as his mother did. Yet they were the air that he breathed, and he could not help but be affected by them. One of his sisters later said, "Perhaps my mother's trust in Sigmund's future destiny played a definite part in the trend given his whole life."[1] As he was growing up, Sigmund did count very heavily on his future success. He was always the top student in his class, and he was an avid reader. Once, when he was four years old, he stained Amalie's favorite chair. When he saw her dismay, Sigmund promised, "Don't worry, Mother. When I grow up I shall be a great man and then I shall buy you another chair."[2]

In later years, Freud admitted that his mother's adoration was the reason for his self-confidence and drive to achieve. As to the stories, he commented, "Prophecies of this kind must be very common: there are so many mothers filled with happy expectations and so many old peasant women and others of the kind who make up for the loss of their power to control things in the present world by concentrating it on the future. Nor can the prophetess have lost anything by her words." Yet, he went on to add, "Could this have been the source of my thirst for grandeur?"[3]

Freud thought himself to be much more like his father than like Amalie. Like Jakob, Sigmund was liberal-minded and skeptical. He had his father's easy humor and gentle warmth. Jakob's optimism and charm, however, were not enough to bring financial success. When the Industrial Revolution brought the railroad to Austria, the lines bypassed Freiburg, a severe blow to Jakob's wool business. New machinery was also changing the face of his trade, and Jakob would not adapt. He had to accept financial help from Amalie's family in order to survive. This was a blow to his pride, and Sigmund slowly began to view his father as a less effective and powerful man.

Almost everyone in Freiburg was hurt by the railroad's bypassing the town. As has been true as long as there have been human beings and hard times, the town's unhappy citizens looked for a scapegoat and found one in the Jews. Life became unpleasant for the Jewish population of Freiburg, and Jakob decided to take his family to Vienna in search of more money and less hostility. Sigmund was still very young when the family moved, but he remembered it as a most unhappy time.

When the family arrived in Vienna after a long train ride, they found temporary living quarters and eventually moved permanently into an apartment with three bedrooms and one guest room. Jakob and Amalie had one bedroom, and six of the children were divided between the two other rooms. As for the guest room, that was for Sigmund alone. Amalie insisted that he would need privacy when he began his formal studies. She also saw to it that Sigmund had an oil lamp, the only one in the household. One of Freud's sisters showed some musical talent and was given piano lessons. But her practicing was a disturbance to Sigmund's studies, and he complained about the noise. The piano was sold; the lessons ceased. The Freud household was centered on Sigmund from the moment of his birth, and Sigmund retained until he died that feeling of being at the center.

Sigmund deeply missed the rural atmosphere, the grass and fresh air, of Freiburg. Vienna seemed cold and unfriendly, especially the dirty and overcrowded Jewish quarter where the Freuds lived. When the family was settled, Jakob seemed no more willing than he had been in Freiburg to find a way to support them. While he sat in the apartment and waited for something to turn up, Emmanuel and Philipp, his elder sons from the first marriage who now lived in Manchester, helped to support his second family.

Later on, Sigmund commented that after the move to Vienna, "long and difficult years followed, of which, as it seems to me, nothing was worth remembering."[4] But remember he did, and Sigmund found himself slowly losing respect for Jakob. Father and son were used to taking long walks together, walks that Sigmund treasured. But he remembered one day in particular, a day when Jakob confided to him about an incident from the past. In Freiburg, years before, Jakob had been walking down the street wearing a new fur cap. Someone had knocked his new cap off and spat out, "Jew, get off the pavement."[5]

When Sigmund heard this, he asked Jakob what his reaction to the insult had been, thinking that he would have struck the offender down. He was appalled to learn that his father had simply gone into the street, retrieved the cap, and gone on his way. This response was a great disappointment to Sigmund, who longed for a show of heroism from his father. This loss of admiration coupled with Sigmund's resentment of his father's place in Amalie's heart combined to make him feel guilty. He was confused and mystified by the complexity of his emotions. His love for Jakob was genuine, but so was his resentment and disdain.

His relationship with Amalie was no less complicated. Mother and son were never separated emotionally, and it was his overpowering feeling for her that led him to try to make sense of the maze of human emotions. In 1932 he wrote in *The Psychology of Women*, "Throughout the ages, the problem of women has puzzled people of every kind"[6]; his mother was certainly the central puzzle of Freud's life.

Freud was nervous about train travel for the duration of his life and admitted to being afraid of crowds. When he later analyzed these reactions, Freud traced them to the train trip from Freiburg to Vienna. He had been terribly afraid at the time that he was to be separated from Amalie. Also, it was on the train to Vienna that Sigmund first saw his mother naked and was aroused at the sight. The strength of his feelings for Amalie frightened and confused him. He resented Jakob and the other children for making him share her, but he resented her too, for loving others beside him.

This jealousy and anger, coupled with the power of his strong love, led Sigmund Freud forty years later to discover the Oedipus complex, to see that his experience was not unique but universal. He realized that every child's first love object is its mother, that the first rival is its father, that as an infant, a baby is completely dependent on its mother for its physical and emotional satisfaction. As the baby matures, she, or especially he, wants to be the most important love object to its mother, just as the mother is to the baby. But a human being's infinite desire for love will never, by its very nature, be sated. How one deals with this hard truth, Freud saw, does much to determine the rest of one's life—one's self-image, relationships, and emotional health.

These insights about unconscious wishes and the complexity of human emotions were the linchpin of Freud's philosophy, as he wrote to his friend William Fliess in 1897, "I have found the love of the mother and jealousy of the father in my own case, too, and now believe it to be a general phenomenon of early childhood."[7] Freud taught that the essential foundations of character are laid by the age of three, and that later events may modify but cannot change a person's personality. What of him? Amalie was the most important person in Sigmund's life, yet he did very little actual exploration of the mother's role in child development. It was his successors who did that. As for the information available on Freud's own maternal influences, these had to be gleaned from Freud's own works and his correspondence. Ironically, Freud, the man who "discovered" repression in his fellow human beings, repressed most of his own feelings about his mother. At two points in his life he destroyed all of the personal letters and diaries that may have referred to their relationship, giving his right to privacy as an excuse.

And yet, even had he wanted to, Freud could never have destroyed the traces of Amalie's influence on his character. It was, in fact, *his* discovery that the marks left by a mother are ineradicable. Documents are not necessary to see the seeds of Freud's greatest discoveries in his attempts to figure out his complicated relationships with Jakob and Amalie. Sigmund Freud was the first man to unlock the mystery of the unconscious mind and explore the dark world of sexuality. He was able to do so because he was a genius and a man of great determination and integrity. But for such an arduous task, he needed great passion, and the wellspring of that passion was his relationship with Amalie, the drive to understand his feelings for her.

Apart from his own need to make sense of his emotions, Sigmund's success was the result of self-confidence and a considerable degree of courage. His theories were despised from the moment he first presented them. The Viennese medical community condemned him viciously for being too deterministic, too rigid, too arrogant and gloomy. He could not have withstood such ostracism and disdain had he not had the strength of character to go on working without the acceptance of his colleagues.

Freud himself knew the source of his strength. He said, "A man who has been the undisputable favorite of his mother keeps for life the feeling of a conqueror, that confidence of success that often induces real success."[8] His position as his mother's favorite gave him a security and courage that never deserted him, even in the face of vituperative criticism.

Amalie Freud did not die until Sigmund was seventy years old. In fact, Sigmund went to his mother's house for dinner every Sunday until her death at the age of ninety-five. Amalie's vitality never deserted her, nor did her love for her golden Sigi. Amalie was present for virtually all of her son's life; he died of cancer shortly after his mother's death. But it was Freud's own insight that Amalie would have been very much present in his life even if she had died twenty or thirty years earlier. Freud once wrote to his fiancée, Martha Bernays, that "I know I am someone, without having to be told so."[9] He knew it because Amalie *had* told him so, not just with her words, but with her eyes and her attention and her love.

Sigmund Freud opened the doors of the human mind and discovered all manner of strange rooms. In so doing, he sparked a revolution in the way men and women look at their mothers, the way mothers see their children, and the way humans view their world. By his own admission, the soul of his philosophy was the Oedipus complex, a theory that caused him to be ridiculed and ostracized.

But when he had hit upon this core of truth in the midst of human life, he would not let go. His own experience led him to ask the questions whose answers have so altered the view of the nursery and the world view of the twentieth century, the significance of mothers and the meaning of man. The doors he opened will never again close; the post-Freudian world will never be the same as it was before his discoveries. Freud opened the doors, but Amalie was the key.

CHAPTER TWO

THE MOTHERS OF THE FOUNDING FATHERS

Compared with the rich heritage and deep roots of European history, American history is a mere baby, born only a few hundred years ago. No one can deny that American history lacks longevity, but it is also apparent that Americans are not lacking in pride regarding that history. In most states across the nation, United States history is a required course in the secondary-school curriculum. Though the pride is sometimes misplaced, it often is not; during those early years of the founding of the Republic, a remarkable number of talented and innovative men emerged to help create one of civilization's most equitable and enduring governments. The annals of American history yield fascinating stories of unusually bright and courageous men, men without whom there would have been no Declaration of Independence, no Constitution, no United States as we now know it. Because United States history is part of virtually every child's education, the names and accomplishments of the founding fathers are familiar, even timeworn. Often, much is known of deeds of these great men, much learned by rote and then relegated to the back files of the mind. Perhaps some small insight into the personalities, the characters of these people would infuse those dull facts with new life. Certainly we can find some interesting stories in the relationships these founding fathers had with their mothers, and in so doing we may find some clues to the men they became, men who created and maintained what has been called man's "last, best hope"—representative democracy.

GEORGE WASHINGTON

George Washington is one of the most familiar and least known figures in American history. Much of the most common information about him—for example, the tale of the cherry tree and young George's admirable honesty—is patently false, purposely created to enhance Washington's legend. This was done at a time when it was not universally agreed among historians that you do a man the greatest honor by attempting to report the truth about him. Even in the legends, though, the facts are there: that as a military leader during the Revolutionary War, he was responsible for some of the most significant victories of the war; that he served two terms as this country's first president and refused against the wishes of the people to serve beyond those two terms. He is regarded as a great president, a man ideally suited to be America's first commander-in-chief. But what kind of man lived behind that familiar face? What was his character? To find the answers to those questions, surely there is no better place to begin than with his mother.

Mary Ball's fame undoubtedly rests on the achievements of her son. Her grave was unmarked for years, until then-President Andrew Jackson decided that it should be preserved for posterity. The stone now reads, "Mary, the Mother of Washington." Of Mary's own life, little is recorded. We know that her father died when she was only three years old and that her mother followed nine years later, leaving Mary an orphan. A guardian, Major George Eskridge, was entrusted with Mary's care until she reached maturity.

When she was twenty-three years old, Mary wed a farmer and planter named Augustine Washington, a forty-year-old widower who already had three children. When Mary gave birth to her own child in 1732, just eleven months after the marriage, she named him George, after her guardian, Major Eskridge. After George, Mary had five more children—Elizabeth (Betty), Samuel, John Augustine, Charles, and Mildred, who died shortly after birth. Augustine died when Mary was thirty-five and George was eleven, leaving her to raise five young children alone. Washington had lived the average number of years for the time, however, so his death was not untimely. Also, he had left his family adequately provided for; there were no pressing financial worries.

What kind of woman was Mary Washington? She has been described as reserved, as a self-reliant woman who was not prone to show affection. There was little spontaneous joy in her character. Spontaneity did not yield practical results, and Mary was a practical woman. She respected the call of duty, and she expected her children to do the same. With Augustine's death came an end of George's formal education, after only six or seven years of schooling. After all, Mary reasoned, George was her eldest son and there were responsibilities to fulfill. George's half-brothers had received formal schooling in England, but a fatherless family could no longer afford such a luxury.

Mary had been a good deal younger than her husband, and now she discovered the loneliness involved in being a young widow. Devoid of a husband to care for and worry about, Mary turned her considerable attentions upon George, to his dismay. The remainder of Washington's life involved his attempts to escape Mary's vigilant and critical eye. Children usually crave attention from their mothers, but Mary's attentions more often than not included complaints, commands, and criticisms. The violent factions Washington dealt with so successfully in the Revolutionary War and the Republic's early days were nothing new to him. George had seen and heard much worse from Mary. Unwittingly, Mary was preparing her son to be a fine and tolerant statesman.

George and his half-brothers got along well after Augustine's death. He was especially close to his half-brother Lawrence, and it was Lawrence who told George that he could arrange a midshipman's commission in the British navy. This sounded exciting and adventurous to George's fourteen-year-old ears, besides being an excellent way to escape Mary's iron rule. He started packing. When Mary heard about the plan, she ordered George to start unpacking, telling him in no uncertain terms that he was not joining the British navy. George gave in to Mary's demands. He did not run away and join the British navy. (American history would no doubt have taken different turns with George a member of the British establishment instead of the American rebels.)[1] Why did he give in? Simply because George did love Mary, despite her faults. He respected his mother and would not deliberately disobey her orders. Mary had instilled in her son a healthy respect for authority; at the age of fourteen, George was still under Mary's authority.

When he was sixteen, George got his first formal job, as an assistant surveyor, and one year later he became a licensed surveyor in his own right. By the time he was eighteen he had made his first purchase of land and at the age of twenty, George was made an adjutant general of the State of Virginia, with the rank of major. Clearly, George was not a lazy man. Nor was he under his mother's roof any longer. When his half-brother Lawrence died, George rented his estate at Mount Vernon from his widow. (George inherited the property when Lawrence's widow died in 1761.) George lived at Mount Vernon while his mother lived at Ferry Farm, the property that George stood to inherit from his father upon reaching the age of twenty-one. When George's twenty-first birthday came, however, Mary refused to give him his inheritance. George did not press the matter. He loved the estate at Mount Vernon, and he wanted to keep peace if it was possible. Mary did not leave Ferry Farm until George was forty-one years old. That was fine with George. She could live wherever she pleased, so long as it was not with him.

Mary never lost her desire to interfere in George's affairs, and she never stopped trying to do so. When he was twenty-three, George was offered a position with General Braddock's staff. It was a good opportunity, and George intended to meet with the general in Alexandria to discuss the position. On his way out the door, George ran into Mary, who had gotten wind of the plans just in time. Mary could not believe that George would even consider the offer; she demanded that he refuse it. It would be a dangerous job, but that was not Mary's major complaint. It would involve traveling, which meant it would take George away from Mary and his duty to her.

George realized that Mary would object, but he had not counted on a harangue just before his scheduled appointment. As Mary talked on and on, the minutes ticking away, George could do nothing short of physically kicking his mother out, something he would never do. Of course, George missed his appointment with General Braddock. He later wrote a letter of apology to the general, who excused this unfortunate first impression, and George received the position of aide-de-camp during the French and Indian Wars. George was no longer fourteen years old; he would always listen to his mother, but he no longer felt compelled to comply with her demands.

As a member of the general's army, George was often away from home, but that did not stop Mary from letting him know that she was still his responsibility. At one point during the war, Mary sent a letter to him at the front, demanding that he send her some butter and a dutchman. (A dutchman is a type of cap that women wore at the time.) It must not have occurred to Mary that these were rather silly and unreasonable requests to make of a man who was fighting a war in the wilderness, but it certainly did occur to George. Ever the dutiful son, George kept to himself the first response that must have occurred to him, responding instead that he could not possibly send her some butter because he did not have any butter, much less a dutchman, and had little chance of providing either in the wilderness.

George had served admirably in General Braddock's forces, and he was well thought of by both his contemporaries and his superiors. It was rumored that upon his return from his assignment George would soon be offered the prestigious position of colonel in the Virginia regiment, which meant that he would be commander-in-chief of the Virginia forces for the duration of the French and Indian Wars. Such a position would require the ability to make decisions and to take responsibility, qualities he had in abundance. It would also necessitate travel, and to this Mary objected strenuously. In her inimitable ear-to-the-ground fashion, Mary had picked up rumors of the appointment, and she wrote to her son immediately. She begged him to consider his safety, to stop taking foolish chances with his life. To this George responded that he would decline if it was possible to do so with honor. This response was probably George's way of pacifying his mother, of doing what he wanted to do with his life while provoking Mary as little as possible. George accepted the position. Mary may never have fully realized that her son was no longer a small boy, but George did.

Once his part in the war was over, Washington returned to Virginia, and Mary heaved a sigh of relief. He had spent altogether too much time gadding about the countryside and leaving her to fend for herself, but now he could stay home, be a proper Virginia gentleman, and above all, take care of his mother. So Mary thought.

Washington was a respected man in Virginia. He was not especially learned (he knew little of art, philosophy, or science, and read no foreign languages), and he was not a particularly effective public speaker. Neither was he a warm and outgoing man, yet people spoke of his tolerance, his dignity, and his sense of duty. He was well thought of, and so it was no surprise that he was elected to the House of Burgesses in 1758. By all appearances, George was indeed settling down for good. That same year, he resigned his commission and married Martha Dandridge

Custis. Not long after that, he was chosen as a delegate to the Williamsburg Convention and then as a delegate to the Continental Congress.

Washington had never traveled to Europe; he was not versed in the intricacies of theories of government. He was not steeped in philosophical forays into the concepts of freedom and equality, and yet these developing colonies excited and intrigued him. It was an adventurous time, and Washington embraced the fervor and the possibilities of his environment.

After his marriage to Martha, George spent as little time with his mother as possible. He always loved his mother; he just did not like her very much. He never shirked his duty to her as her first son, and Mary never stopped appealing to this sense of duty. George helped Mary with her financial affairs and offered his advice whenever Mary asked him for it. In 1771, when she was in her sixties, Mary finally decided to vacate Ferry Farm. George purchased a house and garden for his mother near the home of his sister, Betty, and finally took over the estate at Ferry Farm, twenty years after he had inherited it, in addition to some nearby land that his mother owned. In return for the use of Mary's land, George agreed to pay rent. Mary made certain that George never took advantage of her; it did not seem to occur to her that George would probably never even think of it. On the other hand, Mary felt perfectly free to take anything she wanted or needed from Ferry Farm—not buy, not rent, but take. After all, she reasoned, she had lived there for years. Anyway, she was George's mother. More often than not, she also asked her son for money. He always gave it to her.

In 1775, George Washington was appointed commander-in-chief of the American army. He was an important man, and his reputation was spreading as a man of determination, perseverance, and cool judgment. People who praised Washington in Mary's presence, however, were probably astonished at her reaction. Mary cared not a whit for her son's fine reputation. As far as she was concerned, he was off meddling around in affairs that were none of his business while his poor mother starved. Mary was, of course, far from starving. Very few penniless widows own houses and enough land to collect rent.

The facts, however, did not deter Mary from her fear of

poverty. During the Revolutionary War, while George was taking care of responsibilities other than his mother's welfare, she petitioned the Virginia legislature for a pension because she was in great need. Surprised by such an appeal from the mother of the United States Army's commander-in-chief, the legislature decided to grant Mary's request but wrote a note to George informing him of the situation. Appalled and embarrassed, George immediately wrote back to the legislature and requested that this not be done, informing them that Mary's children were willing and able to provide for their mother. George knew very well that Mary had an ample income of her own. But her stunt had produced the result that Mary had probably sought all along: attention, even if exasperated, from her son.

George took some time off from his duties to attend to the problem of his mother. He wrote to his brother Jack and asked him to keep an eye on her, because her welfare was threatening to become an article of public debate. He continued:

> ''. . . you may inquire into her real wants; and see what is necessary to make her comfortable. If the rent is insufficient to do this, while I have anything, I will part with it to make her so.''[2]

Remarkably, the United States won the Revolutionary War. Much of the credit for that victory must go to the American army's commander. The Battle of Trenton was certainly one of the turning points of the war and was probably one of the most important victories in American history. George Washington was never a brilliant military strategist, but he was a leader of dogged perseverance. When the troops crossed the Delaware, his advisors recommended that he call off the maneuver: It was cold, it was raining, and only one of three columns had made it to the muddy bank on the other side of the river. Washington would not give up. Revealing a touch of his mother's iron determination to have her way, he demanded that the troops press on. The Battle of Trenton was won, and the victory breathed new life into the revolutionaries at a crucial juncture of the war.

After the war ended, Washington returned to his beloved Mount Vernon. Mary wasted no time writing to her son to tell him that she wished to live with him there. George was on the receiving end of a great deal of attention, and Mary did not want to miss out on one bit of it. If there were to be a party, she did not merely want to join it, she wanted to be at the center of it. After all, she was the mother of this important man.

George's reply to Mary's request was diplomatic and pointed. Happy as he and Martha would be to have her, he responded, it probably would not be a good idea for Mary to move to Mount Vernon. He did not see how she could be happy there. As he put it,

> *If an inhabitant you will be obliged to do one of three things:*
> *1. Always dressing to appear in company;*
> *2. Come into the room in dishabille;*
> *3. To be, as it were, a prisoner in your own chamber.*[3]

It worried him, Washington went on, that as an inhabitant of his residence Mary would never enjoy a moment's peace. The letter produced its desired effect. Mary elected not to come to Mount Vernon after all.

Many mothers center their attention on their children, to the exclusion of all else. This attitude often leads to trouble for the children and heartbreak for the mother. Some mothers, Mary Ball among them, have a different attitude. They expect their children to focus all their attention on them and resent anyone and anything that might prevent this. Mary's jealousy of her son's public career drove out any pride or joy she might have had from his success, and their relationship was the poorer because of it. Many must have been the times when George was forced to laugh at his mother's antics because otherwise he would scream.

Mary aged well, maintaining her mental acuity and her strong constitution well into her seventies. At the age of eighty-one, an uncommon age to attain in the eighteenth century, Mary developed breast cancer. Despite a great deal of pain, she remained strong-willed and obstreperous to the end, even to the point of putting up a fight every time she was supposed to take her medicine.

Mary died in 1789, leaving most of her possessions to George, including some land, her best bed, and her best looking glass. For better or worse, Mary had always felt closest to her eldest son. Washington refused the inheritance but not because he did not value it or her. He did not need anything and so would not take anything from her estate, but as for the material items themselves, Washington said that he set a value on them much beyond their actual worth.

Perhaps George did not accept the physical bequests of his mother because he realized what his real legacy from Mary was. It is true that much of Mary's effect on George was indirect; he developed many of his best diplomatic tactics in trying to escape from Mary's determined grasp. Beyond that, however, Mary had left her footprints in George's soul. She had instilled in him a sense of duty and responsibility that led him to serve his country for some twenty-odd years. She had passed on to him her uncommon perseverance and strong will. Washington had an exasperating mother, and he knew it. But he loved Mary, and he owed her a great deal. He knew that, too. Few men could have accomplished what George Washington accomplished, but then, he had had a role model. Not many women could have raised five children alone in a man's world, but Mary had done it. All this was her real bequest to her son, and George never forgot it.

ALEXANDER HAMILTON

Few figures in American history are as intriguing as Alexander Hamilton. Most people recognize the name and realize that he was a figure of some importance during the early days of the United States Republic and that he died in a duel at a time when duels were rather uncommon affairs. He is often portrayed by historians and biographers as a dashing, doomed hero of American history. To delve behind the interpretations to the facts that lie beneath them is to discover that the myths are not fabrications. Hamilton's story has all the stuff of a tragic epic, and it reads like one.

Almost every history book details the man's accomplishments: He was the United States' first secretary of the Treasury and defined the considerable power of that office; he was a dynamic and rebellious force throughout the administrations of the first three presidents—Washington, Adams, and Jefferson; his ideas on economy, on manufacturing, on the degree of power, were a strong undercurrent that gave rise to this nation's first seriously destructive philosophical disagreement. The scope of his effect on United States history cannot be overestimated, and his character is as complicated as it is interesting.

Alexander Hamilton is almost universally acknowledged as one of the geniuses of the early days of the nation. By the time he was twenty-two years old, he had received an appointment to George Washington's staff. At twenty-six, he commanded a raid on Yorktown, and after the Revolutionary War ended, Hamilton passed the New York Bar and began a distinguished career in law. At the age of twenty-seven, he was appointed by President Washington the first secretary of the Treasury.

This reads like the biography of a man who was "to the manner born," who rose through a genteel system of aristocratic connections to assume his place of power and influence, with the likes of Thomas Jefferson and John Adams. Nothing could be further from the truth. The harshness of Alexander's childhood was paralleled only by the harshness of the life of his mother, Rachel.

Rachel Faucet was the daughter of a respectable French Huguenot family. The sorriest failing of the Faucet family was its inability to arrange decent marriages for its members. But what the Faucets lacked in judgment, they made up for in speed. Despite the fact that her own marriage had already failed, Rachel's mother decided when the girl was only sixteen that the time for marriage had come. It was during a visit to St. Croix with her mother that Rachel had the ill fortune to meet her future husband.

John Michael Lavien was a good deal older than his young bride, and Rachel found him physically repulsive. But at that time, much to Rachel's misfortune, matches were not made in heaven. With no choice in the matter, she became Rachel Lavien. The couple's first son, Peter, was born one year after the marriage.

The union was not a happy one. John was so repugnant to her that Rachel continually threatened to run away. After five years of such threats, John had his wife jailed on the charge that she was an indecent and suspicious woman. Clearly, relations were turbulent in the Lavien family. Lavien's only purpose was to frighten his wife into meek and dutiful submission. He informed the jailer that Rachel could come home as soon as she promised to obey him and be faithful to him.

Those terms were too high for Rachel. Her response to her husband was a flat "No." Rather than return to a miserable life with a husband she despised, Rachel escaped from St. Croix and returned to her home at Nevis Island. There Rachel met and fell in love with James Hamilton, son of Alexander Hamilton, Laird of Grange, Ayrshire, Scotland. Hamilton was enamored of this impulsive and high-spirited young lady, and Rachel found in James a focus for all her passion and intensity.

As divorce was out of the question at that time for a woman in the British Empire, Rachel and James never married. They lived together as man and wife, sharing everything but a name, and two sons were born of their union—James in 1753 and Alexander in 1757. In 1759, Lavien sued Rachel for divorce, on the grounds that she had abandoned him for nine years and had spawned two bastards. Time had done nothing to lessen the enmity between Lavien and Rachel. The divorce was granted, with the stipulation that Rachel could never remarry, although Lavien could do so at any time.

Rachel and James lived together for about thirteen years and by all accounts were as happy as any married couple. Young James and Alexander received formal education during this period, but it was Rachel who taught them to read and write. Alexander was the more precocious of the two; he was sent to a school that was operated by a Jewish woman on the island, and he was one of the youngest children who could recite the Ten Commandments in Hebrew.

James Hamilton Sr. had a good name but little luck in financial affairs. The Hamiltons' existence was always marginal; by 1765 Hamilton was totally bankrupt. Unable to bear the disgrace, he abandoned his family and went to St. Kitts. He communicated with Rachel for a while, but he never returned to her or contributed to the support of their children.

Rachel was no stranger to bad fortune, and she did what she had always done before: She used her wits and coped. Fate had not given Rachel much luck, but she had plenty of resolve and an iron backbone. She rented a house for herself and the children, opened a retail store, and sold food and imported items. At the same time, she made arrangements for thirteen-year-old James to be apprenticed to a carpenter and saw to it that nine-year-old Alexander was hired as a clerk by an import–export firm. Rachel needed their wages if the family was to survive.

The small family lived this way for two years, when Rachel caught tropical fever and died. James and Alexander, first abandoned by their father, were now without their mother. Worse, they had an active enemy in John Michael Lavien. When Lavien heard of Rachel's death, he claimed her entire estate for her legitimate son—Peter. The fact that Peter Lavien was the fruit of Rachel's misery did not change the law.

Peter inherited everything Rachel had. Her illegitimate sons received nothing. Her estate was hardly worth collecting; Rachel had been too busy trying to stay alive and feed her two sons to amass many possessions. But she did own thirty-four books, an amazing number for a woman of her small means. She had always cared deeply for learning, and she never let go of her love for the life that her books offered. When Lavien auctioned off Rachel's personal belongings, caring nothing about them or their owner, her nephew bought the books from the estate, thus preserving the only meaningful possessions Rachel had. James and Alexander became the wards of Rachel's nephew, but he committed suicide one year later, leaving the boys alone and destitute.

Alexander, twelve years old by now, moved in with the father of a friend and continued to work as a clerk. Alexander had watched his mother work in her store while she was alive, and he had been impressed by her taste for hard work and her efficiency. Some stores at that time were less than clean and sloppily managed, but not Rachel's. The floors of her shop were always scrubbed, and her accounts were correct and up to date. Rachel was a smart businesswoman, and her example was not lost on her son. Young Alexander was such an industrious and efficient young man that when the owners of the import firm where he worked had to be away for six months, they left him, a fourteen-year-old boy, in charge of the business. The firm flourished quite well.

Clearly, Hamilton had no small measure of his mother's business sense and love of hard work. Eventually, this bright and resourceful young man became a topic of conversation on the island. A Reverend Knox, a Presbyterian minister with an eye for good works, raised the money to give Alexander a chance at something better than the life of a bastard in the British Empire.

Knox and some friends raised enough money to send Hamilton to America, and at the age of seventeen, he arrived in New Jersey and enrolled in an academy to prepare for the entrance examination at Princeton. After a year at the academy, Alexander requested that Princeton allow him to advance at his own speed and graduate early. Hamilton had learned quite a lot at experience's knee, and he knew that he was a very old eighteen. Princeton, however, did not see it as he did, and refused his request. But King's College (now Columbia University) in New York did agree to his terms, and it was from King's that Hamilton earned his degree.

Alexander Hamilton became one of the most dynamic figures of his time. As secretary of the Treasury, he wielded a tremendous amount of power; he managed the entire economic life of the United States. His financial policies were as orderly and precise as Rachel's store had been, and his determination to have his way was certainly reminiscent of Rachel's willfulness.

Because of the hardship of his life, Hamilton had been involved in business for a long time, and he knew that it operated on human ambition and self-interest. As he saw it, government must harness and use those energies if it is to succeed. Toward this end, he wanted there to exist strong financial ties between the United States government and its wealthiest citizens. These people must, he believed, wield power and so fortify and centralize the strength of the federal government. Hamilton had plenty of opposition to his belief that the United States government should be strong, its power centralized. His primary philosophical adversary was Thomas Jefferson, who believed fervently in a loose central government and individual autonomy. This country eventually adopted Jefferson's philosophy rather than Hamilton's, but not before Hamilton had made his presence felt and caused trouble more than once for Thomas Jefferson and John Adams.

During his tenure at the Department of the Treasury, Hamilton set standards for truthfulness and orderliness of which Rachel would have been proud. As a result of his influence, a nation that had existed on the edge of bankruptcy acquired a credit rating equal to that of the most stable countries of Europe. But his ideas on government power set off controversies that would ultimately lead, indirectly, to his death at a very early age.

Jefferson believed wholeheartedly in the essential goodness of human beings and wanted the government to safeguard liberty above all, arguing that men would not abuse such a privilege. Hamilton was not so sure. Throughout his childhood he had seen that men are not always noble. Above liberty, Hamilton prized order and thought that government must ensure order, even if at the expense of some individual freedoms. Jefferson was a Republican. Hamilton and those who felt as he did were called Federalists. The Federalists opposed the Republican philosophy throughout Jefferson's administration, and Aaron Burr, Jefferson's first vice-president (he was dropped from the ticket in 1804), had cause for revenge against Jefferson. It was natural that he turn to the Federalists, but Hamilton refused Federalist support for Burr's plans to upend Jefferson. Any hope of a conspiracy against Jefferson dissolved, and Burr was defeated.

Burr was ruined, and he was incensed. Blaming Hamilton, he demanded that Hamilton retract an unflattering remark he had made to the press about Burr. But Hamilton was no more pliant with his enemies than his mother had been. Just as she once refused to apologize to Lavien, Hamilton refused to apologize to Burr. Burr responded by challenging Hamilton to a duel. Hamilton need not have accepted such a challenge, for he had no need to prove himself. Furthermore, he was a married man with a family to support. Yet his pride would not allow him to decline, and demonstrating a touch of Rachel's impetuous nature, he accepted the challenge.

Hamilton had no intention of killing Burr; he merely intended to prove his courage and satisfy his honor. He intended to shoot his gun into the ground, and he was convinced that Burr would miss. Burr did not miss. Hamilton paid for his willfulness even more dearly than Rachel had paid for hers, but his bequest to the United States government—the efficient and respected Department of the Treasury—was every bit as valuable as Rachel's lessons of resourcefulness and survival had been to her son Alexander. Hamilton was the man he was because Rachel had taught him to survive. Her lessons allowed him to be more successful than most people would ever have thought possible. But just as Rachel's strengths—her pride, her backbone, her resourcefulness—were ultimately her downfall, so too did Hamilton pay a high price for those same qualities. The United States would never have had its early financial security without his genius, and Hamilton would never have achieved what he did without Rachel's influence. Lavien demanded all of Rachel's estate when she died, but Alexander Hamilton had already received the greatest bequest his mother could have given him.

JOHN QUINCY ADAMS

The Adams name is a familiar one. Like the Kennedys in the twentieth century, the Adams clan was dedicated to both family and public service. Like the Kennedys, the lives and thoughts of the Adams family have been the subject of innumerable books, articles, and even television movies. Such attention exists for good reason. The dedication of such families to public service naturally throws the spotlight on them, and that spotlight reveals characters as unique and fascinating as any found in fiction. Their accomplishments read like a *Who's Who* of early American history: the key role John Adams played in the American Revolution as a diplomat and as the new country's second president, John Quincy's ascendance from secretary of State to become the United States' sixth president and later a congressman, the key role Charles Francis Adams played as minister to England during the Civil War, the histories and commentaries of Henry Adams. This family tree is loaded with male actions and male deeds, but its roots and sustenance are distinctly female. Of John Adams's mother historians know little (as noted in the Introduction), but such is certainly not the case with Adams's wife and John Quincy's mother.

Abigail Adams is one of the most widely known mothers in American history, primarily because every Adams was a prolific writer and record keeper, but also because she was a strong woman and a clear writer herself. Her correspondence with her husband, John, attests to this. Many historians focus on John the patriarch; to do so is to tell a woefully incomplete story of the Adams family.

Young Abigail Smith had a strong sense of her own importance. She believed with passion that women make history by supporting their husbands and molding their children. Woman's place was not in the world, Abigail maintained, but in the home. There lay woman's power, and from there came the strength to build nations. She never doubted this; doubt of any sort was foreign to her character. Abigail had an excellent self-image and a clear perception of her goals.

By no means from a wealthy or well-established family background, Abigail was the daughter of a simple country minister. Although she did not have formal schooling, she did learn to read and write, and the clarity and beauty of her letters to John Adams attest to how thoroughly she mastered those skills. Abigail was just shy of twenty when she married John, a serious but not spectacularly successful lawyer almost ten years her senior. Possessed of neither money nor good connections, Abigail had more than her measure of ambition and purpose. Such qualities turned out to be more than compensation for what she lacked.

Deeply in love, John Adams and his bride married in 1764 despite her mother's disapproval. Mrs. Smith was sure that her lovely and vivacious daughter could have done better than to marry a schoolmasterish lawyer. But, as ever, Abigail knew what she wanted, and she wanted John Adams. Nine months after the wedding, Abigail gave birth to a baby girl and named her Abigail, nicknamed Nabby. Two years later, John Quincy was born. John and Abigail had five children altogether: Nabby, John Quincy, Susannah (who died in infancy), Charles, and Thomas.

During those early years of raising the children, Abigail was often lonely because John was forced to travel often, first as a lawyer and then as a patriot. But she was happy, for she was exactly where she felt her place to be: at home, rocking the cradle. There was no calling more important than that of wife and mother; Abigail believed that with all her heart, and she poured herself into her task. Her presence was especially important because John was away far more than he was at home.

When John Quincy was a baby, John was frequently on the road looking for clients, and later be became involved in the United States' break with England. After the Revolution, he was sent to the Continental Congress. Clearly, John Adams was an important man at an important juncture in history. But he had little time for raising children. He was a "postal parent," giving Abigail constant advice and continually exhorting the children to study and excel.

All parents wonder at times if they are doing a good job, and John Adams was no different. In his letters to Abigail, he often voiced his guilt and worried about his long absences from home. But, as most parents do, he rationalized: He was teaching his family the most important lesson of all, dedication to one's principles and duty to one's country. These were the foundations of John Adams's philosophy of life, and he was a living example of them. But John was seldom home, and letters do not measure up to a real, loving parent. Abigail, however, was there. She was loving and she was the one who made certain that the Adams children had Adams beliefs bred into the very marrow of their bones, for they were her beliefs too. John may have been a parent *in absentia*, but Abigail made certain that he was ever present in his children's lives. Abigail kept John's image before John Quincy as a role model. The best thing he could do, she told him, was to emulate his father. This physically absent father took on heroic proportions. From a distance, John Quincy could see his father's virtues but none of his human failings. Abigail consciously created this ideal, and John Quincy spent his life trying to live up to that creation.

Like John, Abigail was ambitious and self-disciplined, believing firmly in absolute moral principles and in total dedication to the greater good of the nation. Abigail was a patriot. When John was in Philadelphia during the Revolutionary War, the family lived so close to the battlefields that they could hear the cannon fire. During the Battle of Bunker Hill, Abigail took John

Quincy to the top of Penn Hill, so that the boy would have first-hand knowledge of the Revolution. It was a scene that John Quincy never forgot.

Abigail felt very strongly about American independence from the English, but then, Abigail felt strongly about everything. She was a woman with convictions, and she never hesitated to voice them. Of course, women were not allowed to voice their political opinions during the colonial era. They could not vote, and their presence was not even allowed at town meetings. None of these hindrances deterred Abigail. She never hesitated to share her opinion with John and often gave him political advice. Adams respected his wife and admired her intelligence, and when she spoke he listened. They were a communicative and mutually supportive pair; John shared his thoughts and experience with Abigail and asked for her counsel. Despite her lack of formal education, Abigail became very knowledgeable about the machinations of American government.

Did she mind the lowly status of her sex? Did it chafe at her, that she could not vote while any less informed man could? Any irritation she may have felt was directed toward men who did not treat women with respect and love. She did not think women should move from the home, but she did want men to acknowledge the importance of their role. Abigail remained convinced that a woman's duty was to stand behind her husband and children, that no man became great without a great woman, that no child could leave a mark on the world unless his mother had left her mark on him.

Abigail had the same mission as her husband: to accomplish great things. But whereas John's accomplishments were his own, Abigail's were indirect. Her presence is what made her husband and her son great men, and it permeated every inch of their lives. She would not have had it any other way. She believed what every young woman of the time was told: that God had made woman for the express purpose of giving birth to and rearing children. Any woman who rejected these duties, Abigail wrote, "does not accept the end of her creation."[4]

A woman's duty, then, was to inspire and sustain her husband and imbue her sons with nobility and ambition. Daughters, of course, must be taught sufficient virtue to be wives and mothers to patriots. Why? Abigail's answer was simple and direct: The future of the country depended on mothers, for without the indirect influence of women, there would be no great deeds.

These sentiments were not merely words. Abigail lived them with the same conviction she used to voice them. God had entrusted four souls to her care, and she took her task on with fervor. John Adams wrote to his wife about the importance of education, and Abigail saw to it that they were educated thoroughly and well. Both John and Abigail were true believers in the virtues of self-discipline, piety, and diligence. Abigail endeavored to instill those qualities in her children. Abigail and John expected a lot from themselves and expected a great deal from their children. John wrote to Abigail: "Cultivate their Minds, inspire their little Hearts, raise their Wishes. Fix their attention on great and glorious Objects, sort out every little Thing, weed out every Meanness."[5]

The couple's eldest son took this command very much to heart. Even as a child, John Quincy felt the duty to make a contribution to the world, to embody in his life every moral virtue, to be worthy of his parents' love. His parents' expectations were indelible marks on his soul, and he never felt adequate to fulfill those expectations. As a boy John Quincy was dogged by a sense of not being good enough. With perfection as his goal, he had left himself infinite room for failure.

John and the children were the focus of Abigail's life, and she hated to be separated from any of them. But she believed that self-sacrifice for a greater good was sometimes necessary, as it was when the children were young and John had to be away. When John Quincy was ten years old, she decided that it would help his education if he were to accompany his father to France. The boy was abroad on various trips for the next six and one half years, his most extensive stay at home being four months. To send her favorite child off, especially when he did not want to leave her (Abigail and John Quincy were very close) must have been heartbreaking for Abigail, but she did it anyway, because she felt that it was best for her son.

When he was eighteen, John Quincy decided that the time had come for a regular education at a regular school. In

1785 he entered Harvard and there confirmed his parents' assurance that he was a bright boy. But he took little satisfaction in his successes, for in his eyes his failures far outweighed them. He was also bothered by chronic small illnesses—stomach upsets, headaches, colitis. Despite the moral virtues that Abigail drilled into him so completely, he drank too much at times and flirted with women. Though often depressed and frequently ill, John Quincy nonetheless acquired a reputation for argumentativeness while at Harvard and later at Newburyport. It appeared that his chosen profession—that of lawyer—would suit him well. The boy who was pliant and eager to please his parents, who did not question their expectations or their standards, was feisty and aggressive with everyone else.

While at Harvard and at Newburyport, Adams had the acquaintance of several women, but they were a disappointment to him. None measured up to his standards. Then, in 1790, he found in Mary Frazier a girl (she was only sixteen) he could love. In that same year, Adams passed the bar examination and moved to Boston. His relationship with Mary continued after the move, but four months later Abigail put her foot down. She forcefully reminded her son that he was in no financial position to entertain thoughts of marriage. The young man who never shied from debating with his friends did not argue with his mother. He never felt strong enough to risk losing Abigail's approval. He equated approval with love, and the stakes were too high. John Quincy bid Mary farewell.

Adams continued to practice law in Boston, meanwhile gaining himself a reputation as an articulate and intelligent debater. But he was lonely and often depressed. It came as no surprise when in 1794 George Washington appointed him minister to the Netherlands. Pleased and flattered, Adams accepted, and not long afterward on a trip abroad, he met Louisa Catherine Johnson. This time, John Quincy resolved not to let his mother sway him. Louisa was part English, which did not sit well with Abigail. Even worse, John Quincy was talking about giving up his career in law and government, because Louisa's father owned property in Georgia. That was too much. Abigail could put up with the marriage, but John Quincy was not to put his duty aside. Adams and Louisa were married, but John Quincy remained in law and politics. Duty to country was as natural to him as breathing. Abigail had seen to that.

In 1801 John Quincy and his bride returned to Massachusetts, to the detriment of Louisa Catherine. Abigail was all of the things Louisa was not: a good manager and a crisply competent and, above all, confident woman. Proximity made comparisons seem only natural, and Louisa always felt that she did not measure up to Abigail. She loved John Quincy, but that did not seem to be enough. John Quincy fostered his wife's feeling of inadequacy by continually praising Abigail's cleverness, her ability to organize and keep a home running smoothly. Subtly (and sometimes not so subtly) Adams pressured Louisa to be more like his mother, to *be* his mother.

Louisa, of course, resented Abigail. Rather than distance herself from her favorite son, Abigail actually encouraged John Quincy in his attitude, because deep down she agreed with him. Abigail felt that she embodied the finest virtues of wife and mother. Wherever Louisa digressed from Abigail's standards, she was failing in her role as John Quincy's wife. Love was all well and good, but it certainly was not enough. After all, Abigail reasoned, a man's success depended on the woman behind that man. John Quincy Adams was destined to be a great man because he had a great mother. But he needed an ambitious and intelligent wife. Abigail simply did not think Louisa had it in her to make a man great. Louisa may have been loyal to her husband and a faithful companion, and that would have been enough for an average man. But John Quincy Adams was no average man. He was Abigail's son, the son of John Adams. Abigail feared that his wife would only drag him down by being satisfied with him the way he was, by loving him for himself and not expecting—indeed, not demanding—more of him.

John Quincy had taken a stand against his mother when he married Louisa, because his loneliness and despair had become more frightening than his mother's disapproval. But his feelings of self-doubt and anxiety never left him, even when he had a marriage and family of his own. John and Abigail were certain that their children would excel, simply because they refused to settle for anything less. John Quincy did become a respected public man, but he was always a failure in his own eyes.

The other three Adams children fared no better in living up to their parents' expectations. Nabby's marriage was a disaster. When she fell in love with a young man named Royall Tyler, her parents did not approve. A woman's most important decision, by Abigail's lights, was her marriage, and Tyler simply was not good enough. (Ironically, Tyler later became a renowned judge, serving as chief justice on the Vermont Supreme Court.) Nabby, like John Quincy, did not have the strength to risk her mother's disapproval. She cut off her relationship with Tyler and began seeing a Colonel William Smith. John and Abigail considered him fine husband material. Smith was handsome, educated, polite, and had "good connections." What more could their daughter ask for? As it turned out, a lot. Colonel Smith had plenty of charm but very little ambition, good looks but no integrity, good connections but no job.

John Adams tried very hard to help the young couple. At Abigail's insistence, he found jobs in government for his son-in-law, to the point of being accused of nepotism by his colleagues. But Smith was unlucky, irresponsible, and a failure at everything he attempted. His greatest accomplishment was his marriage, and even in that, he failed to make his wife happy.

Government is an arena of constant temptation for men of little integrity, and Colonel Smith was possessed of almost none. It was not long before his greed led him to use his position for illicit ends, and eventually he landed in prison. Nabby, who had been brought up to believe that a wife's duty was to remain faithful to her husband, remained at Smith's side, even sharing a cottage with him on the prison grounds.

Nabby was not a lucky girl. She learned early that virtue does not always win fortune's favor. She developed cancer of the breast and had a mastectomy, but the cancer reappeared soon after, and Nabby knew she was dying. Although she was three hundred miles away from Abigail and John at the time, Nabby went home to die.

Charles, the third child of John and Abigail, rebelled against his parents' great plans for him, but he never escaped from them. He had inherited his mother's charm, but little of her ambition. Charles did graduate from law school and managed to be a successful attorney for a while, but without the self-discipline and moral rigor he had rejected, he could not succeed. Eventually, his taste for alcohol became an obsession, and, as Abigail phrased it, "vice and destruction swallowed him up."[6] He died from alcoholism, disowned by his own father as a "reprobate, a beast, and a rake."[7] Abigail never deserted her son, but when she received the news of his death, she wrote that her mourning over Charles had begun long before his physical death.

Thomas, Abigail's baby, never left the comfort and shelter of being under his parents' wing. He was shy and lacking in self-confidence, always convinced that he was not living up to Abigail and John's standards. He remained dependent on his parents for most of his life, and he too was eventually overtaken by alcoholism.

John Quincy was Abigail's most successful child. He served as minister to various countries, served in the Massachusetts Senate and the United States Senate, was a professor at Harvard University, negotiated the Peace of Paris, became secretary of State, president of the United States, and later a member of the House of Representatives. In the course of his public career, he drafted the Monroe Doctrine and worked hard for the abolition of slavery. Despite this impressive list, John Quincy wrote, "I have done nothing. I have no ability to do anything that will live in the memory of mankind. My life has been spent in vain and idle aspirations."[8]

Abigail Adams, possessed of such a good self-image herself, had not engendered a sense of identity in any of her children. All four Adams offspring lacked the emotional independence and unconditional parental love that is required for a strong self-image. John Quincy Adams was a man of integrity and responsibility; as John Kennedy (who was familiar with high parental expectations) wrote in *Profiles in Courage:*

> *John Quincy Adams carried his somber sense of responsibility toward his creator into every phase of his everyday life. . . . He possessed an integrity unsurpassed among the major political figures in our history.*[9]

Believing always that her task was to carve virtue and excellence into her children's souls, Abigail never gave up trying to advise her children, to guide them toward the right choices. Nabby took her mother's convictions to heart and remained obedient to Abigail's wishes, but Nabby's life was heartbreaking and brief. Thomas and Charles rebelled against their mother, but never realized that rebellion is simply one variation of enslavement. They were never free of her.

Abigail pointed to her eldest son, however, with pride. She had been determined to raise a son destined for greatness, and in that she succeeded. But in John Quincy's case, the price was his own happiness. She never quit trying to run her children's lives. Even when John Quincy was a respected member of the United States Senate, he received the following missive from Abigail:

> *I think a man's usefulness in society depends much on his personal appearance. I do not wish a Senator to dress like a beau, but do want him to conform so far to the fashion as not to incur the character of singularity, nor give occasion to the world to ask what kind of mother he had.*[10]

There is no doubt that Abigail did the very best she could to raise her children well. Marriage and family were the focus of her entire life. But Abigail valued achievement over happiness and obedience over independence. In her desire to be matriarch of a perfect family, Abigail forgot that no human being is perfect. In constantly focusing on her family's appearance, she ignored their needs. Her children confused love and approval, because Abigail confused achievement and success.

Abigail died in Quincy, Massachusetts, just before her seventy-fourth birthday, not having lived long enough to see her son become president of the United States, but long enough to see two of her children buried and one swamped in alcoholism. Neither of her surviving children was at his mother's side when she died, Thomas because of health, and John Quincy because of pressing duties as secretary of State. When informed of her death, however, he was stricken with grief, and he never let Abigail's image fade from his own children's minds, constantly reminiscing about her strength, her wisdom, her love for her country. John Quincy Adams loved and respected his mother until the day he died. But he never loved or respected himself. W. H. Auden wrote in his poem "The Unknown Citizen":

> *Was he free? Was he happy? The question is absurd:*
> *Had anything been wrong, we should certainly have heard.*[11]

He might just as well have been writing about John Quincy Adams.

ANDREW JACKSON

The founders and shapers of the United States of America—Washington, Jefferson, Adams—were men very much alike in temperament and outlook. From the inauguration of George Washington through the presidencies of Adams, Jefferson, James Madison, and James Monroe, the character of the United States government remained essentially the same—intellectual and aristocratic. All that changed with the election of Andrew Jackson, a common man who symbolized the emerging diversity and energy of the American people. Jackson exercised more influence on the presidency and on the United States government than any president since Washington. His term of office set the tone for every administration up to the Civil War, and the effects of his policies are still in evidence today.

Was he a good president? Historians are divided on this question. Some rank him just shy of great. Others consider him a disaster. But all agree that he was one of the most influential presidents ever to hold office.

Jackson, known as "Old Hickory," was a simple and forthright man, a rough-hewn character from the frontier who had no connections and no noble family pedigree. His parents were immigrants from Northern Ireland who had followed so many of their countrymen into the "land of opportunity." Elizabeth and her husband, Andrew Jackson, had emigrated to Waxhaw, South Carolina, in 1765 with their children—two-year-old Hugh and six-month-old Robert. Soon after their arrival, Elizabeth discovered that she was pregnant. When she told Andrew, he decided to build a bigger and better homestead for his growing family. They had not done wrong, the couple felt, in coming to America. Here they could build a future for their children.

Elizabeth's hopes were shaken and her happiness shattered when Andrew died suddenly at the age of twenty-nine, while working on the very home that had been the focus of their dreams. At the time, Elizabeth was seven months pregnant, and what had been a source of joy was now a source of worry, for she was now on her own. But Elizabeth Jackson was possessed of a characteristic Irish trait—she adjusted, and she survived.

In times of trouble or need, the Irish invariably turn to family, and Elizabeth was no exception. She and the two children moved in with her sister Jane Crawford and her family. Because Jane was an invalid, Elizabeth assumed the duties of running the household, which now included ten children. When Elizabeth delivered her third child prematurely, she named him Andrew in memory of his father and went back to the work of caring for eleven children.

Elizabeth had little time or energy left at the end of a day's labor. But she forced herself to take time with her children, to make certain that they never felt deprived or unloved. She made it a habit to read to them, relying on Shakespeare and the Bible. She sat them on her knee at the end of a day's work and told them stories. Rather than fairy tales or religious parables, Elizabeth told her sons about the Irish, about their fierce pride and staunch courage, about the cruelty of the British. The boys listened avidly to adventure tales more exciting than any fiction: the British attempts to subjugate the Irish and break their spirit, the independence and loyalty of the Irish patriots. The boys ate up every word and never forgot their mother's pride in her homeland, nor her hatred for the British "nobility" who tried to destroy that homeland.

When Andrew was thirteen and Robert fourteen, they joined the Dragoons, a branch of the American Revolutionary Army, as mounted orderlies and errand boys. Jackson liked excitement, and the American cause appealed to him: Once again, a heroic and courageous people struggled against a British aristocracy. Unfortunately, the British captured both boys before long, and they were imprisoned in Camden, South Carolina. Their brother, Hugh, was already a casualty of the war.

Conditions in the prison were abysmal—the small, over-crowded space was overrun with filth and germs. Disease spread like fire and killed just as surely as British bullets. Both Robert and Andrew contracted smallpox. Few who caught the infection survived in the crowded and dirty prison. But Elizabeth was determined not to lose her sons, having lost her husband and eldest boy already. She arrived at the prison in Camden on a day when prisoners were being exchanged and successfully secured the release of the two boys.

Camden was forty miles from their home, and Elizabeth had brought two horses with her. Robert was by far the weaker of the two, so Elizabeth strapped him on one of the horses. Andrew insisted that his mother take the other horse, saying he felt strong enough to walk. Walk he did, the entire forty miles. Both Robert and Andrew survived the trip, but the strain had been great. Robert died two days after he arrived home. Elizabeth threw herself into nursing her last surviving son back to health, and Andrew slowly recovered.

Just as the end of Andrew's convalescence neared and life was returning to its normal pattern, Elizabeth heard the news that two of her relatives on a prison ship in Charleston were ill with cholera. She probably hesitated to leave her still-recuperating son, but Andrew was almost fully recovered, and the Irish are irresistibly pulled toward family. Two members of her family needed her help, and Elizabeth could not ignore them. She left Andrew in the care of relatives and set out for Charleston.

While on the ship, Elizabeth, her resistance to infection finally worn down, contracted cholera and died. Fourteen-year-old Andrew, now on his own in the world, received the news that his mother had died and was buried in an unmarked grave. Along with that message came her few possessions. He went to Charleston and searched for his mother's grave, to no avail. He had no monument, no marker to hang onto as a concrete symbol of his mother's life. What he did have, as he said much later, was "the memory of my mother and her teachings."[12]

Elizabeth's dream for Andrew was that he become a minister; she wanted him to have status and the respect of society. She and Andrew's father had emigrated so that their children would not be denied their chance for success. Andrew Jackson did not become a clergyman, but he did attain the status and success his mother desired for him. In fact, he probably accomplished more than Elizabeth would have dreamed possible.

Jackson entered the field of law and established a successful law practice in Tennessee. The child of the Carolina frontier became fairly well-to-do. In action reminiscent of his forebears', he used his modest wealth to buy land. Eventually, he was elected to represent Tennessee in the United States Senate. But Jackson made his reputation as commander of the Tennessee militia, for it was here that he kept the "Red Sticks"—the Upper Creek Indians—safely contained.

Jackson's distrust and dislike for the British flared again in 1812, when the United States and Britain once again went to war. The British had scored a coup by overrunning Washington, D.C., and burning all the public buildings, some to the ground. Jackson had already performed a valuable service by keeping the Indians at bay, thus preventing the British from having a powerful ally. But the British objective was now to capture New Orleans and encourage Louisiana and the surrounding gulf territory to secede from the United States to become a British satellite.

Jackson, now General Jackson, was at the forefront of the fight to stop the British. He remembered only too well his mother's tales of British atrocities and the deaths of his two brothers in the Revolutionary War. As the British headed toward New Orleans, it was Jackson's job to halt them in their tracks. The British contingent consisted of about five thousand men and fifty ships. Jackson had three thousand men and seven ships. Just after dawn on January 8, 1815, the Battle of New Orleans was underway. When it was ended, the British had lost their top three commanding officers, in addition to having suffered two thousand casualties. Thirteen of Jackson's men were killed, and about fifty wounded. The British withdrew.

As it turned out, the victory was a moral one. The peace accord had been signed days before, and the news had not reached New Orleans in time to stop the attack. But the victory was a popular final *coda* to the War of 1812, and Andrew Jackson had his own reasons for satisfaction. Later, when he remembered the battle, he recalled thinking of his mother when it was over: "How I wish she could have lived to see this day!"[13] He had exacted his small amount of revenge for what the British had done to his mother, his brothers, to the Irish people of whom Elizabeth had told him stories into the night.

Andrew Jackson was fast becoming a popular hero with the American people. He represented the hopes and desires of many, because he had achieved success through his own initiative and boldness, rather than his family background. He continued to augment his reputation as trouble heated up on the border of Florida, which was then a Spanish province. British traders were stirring up dissension, breeding rebellion among the Seminole Indians.

Jackson and the Tennessee militia charged over the border, tore down the Spanish flag, and captured and executed the two British traders who were causing all the unrest. The British press howled, calling Jackson a ruffian and a murderer, but the British government knew what the two "traders" had been up to, and reacted more mildly. The whole affair convinced Spain that its New World holdings were becoming a long-distance headache, and the Spanish sold their province to the United States for five million dollars.

Jackson was now a full-fledged hero, a good-looking man who had risen from a lowly background to educate himself, establish a profession, become a landowner, serve in the Senate, fight the Indians, and beat the British at their own game. He represented all that was right with America. The time was ripe in American politics for an infusion of fresh blood, and Andrew Jackson was just the man to provide it. He ran for president in 1824 and received more votes, both electoral and popular, than any of the other candidates. However, none of the four candidates won enough electoral votes to capture the presidency, so the election was turned over to the House of Representatives, as the Constitution dictates.

After a great deal of wheeling and dealing, John Quincy Adams was elected, amidst cries of "foul!" from the Jackson camp. Feeling outmaneuvered and robbed, his Irish temper now ignited, Jackson set his sights on 1828. Another Irishman, John F. Kennedy, when in a similar situation, spoke for Jackson's reaction also: "Don't get mad; get even." Jackson wanted to "get even" in 1828.

The election of 1828 was the first truly dirty campaign in the United States. Mud was slung freely on both sides, and neither Jackson nor John Quincy Adams escaped. There was no burning public issue at the time, so personalities became the barometer of public opinion. The Jackson camp accused Adams of bringing gambling to the White House, because he had furnished it (at his own expense) with a billiard table and chess set. Adams was further denounced as a pimp for the Russian czar, because while a diplomat in the United States, he had introduced the czar to a chambermaid.

The Adams camp was also busy. While their candidate was being attacked, they circulated handbills accusing General Jackson of coldbloodedly executing six of his own men. They dug up information that Jackson's wife, Rachel, had not been properly divorced from her first husband when she married Jackson. It had been an honest error that the couple had rectified, but the Adams press decried Rachel as an adultress, unfit for the company of society, much less the White House. Jackson was pained and angered by these attacks, which were undermining his beloved wife's health, but the worst was yet to come.

When Jackson read in the press that his mother, Elizabeth Hutchinson, was "a common prostitute brought to this country by British soldiers," that she "afterward married a mulatto man with whom she had several children, of which General Jackson was one,"[14] he wept. He thought of his mother, who had worked so hard and gained so little. He did not even have a monument for her, had not been able to give her a proper burial. All he had was his memory of her life and character, and now that was being splashed across newspapers, twisted and filled with lies. It was at that moment that Jackson knew that he had to win the election. She would never know it, but Elizabeth's son would be president of the United States.

Jackson did win the election of 1828, and the election of 1832. To the horror of Jeffersonian Republicans, he brought sweeping changes to the operation and character of the United States government. In retrospect, many changes wrought under "Old Hickory" had unfortunate consequences. Politics was no longer the exclusive arena for educated, aristocratic men, and the "new breed" of politician may have been a much-needed infusion of fresh blood. But with that fresh blood came some degrading and vulgar practices: the appointments of incompetent, corrupt men to political office, the herding of drunks and illiterate immigrants to vote for a chosen candidate, and the establishment of the spoils system, whereby a newly elected official appoints cronies and allies to government positions, using the civil service to repay public debts.

Jackson himself was not directly responsible for much of the corruption surrounding him. He was a man of honor, and he did not sink to the low levels of some of his contemporaries. However, he did allow, and even condone, the spoils system. His reasons were probably personal and instinctive; he had learned very early that a man should "look out for his own." His mother had believed in "family first," and her life had echoed that conviction. When Jackson was elected president, he believed that any man of average intellect and common sense could handle a government position, so it was just as well to "take care of" his friends. The unfortunate results are apparent even today: a steady turnover in the government, making consistent policy nearly impossible, and a lack of job security in appointed positions, leading to inefficiency and low production.

Jackson was perhaps a better man than politician, but his administration did open the government to all Americans. Only under Jackson did the United States truly become a democracy, embracing men of all social and intellectual classes. The poor and the "common folk" worshipped Jackson, not so much because of what he accomplished as for what he symbolized. He proved that a man can rise to the country's highest office simply by virtue of his own ability and character. Jackson himself was a lonely man. He desperately missed his wife, who died soon after the election of 1828, her health and happiness destroyed by all the adverse campaign publicity. Jackson never got over Rachel's death. But like his mother, he survived.

Elizabeth Hutchinson's grave was never found. But Andrew Jackson, her only surviving son, made his life a fitting monument to her memory.

CHAPTER THREE

MOTHERS OF A HOUSE DIVIDED

Americans in 1860 believed that they lived in the best of all worlds. Their young country was prospering, and most people lived on farms or in very small towns. A man could live on his own piece of land, or learn a trade that would earn a good wage. Life was good.

But only the most resolute could ignore the rumbles of trouble, of change approaching. As the United States developed, so did regional tensions, especially between North and South. Those tensions were reaching fever pitch and would soon become irreconcilable. The reasoned approach had not resolved sectional differences, for the issues of contention—slavery, but more important, a state's right to govern itself—were not simply rational issues, but emotional ones as well.

War is a notoriously unlucky way to resolve conflict. Not only does war often fail to solve the original problem, it usually creates new and even thornier ones for the future. Nevertheless, war is what men most often resort to, and Americans in 1861 were no different. With all attempts at compromise exhausted, the United States embarked upon the most devastating and destructive war in its history.

The Civil War was fought by boys. When it was over, the United States had lost more young men, proportionate to its population, than France did in World War I—200,000 killed in battle and 400,000 felled by disease. From the distance of over a century, it is too easy to gloss over the horror of Americans killing Americans. Foreign enemies often serve to unite a nation, but here the enemies were fellow countrymen, and such a war can only divide. Though vastly outnumbered, the South had great emotional fervor, for it believed itself to be fighting for the rights to which the founding fathers had devoted their lives: the rights to freedom and self-government. The central issue of the Civil War was not slavery. The slavery question was a symptom of a far deeper division. In seceding from the Union, the Southern states were declaring their right to self-determination. In declaring war, the North was declaring its conviction that the preservation of the Union must take precedence over all regional issues.

Unlike the Revolutionary War, the hostilities with Mexico, even the War of 1812, the Civil War was the first all-out war that Americans fought. It was the first war that involved total commitment on both sides, in both financial and emotional terms. The Civil War was also the first modern war; it inspired new technology, sophisticated weapons, advances in transportation and industry. For the duration of the war, what had been the United States of America was virtually divided into two separate and hostile countries. Had there been no war, or had the North lost, there would be no United States today. There would exist instead a series of small nations with many territorial squabbles and little prosperity. But there was a war, and the North was the victor. By the time the last shot had been fired, the serene agrarian nation that America had been was a fact of history.

The new technology created by the war promoted mechanization of farms and factories. Industry boomed in the North, and the sleepy farm town became the exception rather than the rule. With men involved in killing one another, women found themselves in new positions of power and productivity, and having found new freedom, they demanded more recognition. Avenues previously closed were now open to them, as they took on jobs in industry, went to college, became nurses and social workers. Women were not the only emerging social class created by the war. The slaves were freed, unleashing a wave of unemployed men and women who now demanded their share of the American dream.

The final scene of the Civil War took place in the tiny village of Appomattox Court House on April 9, 1865. But the war did not end with the firing of the last shot. The North won the war, but the issues that divided North and South did not "pack up their tents and steal away" when the hostilities officially ceased. The conflicts that led to the war—questions of states' rights, of federal power, of individual autonomy and human rights—are still very much alive today. More than a century after the end of the war, there are still deep scars, psychological divisions between North and South. It would be impossible to make sense of American history without some understanding of its bloodiest and most divisive conflict. The facts about the war—its battles, number killed and wounded—are available in any United States history text. But perhaps the best way to gain insight into this drama from America's past is to look at the men who played major roles—and at their mothers.

ABRAHAM LINCOLN

What do most people think of when they hear the name "Abraham Lincoln"? An image usually comes to mind immediately—that of a tall, spare, bearded man in a stovepipe hat and a black suit. What of the man behind the image? For most Americans, Abraham Lincoln has evolved into the very symbol of integrity and dignity. He is, for them, the embodiment of those words, "liberty and justice for all." Abraham Lincoln is the man who freed the slaves, who rose from a humble birth to become one of this country's greatest presidents, the man who won the Civil War. When such an aura of myth springs up around a historical figure, it is sometimes difficult to find the facts. But scholars and historians have found in Lincoln a treasure trove of material, both factual and mythological. The man fascinates simply because he is fascinating. And although they are false, the myths retain their power, because they do reveal truths about this enigmatic and charismatic man.

It is popular lore that Lincoln was born in a log cabin and raised in abject poverty. Lincoln himself would have disputed this. Thomas Lincoln, Abraham's father, was a respected and industrious member of his community, and the Lincolns were not poor. Measured against today's standards, their possessions were meager, but in the America of the nineteenth century, the Lincolns could hold their heads high. A carpenter and cabinetmaker, Thomas was a skilled craftsman, and the much-discussed "log cabin" was in fact comparable to the other homes in the community—it was the "suburban tract home" of the nineteenth century.

Abraham Lincoln, born February 12, 1809, was Nancy Hanks Lincoln's second child and her only son. Her son was not a demonstrative child; he did not readily give or show affection. His curious reticence is evidenced in Lincoln's later descriptions of Nancy. He remembered her as a "woman with withered features" and "wrinkles," "a want of teeth," and in general a "weather-beaten appearance."[1] At another time, though, he admitted that it was Nancy who taught him his letters. Nancy could read, but she could not write. Nevertheless, she made certain that Abraham knew the alphabet by the time he was five and could read when he was eight. She read to him regularly, invariably from the Bible. When that seemed a little dry, Nancy would close the book and improvise, telling Abraham the same stories in colorful but simple terms. Abraham was profoundly impressed by those tales, and he credited them with the formation of his own moral character.

It is possible that Abraham was close-mouthed on memories of Nancy because she died when he was only nine years old. Although Nancy was just thirty-five and reasonably healthy, she succumbed to "milk-sick," an epidemic that swept the community whenever the cows ate snakeroot, which poisoned their milk. There was no cure for the disease, so Nancy knew as soon as she saw the telltale milky coating on her tongue that she was going to die. She tried to prepare her children by telling them that she was going to leave them soon, but Sarah and Abraham were too young to grasp the import of their mother's words.

When Nancy died, Thomas built her a coffin, but until the coffin was finished, her body lay in the same room in which Thomas and the two children slept and ate their meals. When she was finally laid to rest there was no ceremony, because no minister was in the area at the time. She was buried in an unmarked grave, and Lincoln never bothered to place a monument there himself.

Twelve-year-old Sarah, Lincoln's sister, tried as best she could to keep up with the housekeeping and the cooking, but it was an overwhelming task for a child. Thomas felt that his children needed a mother to care for them. He remarried just fourteen months after his first wife's death. Sarah Bush Johnston, known simply as Sally, had also lost her first spouse through death. When Sally moved into the Lincoln household, she brought three children—aged twelve, eight, and five—a small dowry, all her possessions, and some much-needed warmth and joy.

Sally Lincoln was by nature affectionate and cheerful, and she loved her two stepchildren spontaneously. When she realized that Abraham was a very bright child, she wanted him to attend school regularly, but it was not financially possible. There were no public schools in Indiana, where the Lincolns lived. A student who wanted to learn had to hire the teacher and pay a fee. The family did not have enough money to pay a teacher regularly, and so Lincoln had less than one year of formal education.

Sally could not stand to see such a good mind atrophy for want of money. She noticed that Abraham picked up knowledge easily and retained it thoroughly. She saw him grasp difficult problems quickly and penetrate to the heart of questions and knew that Abraham was a child of intellect and insight. She encouraged Abraham's desire to learn and study and helped him whenever she could. Lincoln later credited Sally for her encouragement, but resented the fact that his own father did not help him reach beyond his limited environment. The best Sally could do was persuade Thomas to keep from disturbing Abraham when he was reading.

Abraham left home when he was about twenty-one years old and got a job as a store clerk in New Salem, Illinois. The work was mindless, but it paid a living wage and allowed Lincoln to study and read in the evenings. His interest in history increased as his knowledge grew, and Lincoln found himself fascinated with the dynamics of American government. Eventually, he decided to get some first-hand experience in politics and ran for the state legislature. What Lincoln learned was that he still had a great deal to learn about campaigning. He finished eighth out of thirteen candidates. It was back to the less fickle world of business.

However, Lincoln had enjoyed that small taste of politics, and its intrigue did not lessen with time. He left the business world and became postmaster of New Salem. Eventually, he ran for the legislature again. This time Lincoln won. His seat on the state legislature convinced him that if he wanted to move into bigger political circles, he needed more than his eclectic but spotty self-education. Lincoln began a systematic study of law. He did not enter a prestigious law school; he learned the law simply by reading it. The quick mind and sharp perception that Sally had seen so early was still there. Abraham passed the bar at the age of twenty-seven, having had no formal legal training.

Abraham Lincoln was an outstanding lawyer, adept and quick-witted. As a boy, he had been unable to express emotion or let his needs be known. As a man, this inability became an advantage, as Lincoln was able to dismiss the personal and focus on the broader context, the bigger picture. Lincoln never got bogged down in trivial concerns, the downfall of so many statesmen, and his ability to disregard the personal and see the wider perspective of history would play a crucial role in both his own development and the fate of the country.

The lessons that Lincoln had learned by working with the intricacies of the legal system had made him a more confident and able public speaker. Law shares some characteristics with politics. Both require the ability to think quickly, to grasp the essentials of an argument, to sway people with both reason and sentiment. Lincoln enjoyed his life as a lawyer, but it had always been a means rather than an end. His heart remained in statecraft. He ran for the House of Representatives and won. This was the life he wanted, and he pursued it with single-minded determination. The aristocratic families in Illinois found this tall, taciturn congressman fascinating, and Lincoln was received in many of the "best" homes. Eventually, he married Mary Todd, a relative of one of these elite families. He was on his way.

It was during this period that Lincoln became particularly disenchanted with his own background. He was ashamed of his mother because of her suspected illegitimacy and resented his father deeply. Lincoln had never been open in his affection for either parent, but now whatever love he did feel was swallowed in recrimination and old sorrows. Thomas, he felt, had never encouraged him in his desire to learn, nor helped him in any way to get an education. Nancy had left him when he was too young to comprehend her reasons for leaving. Lincoln did not even allow himself to feel anger toward his parents. He simply distanced himself emotionally until he felt nothing at all.

When Thomas Lincoln was dying, Abraham's step-brother, John Johnston, wrote to him and told him that their father wanted to see Abraham before he died. Thomas was by then a broken man. He had lost properties and most of his possessions. But Lincoln was not moved. He wrote back to his brother that since he had nothing to say to Thomas, he saw no point in making the trip. Thomas died without seeing Abraham, and Abraham did not attend his father's funeral.

Sally Lincoln was another story. Despite the fact that he was not tied to Sally by any bonds of blood, Abraham had more loyalty to Sally than to either of his biological parents. He never forgot her efforts to see that he was educated, and although he rarely displayed open affection for his stepmother, he welcomed and was grateful for her steady love for him. Lincoln tried to keep watch over her affairs even though he was usually away and seldom visited her.

Thomas had left only a small inheritance, but Lincoln tried to ensure that even that small sum would not be wasted by his shiftless stepbrother, John Johnston, who wanted to sell the family farm and move to Missouri. Lincoln's concern for Sally is clear in his reply to Johnston's request:

> *. . . you are lazy, because you have not bothered to even put in a crop, because you "have* idled *away all your time." . . . The Eastern 40 acres I intend to keep for mother while she lives—if you* will not cultivate it; *it will rent for enough to support her—at least it will rent for something.*[2]

Lincoln had called Sally "mother" since he was nine years old, and he considered her more a parent to him than either of his natural parents. As he rose to national prominence in American politics, he saw her less often, but he never distanced himself completely, as he did with his father, seeing to it that she had sufficient money and concerning himself with her well-being. After he was elected to the United States presidency in 1860, he finally went to visit her on his way to Washington.

Lincoln had seen little of Sally in thirty years, and he was shocked at the change in her appearance. The cheery, efficient woman of his youth had withered into an old, wrinkled, and fragile woman. But she still embraced her reticent stepson with vigor and gave him her love with no expectation of demonstrated affection in return. She realized that Abraham expressed his emotions differently, that he found his outlet in broad sweeping issues rather than personal relationships. Nevertheless, when Abraham left Sally for the inauguration in Washington, he hugged her. That was the last time Sally and Abraham were together.

Abraham Lincoln was sworn in as president of the United States on March 4, 1861—a cold, bleak, windy day. The country was edging into civil war, and few people had faith in the spare, solemn man with the squeaky voice who was promising to "up-hold, protect, and defend the Constitution of the United States." But Lincoln had a deep and abiding confidence in his own abilities and in his mission to preserve the Union and its Constitution.

It was not long before Lincoln had to deliver on the promises he made in his inaugural address. At 4:30 A.M. on the 12th of April in 1861, militia men in the seceded state of South Carolina fired on the Union soldiers at Fort Sumter, and the war between the States was underway. For Lincoln, the war had one purpose. As a boy, Abraham had fallen in love with the dignity and vision of men like Washington, Jefferson, and Adams, and he took it as his task to keep intact the Union they had fought to establish. To them, and to him, the Union had come to represent the world's best hope for freedom, dignity, and life. As a student of history, Lincoln had come to believe that destruction of the Union would deal a fatal blow to human rights everywhere on earth.

When he took office as president, Lincoln did not have the stature of the former presidents he so admired, but he had more than his measure of greatness by the time his tenure came to an abrupt halt. His self-confidence never deserted him; nor did the solemn reserve he had had since he was a boy. His refusal to get involved in matters of personal emotion served the country well, for Lincoln did not allow the war to become merely a fight over the emotionally charged issue of slavery. Lincoln did not condone slavery, but he did not consider abolition the focal cause for which the North was fighting. He rose above the regionalism and divisiveness of the slavery question, to keep preservation of the Union at the forefront of Northerners' hearts and minds.

It was his self-confidence, combined with his unwavering dedication to the task of keeping the Union intact that led Lincoln to use the executive power freely, even recklessly, to the point of violating the Constitution at times. During the Civil War, Lincoln had opponents of the war arrested and often suspended their right to trial; over 13,000 Americans were deprived of their constitutional rights. Lincoln felt that he had to sacrifice parts of the Constitution for a while, in order to preserve the whole. When a man is drowning, he believed, you save his life first even if you break his arm dragging him to shore.

Sally was alive during all this tumult, but she was too

infirm to comprehend the significance of events around her. She did not really understand all the issues; in fact, the horizons of her world had shrunk to the basic daily battle to survive. Abraham did not forget Sally. He sent money for her care, and inquired as often as he could about her health. But Sally received little of the money Lincoln sent her. Most of it ended up in relatives' pockets, and Sally never had the clothes and shoes Abraham directed them to buy for her. The importance of her stepson's role in American history was lost for her, but Sally knew enough to be proud of Abraham. She cried like a child whenever someone mentioned his name to her, and she cried again when he was shot to death by an assassin in 1865.

Many cried with her that day, for with that bullet the world lost one of its greatest leaders and orators. Sally did not cry, however, for the loss of the man who won the Civil War, who preserved the Union and freed the slaves. She cried for the boy who looked so forlorn when he was nine years old and she came to stay, who worked so hard all day and studied so long, far into the night, who had overcome his dislike of displaying affection on a chilly day in 1861 and hugged her fiercely before he left for his inauguration in Washington.

ULYSSES S. GRANT

When Confederate soldiers attacked Fort Sumter in April 1861, their gunshots marked the beginning of the Civil War. At that time Ulysses S. Grant was living in Galena, Illinois, working as a clerk in his father's leather goods store, having been forced to resign from the United States Army under a cloud of rumored drunkenness, and having already failed at farming and business. His life up to that point had been one failure followed by another. He was fit for nothing, respected by no one except his own wife. The outbreak of fighting changed all that, for Grant found his gift and his calling: military leadership. He headed a group of volunteers in the Union Army.

By the time the war was over, Ulysses Grant was a hero, going from there to serving two terms as president of the United States. The Union may well not have won the Civil War without

Grant, and Grant would have lived out a life of humiliation and petty failure had the Civil War not occurred when it did. What sort of man was this flinty, hard-drinking, wily general who made history and used the tide of history to make himself?

Grant was born in Point Pleasant, Ohio, on April 27, 1822, the child of Jesse and Hannah Simpson Grant. Very little is known about his early years, but the few incidents that Grant did later recount are broad brushstrokes that suggest a portrait. Jesse Grant made an adequate living as the owner of a tannery and as a now-and-then politician—at one point, he served as mayor of Bethel, Ohio, and later was appointed postmaster in Covington, Kentucky.

Jesse was a boastful and opinionated man who was used to ordering people around. He treated his wife much as he treated his employees, and Hannah had no recourse but to follow his will. One month after her son was born, the family had a cere-mony to select the baby's name. Each invited relative wrote his or her favorite name on a piece of paper, and the papers were read and discussed. Hannah wanted to name the baby Albert. Her father liked the name Hiram, and Jesse favored Ulysses. The baby was named Hiram Ulysses, an indication of how much sway Hannah's opinion had over family matters.

Grant had five brothers and sisters. Hannah's main func-tion in the Grant household was childbearing, but her lack of any other power did not bother her. Whatever Jesse did not control, Hannah believed, was in the hands of God. She saw the direct will of God in every event, from the birth of a healthy child to whether it rained on washday. When Ulysses was three years old, he toddled off to the stable to play. A neighbor watched him sit down directly under the hoofs of one of the horses and shouted a warning to Hannah. She was unperturbed, telling the neighbor that the baby could take care of himself, and if he could not, well, that was the will of God.

Hannah was not a demonstrative mother, but her lack of affection did not seem to bother Grant, probably because his character was similar to hers. When Grant was a young man, he coolly informed his father that he could not work at the tannery, because he could not stand the sight of blood. Jesse responded by securing an appointment for his son to West Point. The irony of preparing Ulysses, who sickened at the sight of blood, for a career in the army was apparently lost on Jesse Grant.

When Grant left for West Point, his trunk was marked with his initials: H.U.G. When he noticed this, Grant was embarrassed, fearing that the others would make fun of him and label him a sissy. To prevent this, he reversed the letters and became U. H. Grant. When he arrived at West Point, his registration form had dropped the Hiram completely, listing him as Ulysses Simpson Grant. Hannah's opinion had counted for nothing when Grant had been christened; ironic, then, that he should end up with Hannah's maiden name as his own.

Grant missed his mother while at West Point, writing to her that he felt alone in the world without her. He promised that if any honors should ever be his, he would share them with her. Though Grant's sentiments were laudable, his career at West Point was undistinguished.

Grant's first military experience was in the Mexican War, and he performed adequately. However, when the war ended, his sense of purpose disappeared and he turned to alcohol. In 1854 he was forced to resign his commission to avoid court-martial on charges of drunkenness. He tried his hand at farming and failed. He tried real estate and failed. Thus did the outbreak of the Civil War find him clerking in his father's store at the age of thirty-nine.

Grant found his calling in the war. He was a brilliant strategist and clever tactician. With the exception of Grant, the Union Army was plagued with incompetent generals, and President Lincoln was lucky to find in Grant a man with an overall scheme of the war, a man who knew how to disregard the pomp and circumstance surrounding a battle and concentrate only on winning. Grant disliked the trappings of war and often ignored military routine, but he knew what was necessary for the Union to win the war, and he was willing to do it.

One distinct advantage the Union had was manpower. As the war dragged through its second, then its third year, Grant showed that he was more than a clever strategist. He had the single-mindedness to persist against heavy odds, to attack when other generals would surrender or retreat. More important, he had the respect of the men he commanded, for they followed him into battles where their odds for survival were bleak.

The loss of human life in Grant's regiments was staggering. He was willing to use his greater manpower as an advantage, which meant fighting a war of attrition, eventually exhausting and overwhelming the South with a new soldier for every one that fell. The boy who had sickened at the mere sight of blood in his father's tannery was now willing to let a massive amount of blood be shed for the Union cause. Grant was unlike other generals in his persistence; he was also unique in his insistence that at battle's end, the wounded on both sides be carried to first-aid stations. It was common practice at the time to leave the wounded to die in the fields.

The Eastern press despised Grant and lambasted him regularly as a drunkard and an ignoramus. But Lincoln respected Grant and refused to hear the clamor to remove him from command. In March of 1864 Lincoln appointed him general-in-chief of the Union Army and invited him to Washington. Grant detested the political atmosphere of the Capitol, but he wanted to meet his commander-in-chief and so went and accepted his commission.

Eventually, the South had to succumb to its overwhelming losses and desertions. Surrounded and starving, the Confederate Army, led by General Robert E. Lee, surrendered at Appomattox Court House to General Grant's army on April 9, 1865. Grant was as magnanimous in victory as he was hard-hearted in battle. When the two men met, he treated General Lee with respect and dignity. The surrender terms, written out by Grant himself, were generous. Grant never forgot, as so many other Union officers did, that the defeated enemies were also countrymen and brothers. His first action after the surrender was signed was to rush Union rations to the starving Confederate soldiers, and he refused to consider a colleague's suggestion that Lee and the rest of the Confederate generals be arrested as conspirators.

General Grant was the conquering hero of the Civil War, the first four-star general in American history. After the official surrender, he returned to his family's home. Upon seeing her son, the ever-unemotional Hannah said, "Well, Ulysses, you've become quite a great man, haven't you?" and with that returned to her housework.[3]

After Lincoln's assassination, Andrew Johnson became president, and the kindest thing to be said of his administration was that it was mediocre. In 1868, both parties wanted as their nominee a popular, strong, charismatic man. Both parties wooed General Grant, a respected national hero. Grant accepted the Republican offer and was elected. Grant invited his family to the inauguration but wrote and told them that his house would be full. Hannah wanted very much to see her son sworn in, and Jesse wrote and asked if some arrangements could be made to accommodate her. As Grant saw it, however, a full house was a full house.

When Jesse arrived in Washington, Hannah was not with him. When reporters asked him where she was, he replied that Hannah had refused to come. When Ulysses S. Grant took the oath of office, he was surrounded by his wife and children, his father, and his in-laws. No one knows if he missed his mother, or if he thought of his promise at West Point to share his every honor with her.

Unfortunately for the country, Grant's consummate skill as a general did not carry over into his presidency. The simple and taciturn character that had served him so well in battle hurt him as a politician. Grant was the last professional soldier elected president until Dwight D. Eisenhower in 1952, and if Grant's two terms in office proved anything, it was that good generals can make bad presidents.

Any similarities between a battlefield and the arena of politics is superficial, as President Grant soon discovered. He chose his cabinet as he would have chosen his military staff and ended up with yes-men and corruptible businessmen rather than statesmen. Grant knew virtually nothing about government, and his ignorance, combined with a weak administration, resulted in a puppet government run by special-interest groups and dishonest party politicians.

From the day of her son's inauguration, Hannah kept her thoughts to herself. She would not say a word about Grant, good or ill, though she had ample opportunity. An aura of mystery eventually developed around the president's mother, and a reporter decided to try to break Hannah's silence. On the pretext of asking her to verify a picture of Grant, the reporter succeeded in getting Hannah to open the door of her home. But he had underestimated Hannah's ability to remain silent if she wanted to. When the reporter attempted to dig information out of her, Hannah drew her slender figure erect and fixed him with a stern glare. The reporter got nothing for his trouble except a few curt monosyllabic responses to questions. Hannah lived to see her son step down after two terms as president, but she died too soon to see him fail once again as a provider and a businessman. She died in 1883 at the age of eighty-four.

Former presidents were not provided with pensions at that time, and so Ulysses was forced to try his hand once again at business, with no more luck than he had had fifteen years before. Grant had been an incompetent president, and now he was an incompetent businessman. The investment firm he started went bankrupt, and Grant had no way to support his family. Just when the debts were piling high, he discovered he had cancer of the throat. Grant's persistence, first evident when he was a general, continued. In order to pay his bills and leave his family with some money, he wrote a book detailing his version of the Civil War, fighting the intense pain of his disease as he had fought the Confederate Army. Grant died on July 19, 1885. The book's final chapter had been completed four days earlier. He had won his final battle of attrition.

ROBERT E. LEE

War is a tragedy that creates both heroes and villains. Usually, the winning side boasts of the heroes, whereas the losers become the villains. The winners write up the accounts, and as Napoleon once remarked, "God is on the side of the strongest battalion." But there are exceptions to this general rule. There are men who command respect and affection for their nobility and allegiance, even if it is to the "wrong side." One such man was Robert E. Lee. The brilliant general who led the Confederate troops against the Union Army stands as tall in history as he did in life. His cause was a losing one, but that only serves to make his loyalty and dignity more bittersweet. President Lincoln said, upon seeing a picture of Lee after the war had ended, "It is a good face. I'm glad the war is over at last."[4]

Robert E. Lee was a man who belived that duty mattered before all else. But duty did not signify to him a leaden, unwilling "ought." The word was as simple as trust, as important as loyalty, as natural as affection. Lee believed it was the ability to make commitments and honor them that raised men above beasts, and he realized that his life was his commitment, or it was nothing. For this reason, Lee is often taken as a symbol of the Southern gentleman, of the way of life that created such men, a way of life that took its final bow at Appomattox.

Anne Carter Lee would have been proud of her son. His defeat would have mattered to her far less than the dignity with which he bore it. Anne understood that human beings cannot always control what happens, but she knew that they can always control their reactions to what happens. It is there that gentlemen are made or broken, and Anne's son was a gentleman to the last.

Robert was Anne's youngest son. When Anne discovered she was pregnant with Robert, she felt no joy. Her husband was already deeply in debt, and another baby, she feared, would only add to the burden. Anne's father, Charles Carter, had warned her before she married that her future husband was financially inept, but like many strong-willed young ladies, Anne listened to her heart rather than her parent.

Anne had grown up in an atmosphere of wealth and ease. Charles Carter was one of the richest men in Virginia, the owner of 25,000 acres and thousands of slaves. Charles was as rich in family as he was in land—his two wives bore him twenty-three children, enough so that the family had its own school on the Carter estate.

Anne was only twenty when a handsome man named Lighthorse Harry Lee swept into her life. Anne loved Lighthorse Harry; he was gallant and charming. Furthermore, he was a distinguished patriot, a commander in the Revolutionary War and a favorite of George Washington's. It was common knowledge in

Virginia that at Washington's funeral, the dashing Commander Lee had spoken the eloquent words, "First in war, first in peace, first in the hearts of his countrymen."

Still, Harry was seventeen years older than Anne, a widower with two children. Worse, he had already squandered his first wife's estate, despite the fact that she had known Harry well enough to bypass him in her will and leave everything to her two children. In addition to his wartime heroics, Harry had served on the Virginia legislature and as that state's governor, but he was a financial incompetent. Everyone knew it and had doubts about Harry as a result. Everyone, that is, except Anne.

On Harry and Anne's wedding day, Harry was hopelessly in debt, his career in a state of collapse. But in marrying this beautiful girl, Harry believed that the wealth and fortune Anne lived in would somehow rub off on him. Likewise, Anne had lived with wealth for so long that she could not believe she would ever need for anything. Unfortunately, both of them were wrong.

Anne and Harry's first child died at the age of fifteen months, but she had another baby nine months later, and one every two years after that. Harry's financial luck did not improve, and the family teetered on the edge of bankruptcy. Thus it was that when Anne, by now thirty, discovered that she was to have her fifth child, she was not happy. The girl who had wanted for nothing now lived with worry, fearing that Harry would end up in debtor's prison and she and the children would be alone.

At that time, the family was living on an estate in Virginia that Harry's first wife had left to her son. It was a beautiful home, but it was a temporary solution, and both Harry and Anne knew it. They had already sold the furnishings, right down to the paintings off the walls. When Charles Carter died, Harry had some hope of reprieve, but Charles's will dashed that hope. Harry could not touch the money in the Carter estate, and there was nothing Anne could do about it.

When her fifth child was born, Anne named him Robert. Despite her misgivings about having any more children, Robert was her favorite child, a source of contentment and pleasure in her increasingly worry-fraught world. When Robert was two years old, Anne's fear came to pass: Harry was sentenced to one year in debtor's prison. When he was released, the family moved to Alexandria and lived as close to the bone as possible. Anne was determined that none of her children would grow up to be as irresponsible as Harry, and she labored to instill in each of them the powers of self-control, economy, and self-denial.

When Robert was five, Harry got into trouble again. Convinced that another war with England was foolishness, he opposed the War of 1812 and was hurt in the Baltimore riot against the war. To avoid reprisal for his role in the riot, Lee petitioned President James Monroe to send him out of the country. His request was granted, and in 1813 Harry fled to Barbados. Anne and the children never saw Harry again. He wrote to his family often while he moved from island to island, but Anne seldom replied. Five years after he had left them, Harry decided to return to his family and his responsibilities, but he died before he reached Virginia.

Anne had never been physically strong and the five years of Harry's absence had been especially debilitating and trying. After five pregnancies and constant worry, Harry's abandonment was too much. By the time Harry died, Anne was an invalid, confined to her bed. Robert, the child she had welcomed the least, was now the one she treasured the most. Robert cared for her and loved her and made her feel less alone. He was a dutiful son, not because he had to be, but because he realized that duty is part of love.

Anne did not let the failure of her marriage destroy her. She concentrated her energies on raising her children with love and dedication, and her youngest son is testament to her success. She needed Robert as much as he had once needed her, but she did not let need become an obstacle to her son's success. When Robert was eighteen, he left for West Point, with Anne's blessings and encouragement. Her enthusiasm masked her fear of life without him; she wrote to a friend, "You know what I lost? He is son, daughter, and everything to me."[5]

Lee returned home each summer to be with Anne and care for her. Her health was failing, and when he graduated from West Point, second in his class, Anne was on her deathbed. Lee went to her side as soon as the ceremonies ended, and he cared for her until she died soon after. Anne was only fifty-six when she died, but she considered her life well spent. She had married for love, and even desertion did not make her regret the failure of her marriage. She had given her heart to her children, and in Robert she saw her hard work bear fruit. She died knowing that he would grow into a strong and able man.

Anne was right. Robert E. Lee set a standard of nobility that has seldom been met in American history. When the Civil War broke out, Lee thought that the Union's dissolution would be a disaster, a tragedy. But he did not think that weapons and threats would ever keep the states united. His loyalty to Virginia, his home and the home of his family, led him to join the Southern cause and lead the Confederate army against the North. His fight was not for secession, of which he disapproved. It was not for slavery; Lee had emancipated his own slaves. Lee was fighting for a way of life that the South symbolized for him, a way of life that included respect, dignity, and honor.

The union generals liked and admired their adversary. General Grant had fought alongside Lee in the Mexican War and knew that he was an excellent general, a clever strategist, and a natural leader. When his men were starving, Lee starved alongside them. When the only fare day after day was cabbage, Lee refused his privilege of eating meat and ate cabbage. He was renowned for his courtesy, even to those who failed him. But loyalty and courage alone do not win wars; troops and weapons do. Eventually, the North's advantage in both proved to be too great, and Lee was forced to surrender. Historians record that few eyes were dry at the sight of General Lee, in full dress uniform, as he rode to meet General Grant and acknowledge defeat. But Lee had learned an important lesson from the example of his mother: He could not control what had happened, but he could control how he reacted to it. Lee's reaction to the defeat of his beloved South stands in American history as a paradigm of dignity, valor, and honor. The United States can be proud to call him a citizen, as Anne Carter Lee was proud to call him her son.

JOHN WILKES BOOTH

The writers of history books usually try to be neutral in their attitudes, to present both sides of a situation to their reader and let that reader come to his own judgment of events. Sometimes, however, even the best historians are faced with an event that rules out neutrality, a situation in which objectivity seems obscene, if not impossible. One such event in American history was the assassination of Abraham Lincoln. Faced with the specter of John Wilkes Booth's senseless and devastating act, even the finest historians put aside rationality and neutrality. Witness Samuel Eliot Morison's words in an otherwise straightforward college text: "10,000 curses on the memory of that foulest of assassins, John Wilkes Booth!"[6] or, again, this passage from a noted Civil War historian, Bruce Catton's *The Civil War:* " . . . he [Booth] conspired with a weird group of dimwitted incompetents who could hardly have carried out a plan to rob the corner newsstand."[7] Clearly, Booth is a man who inspires even the coolest, most reasonable minds to hatred and despair.

No one will deny that John Wilkes Booth changed the course of events, to the detriment of the South and of the nation, when he shot Abraham Lincoln in Ford's Theater on April 14, 1865. But Booth believed that he would be welcomed as a hero in the South. He never realized that Lincoln's murder would unleash forces of hatred and vengeance that would do damage to the South and its people as great as that in any battle. Booth has been variously described as a "crack brain," "insane," "perverted," "twisted," "inadequate," and a "coward." If Booth was insane, he came by it honestly—his father, Junius Booth, was given to bouts of madness.

Like all his sons—Junius Jr., Edwin, and John—Junius Brutus Booth was an actor. Junius was a genius at his craft, a talented and acclaimed professional. It was during an engagement with the Shakespearean Acting Company that Junius met Adelaide, the woman who would become his first wife. It was common practice at that time for actors on tour to board in the homes of willing townspeople, and when Junius left the home of Adelaide's mother to return to London, he took the daughter with him. Adelaide wrote to her mother and told her that she had been married by a curate, in 1815, and promised her mother that she and Junius would be married again by a Catholic priest as soon as they had the money. That promise was never fulfilled.

In 1819 Junius and Adelaide had a son and named him

Richard. Junius' career was skyrocketing; his acting received consistent critical acclaim, and he was the toast of London. His life settled into an agreeable and altogether pleasing pattern that lasted about seven years. Then, as he walked out of the theater at Covent Garden one night after a performance, he spotted a beautiful young girl selling flowers. Booth was enchanted. He walked over and spoke with her, finding out that her name was Mary Ann Holmes and that she was eighteen years old.

Mary Ann and Junius, the lovely flower girl and the flamboyant actor, started seeing each other every night after Booth's performance. When the company's run at Covent Garden closed, Junius told Adelaide he was scheduled for another tour and took Mary Ann to France. He returned home to Adelaide long enough to circumvent suspicion and then set off with Mary Ann on another "tour"—this time of the West Indies. It was there that Mary Ann told Junius that she was pregnant. Junius knew that he had to make some plans, for Mary Ann could no longer continue to sell flowers on the street. He booked passage for both of them on a ship bound for America.

Once in the United States, Junius leased a farm in Maryland for Mary Ann and stayed with her until the baby—a boy— was born. He wrote occasionally to Adelaide, assuring her that he would soon be returning and sending her money. Meanwhile, he was touring the United States with a company and playing to packed houses wherever he appeared. Booth wanted no one—no reporters, no colleagues, certainly not his wife—to know of his involvement with Mary Ann, and the strenuous efforts of a double life began to take its toll. Mary Ann got pregnant again and had another baby. Booth began to drink heavily. But American audiences continued their love affair with him, and his talent continued to bring them to their feet.

After four years on the circuit, Booth had played every major city in the United States. It was time to return to England, and Booth knew it. He could not bear to leave Mary Ann, and so he packed her up, along with the two children, and sailed back to England. Once there, Mary Ann and the two children stayed with her mother. Junius returned to Adelaide and Richard, his six-year-old son. Booth played his role of devoted husband and father with aplomb, but he soon wearied of the pretense. His heart was with Mary Ann, and he sorely missed living with her. Before long, he went on another "tour" in America, and he and Mary Ann returned to the farm in Maryland.

This time the "tour" was extended. In the following six years, Mary Ann had three more children. Booth was again feeling the pressures involved in living two lives and returned to drinking heavily. This time the drinking was accompanied by bouts of madness, periods in which Booth would be incoherent, rambling, raging, and uncontrollable. These episodes frightened and depressed him, and bad fortune seemed to plague him— three of his children died in the space of a year.

Mary Ann was left desolate by the losses of her children, and her husband's erratic behavior worried her. She was joyous, however, when she discovered that she was pregnant yet again. She felt as if this baby would compensate for the three who had died, that a new life would somehow ward off the misfortune that was dogging them. When the baby was born, she named him John Wilkes.

Adelaide was in England this entire period, never dreaming that her husband was living with and supporting another family. As the years passed, however, her son began to wonder about this mysteriously absent father. In 1842, when he was twenty-three, Richard came to America to find his father. He found not only his father, but his father's mistress and their children. When Adelaide heard this news from her angry son, she was outraged. For four years she waited for her husband to come to his senses, but it became obvious that Junius liked the situation just as it was. Adelaide had fooled herself for twenty-seven years, but the time for self-deception was ended. Junius was not ever coming back to her, and Adelaide finally admitted that fact to herself. Thus it was that in 1846 Adelaide sailed to America and demanded recognition for herself and her son.

Junius was impervious to her. His days of trying to play two roles were over. He was with the woman he loved, and her children were his children. That was the end of it, as far as he was concerned. Eventually, Adelaide had to give up. Her husband was simply ignoring her demands, and she felt helpless and humiliated. Adelaide divorced Junius in 1851. She never recovered from the blow of discovering her husband's double life. She began drinking heavily and died seven years later in Baltimore. The only mourner at Adelaide's funeral was her son, Richard.

Junius married Mary Ann after Adelaide divorced him. Mary Ann was happy that she was finally Junius' lawful wife, but her real joy was that their children were legitimate. This happiness was short-lived, for fate managed to accomplish what Adelaide could not: Only a year after their wedding, Junius died on his way back from a tour. Booth's immoderate lifestyle had swallowed his actor's salary, and there were no such things as pensions. Mary Ann was left with several children still at home to care for and no money with which to do it.

Two of Mary Ann's sons, who were now old enough to live out on their own, sent money to their mother whenever they could. It was not very much, however, and Mary Ann struggled just to keep herself and her family fed and clothed. Her favorite child, Johnny, was no help at all during this period. John Wilkes Booth was a lazy and demanding child, but he more than any of her other children reminded Mary Ann of Junius. John had inherited his father's good looks and more than enough of his charm. Mary Ann assuaged the pain of losing her husband by concentrating her love and attention on John.

John Wilkes did not want to go to school. Mary Ann did not force him to do so, as she might have forced her other children. Unlike her behavior with the others, she could never bring herself to be firm with John. She indulged his whims, and when he got himself into various scrapes, she protected him from suffering the consequences of his actions. Even when it was Mary Ann herself who was hurt by John, she forgave him without punishment. Mary Ann did not like violence, and John Wilkes was subject to violent outbursts, much as his father had been. Many times, Mary Ann gave in to her son simply to keep peace in the Booth household.

Eventually, as her children grew up and left home to make lives of their own, Mary Ann decided to move to New York. She still missed Junius, but her children were a comfort to her. They had grown into decent men and women, she thought, despite their rocky beginning. Although the children had never gotten along very well with one another, they were all fond of their mother. For that, Mary Ann was grateful. And it pleased her that three of her sons—Junius, Edwin, and John Wilkes—had followed their father into the theater. They had inherited their father's talent; unfortunately, Mary Ann had noticed, John Wilkes had also inherited Junius' unsteady disposition. As his father had been, John was subject to bouts of irrational thinking and wild behavior. Unlike his father, however, John Wilkes did not have to live with the consequences of his actions. Mary Ann always sheltered him from that.

Mary Ann was in New York when she heard newsboys on the streets shouting that President Lincoln had been assassinated. Horrified, she ran outside and grabbed a newspaper, only to read that her son, her darling Johnny, was the suspected assassin. Mary Ann literally could not believe her eyes; she sobbed, "Oh, God, if this be true, let him shoot himself, let him not live to be hung. Spare him, spare us, spare the name that dreadful disgrace."[8]

In one way, Mary Ann's prayer was answered. Booth was not hanged. After shooting Lincoln, he had fled the theater on horseback and been cornered in a barn by the militia. The militia set the barn on fire and dragged Booth out. He had been shot, and he died a short time later. No one knows whether the gunshot came from the militia or was self-inflicted. Mary Ann was on her way to Philadelphia, where her daughter, Asia, lived, when she read the news that Booth had been captured and killed. It was reported that his last words had been addressed to her: "Tell my mother that I died for my country."[9]

This message hit Mary Ann especially hard, because she had watched her son slide into political fanaticism and had been helpless to stop it. She had tried to reason with John, to convince him to stay with acting and forget his notions of political intrigue and plotting, but Mary Ann had never been firm where John was concerned, and he had long ago stopped listening to her admonitions. Mary Ann felt that she should have seen it coming, but in a way, she did. In a letter to John dated just three weeks prior to the assassination, Mary Ann wrote:

> I have never doubted your love and devotion to me; in fact, I have always given you praise for being the fondest of all my boys, but now you leave me to grief I doubt it. I am no Roman

mother. I love my dear ones before country or anything else. Heaven guard you, is my constant prayer.

Your loving mother,
M. A. Booth[10]

John Wilkes Booth died believing that he had done his country and his mother a great service by killing Lincoln. He had expected the fallen Confederacy to hail him as a great savior of their cause. Booth could not have been more grievously wrong. In murdering Lincoln, Booth killed the South's only hope for a fair and friendly peace. Lincoln's only real goal throughout the Civil War had been unity, and that unity mattered far more to Lincoln than punishment and revenge.

When Lincoln died, the lust for retribution against the South was given free reign. Andrew Johnson, the new president, would try to follow Lincoln's policy of moderation during the Reconstruction era, but to no avail. Johnson had neither the intellect nor the charisma of Lincoln, and both were desperately needed at that point in history. Without Lincoln to guide, cajole, and push ideas through Congress, Reconstruction became a tool that the Radicals used to humiliate and crush the old Confederacy. As a result, the Union was reconstructed, but the price was a great deal of injustice and deep-seated bitterness. The wounds created during that period of anger and suspicion are still healing today.

Mary Ann Booth, however, was less concerned about the fate of the country than she was about the fate of her son's body. After he died, Booth's body had been buried in the dirt floor of the Arsenal cell. Mary Ann wanted her son to be buried in the family plot. She wanted her family to be together in death as they had not been in life. It was not until four years later that Mary Ann's request was granted by the United States government. In 1869, Booth's body was moved to the Booths' place of internment, and Mary Ann sobbed as she watched her son's body lowered into the ground. The world had done what Mary Ann had never been able to bring herself to do: John Wilkes Booth had finally paid the price for his actions.

CHAPTER FOUR

CAPITALISTS, COMMUNISTS, AND MOM

JOHN D. ROCKEFELLER

The last third of the nineteenth century is a startling study in contrasts. While Russia was feeling the heavy yoke of czarist rule and a German philosopher named Karl Marx had just perfected his theory of a workers' revolution, the United States was busy expanding and developing into the world's greatest economic power. Fledgling industries were prospering, and money flowed. American capitalists were enjoying their finest hour, oblivious to the imminent doom Marx foretold.

The Industrial Revolution had already occurred, but it was in the late 1800s that its effects were widely felt in America. The greatest advance was in transportation, especially the establishment of the first transcontinental railroad in 1869. The connection between East and West revolutionized farming and industry, as goods could now be transported from producer to consumer quickly and safely. The coupling of transportation breakthroughs with industrial development resulted in an explosive period of growth in America.

This growth was by no means peaceful. The nation's childhood was long past and in the late 1800s the United States entered a stormy and cantankerous adolescence. There were violent labor strikes, cutthroat competitions in business, and financial panics. It was a time before government regulation, before consumer protection, before fair business practice laws. A man could make millions, and consumer beware. The temper of the times was epitomized when William Henry Vanderbilt expostulated, "The public be damned."

One man who made millions was John D. Rockefeller, and the name has now become an American synonym for wealth. At first glance, Rockefeller's background contained nothing that would foretell this, but Rockefeller himself might disagree. That background included his mother, and Rockefeller felt that he learned far more than his letters from Eliza. The world taught Rockefeller the price of everything, and he was an adept pupil. But Eliza Rockefeller knew more than the price of things. She knew their value.

John D. Rockefeller resembled his mother in many ways. Like her, he was a silent, taciturn person. Like her, he most often listened to his head rather than his heart. Like her, he was a devout Baptist. But though her son never did, Eliza trusted, once in her life, her fate to someone else. She married William Avery Rockefeller after a brief courtship. It was a mistake. She taught her children to avoid ever making the same kind of mistake.

William Rockefeller must have appealed to the shy and reserved Eliza, for he was outgoing and good-humored. The word "convivial" comes from two Latin words meaning "with life," and William had the ability to charge whatever room he was in with life and laughter. Eliza longed to enjoy the warmth that spilled over when she was in his presence. Everyone respected Eliza—she was a dependable and industrious girl—but few people loved her, as they loved William.

William and Eliza had six children: Lucy, John, William, Mary Ann, and a set of twins who died in infancy. William was not shiftless. His family was always financially comfortable. His enthusiasm, however, was not matched by his integrity. He worked as a peddler of patent medicines, traveling across the country extolling the virtues of various tonics and creams. In fact, he was known in some parts as the "travelling cancer specialist."

Not only did William Rockefeller claim to cure cancer, but he promoted himself as a man capable of curing every human disease and infirmity. From his father, young John had a first-hand lesson in the importance of successful marketing techniques; he later said that William had taught him how to buy and sell. John also had a chance to see the benefits of entrepreneurship and bombast. William's success was a living example of the fact that the intelligence of the American public, as H. L. Mencken once pointed out, cannot be underestimated.

As John was the eldest son, and his father was away more often than he was home, it was John who kept the family account books and paid the bills. While William was out making money, John was learning how to manage it. If the boy ever had any reservations about the way his father earned his wages, he kept them to himself.

When John was ten years old, his father left home. This time, William was not going off on a business venture. He was escaping the jurisdiction of the New York Court, evading the charge that he raped the family's hired girl. Because William left town, the case was never brought to trial. Interestingly enough, however, Eliza's father changed his will, putting Eliza's share in trust and giving $50 to the girl his son-in-law was accused of raping.

The Rockefellers left New York State for Cleveland in 1853, when John was fourteen. The family saw very little of William. Eliza received a letter from him once in a while, letting her know where to reach him in case of an emergency. Now and then he would come back, but he never told them what he had been doing while he was away. He established a line of credit at the town's general store so that Eliza could provide for the family. Beyond that, Eliza was alone. William, however, was not alone. In 1855, he "married" a girl twenty years his junior, living with her in South Dakota for forty years under the assumed name of Dr. William Livingston.

John never forgot the effect William's long absences had on his mother. He remembered her as "a humiliated, abandoned woman spoken of in backfence gossip, who spent long nights alone in a rocking chair staring at the fire, with a Bible in her lap and a corncob pipe in her mouth."[1]

Young John was impressed by what happened to his mother. He was determined to be very careful about whom he trusted. As far as his future, John knew he would always be in charge of his own fate.

Virtually abandoned by her husband, Eliza concentrated her energies on raising her children; and her children respected her. Eliza had little education, but she had a good deal of common sense and an ability to cut through nonsense and get to the essentials of a situation. The children were raised to believe that success comes from hard work and thrift, not from luck or personality. She did not intend to see any of her children take after William. The image of God hovered over the children at all times, a stern God who loved them but readily punished any transgressions against His will. As God's handmaiden, Eliza stood by to spank soundly anyone who misbehaved. Every Sunday, after she scrubbed and dressed each child, the family attended services in the local Baptist church.

Eliza did not pity herself—self-pity accomplished nothing, and she had a lot of work to do. But she was lonely. John was her eldest son, and she often turned to him for help with the younger children, for support, sometimes for consolation. John welcomed this closeness. He felt sorry for his mother, and he loved her. Eliza trusted his judgment and valued his opinions, as he did hers. Later in his life, John never hesitated to trust his own judgment, and he commanded respect because he believed himself worthy of it.

Living with a barely part-time husband had sharpened Eliza's financial concerns. The family was adequately provided for, but Eliza wanted her children to be able to provide for themselves. She did not want her children to have to depend on someone else for support, as she had. John learned Eliza's lesson thoroughly. He wanted only enough education to ensure him a job. There would be no pursuit of knowledge for its own sake in his preparation for life.

John finished high school and then enrolled in a three-month course at a business school, which was to be the end of his formal education. He was sixteen years old; it was time to find a job. There was an opening in a commercial merchant's produce-shipping firm with pay of $3.50 per week. Even for 1855, these were low wages, but it was a start. John took the job.

When he received his first weekly paycheck, John immediately deducted 10 percent (thirty-five cents) and gave it to charity. Eliza taught him to believe that money was a gift from God, and throughout his life, he referred to his moneymaking ability as a "gift," earmarking 10 percent of everything he earned for charitable causes.

John worked for the produce firm for three years. He left in 1858, after he had requested a raise from $600 to $800 per year and been turned down. In any event, he had learned all that the firm could teach him about the commission business. At nineteen John decided to set up his own firm with a partner. He would be his own boss; if the firm was successful, he would not have to ask another man for a raise in wage. Eliza, he knew, would like that.

John Rockefeller's first business venture soared. His timing was right, for the Civil War began in 1861, and the war was very good for the merchant-commission business. But his success was due to more than timing. Rockefeller was a very clever businessman, because he knew the importance of common sense. His mother had survived because of her common sense, and John thrived because of it.

Rockefeller was drafted by the Union Army, but he had no intention of interrupting his life at such a crucial juncture. The business was still new, and to leave it would risk losing it. He hired a substitute to fight for him, a common practice in the North for those who had the money. Rockefeller had the money, and he intended to have more.

After seven years Rockefeller was ready for a new challenge. He had learned all that he could from the merchant-commission business, the most important being the increasing value of oil. The industrial revolution had given birth to the age of machines, and machines run on oil. At the age of twenty-six, Rockefeller went into the oil-refining business. Once there, he listened, he watched, and he learned.

By 1872 he had learned every facet of oil refining and had started his own oil-refining company, calling it Standard Oil. The company was successful from the start. Rockefeller was respected and feared by his subordinates, for he wasted nothing and surrounded himself with able and talented men. He viewed every potential disaster as a potential opportunity and made the most of those opportunities. No one would ever be able to consider him a victim, if John had anything to do with it.

The respect of the business world was not mirrored by the public. People despised him as a ruthless, grasping "robber baron," who pocketed excessive profits while the workers suffered and competition withered away. Rockefeller was still a faithful Baptist and even taught Bible classes. He continued to give 10 percent of his profits to charity. But the general public objected to the size of those profits and to the manner in which he acquired them.

The United States of the late 1800s was a capitalist businessman's Garden of Eden. The government wanted growth and gave business a free hand in achieving that growth. There was very little government regulation, and the United States economy did indeed skyrocket. But the cost was tremendous in terms of fairness and equal opportunity. Intense competition between companies continually forced prices down, and "gentlemen's agreements" to maintain prices were broken as quickly as they were made.

Rockefeller found this climate intolerable. He saw glutted markets, disorder, and uncertainty in the business community, a sure detriment to a strong and stable economy. The only way to prevent wild fluctuation, as Rockefeller saw it, was to establish a trust—an affiliation of similar companies, with power concentrated in a single board of trustees. Standard Oil became the first such trust in 1879.

What made perfect sense to Rockefeller,however, was not welcomed by the public. Twenty-seven competitive oil companies had turned their stock over to Standard Oil, and John D. Rockefeller controlled all of it. Those companies had been forced to sell out to Standard because Rockefeller had cut prices below cost to squeeze them out. As he saw it, that was only good business, and no law stopped him. Furthermore, Standard Oil had an agreement with the railroads that favored Standard's products over all others. For other oil companies, in 1872, it was a choice of being swallowed by Standard or dying. Many were swallowed, and many died.

The government tolerated this situation, because it brought progress and development. Standard Oil produced improved products and distributed them efficiently. But trusts were sprouting up all over the nation. The doors of individual competition and equal opportunity were slamming, and the public howled. Once competitors were eliminated, companies were free to raise prices as high as they pleased, and no one benefited except big business. Eventually, the government had to act.

Congress passed the Sherman Anti-Trust Act in 1890, outlawing trusts. Most were reorganized into holding companies and corporations. Standard Oil was prosecuted in 1906 and finally dissolved in 1911 into the holding companies that still exist today.

John Rockefeller was a millionaire many times over when Eliza died in 1889. He was with her when she died, and he knew that she was proud of him. Eliza had watched him put to use all of the lessons about the value of hard work and efficiency that she had taught him. That he was wealthy pleased her, for no one would ever be able to treat him as William had treated her. But even more important to Eliza was the fact that John was a conscientious man and a churchgoing Christian. Although Rockefeller had millions, what pleased Eliza was the fact that he never wasted a cent. Nor did he ever forget charity. He contributed $80 million to establish the University of Chicago, founded The Rockefeller University—Institute for Medical Research, and established the Rockefeller Foundation to assist people in need. When he died in 1937 at the age of ninety-eight, Rockefeller's estate was valued at $26.4 million; he had already given $875 million away. That he was one of the world's richest men would have been all right with Eliza. That he was respected, even feared, would have pleased her. She had not endeavored to raise her child to be rich. She had tried to raise him to be his own man, and that he was. It was that independence which would have made Eliza proud.

ANDREW CARNEGIE

There are pictures of them in almost every history textbook— dark, imposing men dressed in black, often as not sporting a stovepipe hat. Capitalists. "Robber barons." It was said that some of them were cruel taskmasters, men who hired young children and flogged them if they did not work quickly enough, who paid workers less than they needed to survive, who lived in large estates peopled with servants, amassing staggering profits at the cost of their employees' health and well-being. John D. Rockefeller's photograph invariably appears in the books, next to words like *trust, monopoly,* and the ubiquitous *robber baron.* The picture next to Rockefeller is usually that of Andrew Carnegie, the King of Steel in the United States. An industrialist. An entrepreneur. A capitalist.

What do these words mean? Was the world of the nineteenth century truly a world in which "capitalists" owned everything, including the right to cause misery for everyone else? Such suppositions are not best answered with general statements. The best way to understand the phenomenon of robber barons in the United States is to study the most familiar of these men. Rockefeller can be more than a photograph in a history book only if one looks for the man behind the money. Andrew Carnegie becomes more than an abstraction if one understands him as a person. It is an old truth that in order to understand what someone *is,* one must look at where he *has been.*

Andrew was the first son of Margaret and William Carnegie. When Andrew was born, his father was a successful and prosperous weaver in Dunfermline, Scotland. But William's days as a craftsman were numbered. The Industrial Revolution was changing the face of the world, and it eventually reached the rural corner of Scotland where the Carnegies lived. The hand loom was destined to become an artifact of a past age, but it was William Carnegie's pride and his livelihood. At the time that automation started to make its appearance in Dunfermline, Carnegie had four looms in constant use. His shop was peopled with apprentices, and his books were filled with orders.

Carnegie refused to see the handwriting on the wall. He simply ignored the changes occurring all around him and clung stubbornly to his craft. Business slackened, orders fell off, and he had to let the apprentices go, one by one. Eventually, he was down to just one loom—his own. Then there was not enough work to keep even his own loom going, and it, too, stopped. His son watched as his father's business crumbled and as his father's spirit was destroyed as well:

> My father did not recognize the impending revolution and was struggling under the old system. His looms sank greatly in value, and it became necessary for that power which never failed in any emergency—my mother—to step forward and endeavor to repair the family fortune.[2]

It was at this point in his childhood that Andrew was first impressed with the strength and character of his mother. As he watched Margaret cope with her husband's business failure, his respect for her grew, a respect he was never to lose. While William Carnegie bemoaned the loss of his craft and mourned an era now past, Margaret searched for a way to survive in the new era just dawning.

The first thing she needed was money. She sold William's

looms. With the profit, Margaret bought a small shop and opened a candy and vegetable store. The Industrial Revolution was changing many aspects of human life, but she figured that people would always have to eat. Margaret rose early every morning and opened the shop in time to sell fresh produce to the village cooks who were planning their day's menu. After a full day in the store, Margaret arrived in her own kitchen to fix dinner for her family. When Andrew was eight years old, she had another baby and named him Thomas. At night, she bound and sewed shoes; the shop kept food on the table, but the extra money she earned at night kept Andrew in school.

Every now and then, Margaret would receive a letter from one of her sisters. They had gone to America, the "land of opportunity," and in their letters they reported that life was, indeed, better on the other side of the ocean. Margaret would read these letters after a long day at the shop and compare her sisters' lives to her own. Surely, she thought, life can be no worse than it is now, barely making ends meet, coping alone with a desolate husband and two growing sons. Margaret decided that the Carnegie family would leave Scotland for America in search of better times. After selling their furniture at auction, Margaret still did not have enough money to buy four tickets. She did what she abhorred: She borrowed money. A childhood friend offered to lend Margaret twenty pounds (about $100), and she accepted the offer. The Carnegies were on their way to America.

When the family arrived in New York harbor on July 15, 1848, Will was forty-three, a defeated and broken man. Margaret was thirty-three and by no means defeated. She did not cherish any hopes for her own life or her husband's. She went to America because she hoped her sons, then aged thirteen and five, would have a greater chance to succeed there. She desperately wanted them to have that chance. From New York, the family moved to an area near Pittsburgh, where Margaret's sisters had settled.

Her sisters welcomed her and promised to help the family in any way they could. Margaret saw that her sisters were happier and more hopeful than they had been in Scotland, and she easily caught their optimistic fervor. The same could not be said of William Carnegie. He hated the new world of machines. It was too fast, too new, too faceless. He had no desire to begin again in

America. His world had been in rural Scotland, amidst his hand looms and his craft. This new "land of opportunity" had no place for him. But, as Margaret pointed out, he had two sons to think about.

Will and Andrew found jobs in a small cotton factory. The pay was meager, and they were expected to work from five o'clock in the morning until six o'clock at night, but it was honest work. When Andrew decided to change jobs and take a slightly better offer from another factory, Will quit too. He had taken the job only to look after the boy, and it appeared that Andrew could look after himself.

Will stayed home. Surely, he thought, people must still appreciate beautiful cloths, finely woven. It was a new and confusing time, but that did not have to mean that people no longer wanted fine things around them. Surely, he thought, the world still had room for quality. Will rented a loom. He began weaving again and produced fine tablecloths, tablecloths that no factory could manufacture. He packed them up and went door to door, up and down the streets of the city, peddling his quality cloths. He did not sell one.

While Will stubbornly worked on his tablecloths, Margaret worried about keeping food in her cupboard. Andrew was bringing his salary home, but it was not enough. She found a job at a local cobbler, binding shoes. The pay was eighty cents a day, for seventeen hours of work. When Margaret arrived home at eight or nine o'clock at night, she did the cleaning, the cooking, and the sewing. Around midnight, she would fall into bed until 4:00 A.M., when she arose to fix her son's and her own breakfast.

Andrew was working in a textile mill, running the steam engine and firing the furnace. Eventually, he moved up to a position of office clerk and took on the additional duties of bobbin boy. He hated the extra job, but the family needed the pennies he got for the added work. While Andrew worked, he watched and listened. He had seen his mother labor ceaselessly to ensure her family's survival. He had seen his father shuffle down the streets in pursuit of a life that was lost to him. Now he saw his co-workers: As exhausted as his mother, as hopeless as his father, they struggled from morning until dark just to survive.

Andrew did not want to meet the same fate. The only way

out, as he saw it, was to get an education. He told his mother that he had to go to school, and Margaret agreed with him, glad that her son wanted to find a way out of the harsh monotony of their lives. Andrew stopped coming home after work; instead, he went to night school and studied double-entry bookkeeping. There were nights he had to struggle to stay awake in class after a fourteen-hour workday, but Andrew figured that if Margaret could fulfill all of her household duties after a full day's work, he could certainly stay awake in school.

In 1849 Andrew quit his job at the textile mill and started working for the Pennsylvania Railroad as a telegraph messenger. He gained a reputation as the best messenger in the company, and as a reward for his diligence, he was promoted to operator. He excelled at that job too, and the company officials grew to respect and like Andrew. The superintendent of the Western Division, Thomas A. Scott, decided to hire him as his secretary and personal telegrapher.

Scott and Andrew had a good relationship, and Andrew liked his new job. Working for Scott gave him the opportunity to meet the country's most prominent leaders, both in the railroads and in industry. Scott was a clever business man, and he advised his protégé on investments. Railroad barons were laying the tracks of America's future, and they required vast amounts of iron. Andrew invested a small portion of his yearly salary of $2,400 in the foundries that produced iron. Through investment, he was slowly moving out of the circle of vicious poverty he saw all around him. Andrew's income, combined with Margaret's pay, ensured that the Carnegies would not only survive but would prosper in America. They repaid the $100 lent to them by Margaret's friend and were even able to buy a home.

The future was beginning to brighten for the Carnegies, but Will was not to be part of that future. He died in 1855, a broken and dispirited man who had long ago lost the love of his wife and the respect of his sons. Will had not proved to be a survivor, and it was a time fit only for survivors. In the years since the family had emigrated, Margaret had begun to treat him with contempt, turning not to him but to Andrew for support and counsel.

Andrew was continuing to move up in the railroad hierarchy. Undersized but handsome, Andrew Carnegie had plenty of charm and enough skill to match his charm. He was put in charge of the Pittsburgh railroad system when he was twenty-five, and when he was only twenty-six, he completely reorganized and updated the telegraph system for the Union Army in the Civil War.

The business of railroads was exciting, but Andrew knew that the railroads were completely dependent on iron. The railroads were necessary to America, but iron was necessary to the railroads. Andrew set up an iron mill in Pittsburgh. By this time, the investments he had been making for the last ten years were paying off handsomely; he had an annual income of almost $48,000, a rich man's income in the 1870s.

In 1872 Andrew Carnegie observed a process that was to change the course of his life and revolutionize American industry. Until that year, railroads had been forced to rely on iron for their rails. Steel would have been more durable and efficient, but it had always been prohibitively expensive to produce. Then, in 1872, Carnegie heard about a new patented method called the Bessemer process, which produced steel cheaply and quickly. The Bessemer process, coupled with the vast ore deposits in the Lake Superior region of the United States, meant just one thing: Iron was the past, steel the future.

Carnegie saw that one day steel would be the metal holding the country together. Steel would be the provider of food, shelter, and transportation for millions of Americans. Andrew Carnegie did not intend to repeat the mistakes of his father. The iron mill was Andrew's hand loom, and he tossed it away before it could drag him down. In 1875 he built a steel mill. The Industrial Revolution had destroyed William Carnegie, but his son Andrew would ride on the wave of it and make himself a millionaire.

Carnegie knew next to nothing about technology, but he capitalized on the qualities he did have, and they proved to be more than enough. He was an articulate writer, a persuasive speaker, and a very effective salesman. Furthermore, he had an ability crucial to any successful businessman: He could spot talent in others, and he surrounded himself with men of the highest caliber. His days in Thomas Scott's office now served him well, for there he ingratiated himself with the railroad barons of the day, and those men remembered personable young Andrew Carnegie when it was time to buy steel.

Throughout his steady climb to the top levels of industrial America, Margaret Carnegie was at her son's side. He relied heavily on her judgment, her Scottish common sense, and her usually sound advice. More important, Margaret gave Andrew the confidence to take risks necessary to success. She believed that her son was the brightest, cleverest, and most trustworthy businessman in America. Margaret's faith in him was a constant fuel for Andrew Carnegie's ambition, and he never forgot that faith.

Margaret and Andrew were inseparable companions. As Margaret grew older, she became possessive of her son, demanding that he devote more and more of his time and attention to her, but Andrew never objected. He wholeheartedly believed that he owed her everything he had and all that he was. It was Margaret who had kept the family alive when Will fell apart, Margaret who had borrowed money to get her sons to America, Margaret who had worked all day sewing shoes and at night cleaning house. He admired his mother, he respected her, and he loved her. Most important, he *liked* her; Andrew and Margaret understood each other. They had come from the same place and they had both fought to escape. They had both survived.

Andrew, who certainly must have been considered a highly eligible man, did not marry as long as Margaret was alive. He courted Louise Whitfield for many years. Louise cared deeply for Andrew and just as deeply resented his mother. At one point, Louise said of Margaret, "She was the most unpleasant person I have ever known."[3]

By the late 1800s, there were thousands of steel mills in the United States. As ever when there are many companies in competition, there was a good deal of ruthlessness and disquiet in the marketplace. Just as there had been in the oil business, there were cutthroat tactics throughout the steel industry—blackmail, vicious price slashing, unfair labor practices.

Andrew Carnegie became the dominant figure in steel. At the pinnacle of his career, he had the entire steel industry well within his grasp. He was unlike other businessmen, however; in fact, he was regarded as the "articulate industrialist." But his hands were not completely clean. Carnegie was not above ruining his competitors when the occasion demanded it. He was also known for his willingness to play his own partners against one another if it furthered his own aims.

Carnegie was widely respected but not universally liked. Some termed him the most inhumane taskmaster in America; it was said "at every Carnegie plant there was a scrap heap for men as well as for metal."[4] His attitude toward labor earned the hatred of the working class, for he judged his workers by the standards of his own career as a laborer, and those were hard standards to meet. Carnegie considered a dollar a day more than an adequate wage: After all, he had worked for $1.20 a week at one point. The workers did not see it as Carnegie did. All they could see was the fact that their boss was earning $25 million a year and expected them to survive on $1 a day.

Carnegie's reputation was not helped by a debacle at his Pennsylvania steel mill during a labor strike. There were 3,800 workers demanding more money and better working conditions, but management was determined to hold the line. Carnegie's general manager, Henry Frick, decided to call in 300 Pinkerton guards to break the picket line. The presence of the guards brought tension to a fevered pitch; someone fired a shot, and a melee ensued. When the dust had settled, three guards and ten strikers were dead, and many more were wounded. The strike had been broken and unionism in the steel industry was seriously injured, but public sympathy surged toward the defeated strikers and against Carnegie Steel.

Horace, an ancient Roman poet, once remarked, "The populace may hiss at me, but when I go home and count my money, I applaud myself!" Andrew Carnegie had plenty of money to count. At the height of his career, his fortune was worth $350 million. In fact, at one point, J. P. Morgan, another wealthy industrialist, sent Carnegie a wire. It read: "Mr. Carnegie, I want to congratulate you on being the richest man in the world."[5]

As for the populace, their hissing was not entirely justified. Carnegie was a hard taskmaster, but he was fair, even enlightened, considering the times in which he lived. He was one of the first business owners to institute an eight-hour day, and he allowed his workers to buy coal from him at cost so that they could heat their homes.

Philanthropy was very important to Carnegie. In fact, it was his only religion. His philosophy, which became known as the "Gospel of Wealth," was that the owner of vast amounts of money was in fact only a trustee of the wealth, and it was his duty to distribute it for the good of the people. To this end, he endowed the Carnegie Institute, which still funds research in science and the humanities, and the Carnegie Foundation, which funds teaching fellowships. His money also built Carnegie Hall in New York City. Other than philanthropy, Carnegie practiced no formal religion. His father had taken him to church when he was young, but it was Margaret whose example he followed. Margaret's religion, she told her son at one time, was "to perform the duties of your life well, not troubling about another."[6] Andrew took this advice seriously, and philanthropy was his way of performing his life's duties well. The results stand all over the world: Around the globe, there are libraries endowed by Andrew Carnegie. One library that Carnegie's money built had special meaning. It was in Dunfermline, Scotland. Andrew traveled to his birthplace with his mother to lay the cornerstone.

Margaret died in 1886. Carnegie was so devastated by her loss that he refused to talk about her. He had everything associated with her removed from his sight. To be reminded of his mother was painful, for he missed her terribly. He finally married Louise Whitfield, his long-time sweetheart. She was twenty-eight at the time, Andrew fifty-two. They had a daughter, and Andrew named her Margaret.

Andrew Carnegie was one of the most spectacular economic success stories history has yet recorded. Until the day he died, Carnegie believed that he owed his success to the strength and character of his mother. In his autobiography, Carnegie wrote:

Perhaps some day I may be able to tell the world something of this heroine, but I doubt it. I feel her to be sacred to myself and not for others to know. . . . [7]

Carnegie was king of the country's largest industry and controller of a great deal of its wealth. It probably seemed ironic to Andrew Carnegie that he should have become as successful as he did in that particular industry. After all, it had been Margaret, not he, who had always been made of steel.

KARL MARX

No philosophy has had a greater influence on the twentieth century than that of Marxism. For good or ill, Karl Marx inspired a political movement that has had a massive impact on the contemporary world. The world view outlined in *The Communist Manifesto* and *Das Kapital* exploded onto the pages of history in the form of revolutionary communism, and both East and West are still experiencing the fallout of that view.

Karl Marx was from an upper-middle-class Jewish background. Both Hirschel and Henrietta Marx were the children of rabbis; Hirschel was Prussian and Henrietta of Dutch descent. However, religion was not a strong influence on Karl. Hirschel was a skeptic, and he wanted young Karl to be rational and enlightened rather than devout.

When Karl was six, Prussia passed a law forbidding any Jew from practicing law in Prussia. Hirschel was an attorney, and a financially successful one. His profession and standard of living were far more important to him than his religion, so he changed his name to Heinrich and converted to Lutheranism. Eventually, Henrietta and the children were also baptized in the Lutheran faith.

Karl was Henrietta's favorite child. He was the eldest son of seven children, and she doted on him and spoiled him, giving him all the material comforts he could ask for. Henrietta was an old-fashioned mother. She valued cleanliness and order and placed a great emphasis on possessions. She was proud of having come from a comfortable background. Henrietta liked to have nice things around her, and she expected her children to appreciate the fruits of hard work and frugality.

Karl was an affectionate child when he was very young, calling his mother "angel mother" or "little mother." But his affection waned as his years increased, when he developed into a truculent and cocksure young man. He was a very bright child, and he began to feel contempt for his mother's lack of education. Henrietta could read and write Dutch, but she never had a good grasp of German. This further separated mother and son, as Karl began turning more and more to his father, whom he respected and with whom he communicated easily.

Hirschel/Heinrich Marx died when Karl was twenty years old, leaving his wife a substantial estate. Henrietta brought her Dutch frugality to bear on it and nursed her inheritance vigilantly, even managing to increase it over time. At the time of his father's death, Karl was studying law in Bonn. He rarely communicated with his mother, and this hurt Henrietta. At one point, she wrote to him complaining that she did not even know whether he had received his degree.

Henrietta loved Karl, but she could not understand him. She realized that she was not cultured or intellectually gifted, but she believed that she could instill in Karl the values she thought to be really important: industriousness, tidiness, and an appreciation for money.

Nothing could have been further from Karl's heart or mind than Henrietta's values. After completing his legal studies he moved on to Berlin, where he began working toward a doctorate in philosophy and history. He was a self-confident but quarrelsome young man with few friends, an avowed and vocal atheist interested in radical causes. He was slovenly in his personal habits, careless with money, and exceptionally lazy. His whole style of living was a deliberate sneer at everything for which Henrietta stood.

Henrietta never quit trying to advise Karl. She wrote to him at school, asking him if he was keeping his quarters neat and spending his money wisely. In one letter, she promised, "If you wish for anything at Christmas that I can give you then I shall be happy to do it." Henrietta's letter went on, "so goodbye my dear Karl, be a good boy, thinking always of God and your parents."[8]

Karl received his doctorate in 1841. An academic career was out of the question because of his militant atheism. He worked for a newspaper, but it was not long before his distaste for the autocratic government of Prussia became so great that he moved to Paris. His only communications with Henrietta were requests for money. Karl was perpetually broke and usually in debt.

For her own part, Henrietta could not understand why Karl, with his Ph.D. and fine mind, was not the one giving her money. She was, after all, a widow with five unmarried daughters and a sickly son. Karl never displayed any concern for her well-being. The young boy who had called her "angel mother" now referred to her with contempt as "the old lady."

When Karl decided to marry, Henrietta advised against it. As she saw it, a young man with no money and no regular job had no business taking a wife, much less an aristocratic one. Karl treated this objection just as he treated all of Henrietta's advice. He ignored it. He continued asking his mother for money and was incensed when she refused to advance his father's inheritance to him.

While in Paris, Marx met and became friends with Friedrich Engels, a well-to-do businessman who was concerned about the hardships that the Industrial Revolution had visited upon the working class. The two men were of very different character, but they shared the same vision and decided to work together. Thus began the most important literary partnership in modern history. In 1848 the two published *The Communist Manifesto*, which urged all workers of the world to throw off the yoke of industrial capitalism and establish a classless society.

The revolution he was encouraging, Marx believed, was actually only a matter of time. Before long, as he saw it, workers would recognize their power and realize that economic production is the substructure of every society and all institutions. Then they—the "have-nots"—would see that in controlling production they controlled the economy, and the bourgeois capitalists— the "haves"—would be dethroned.

Marx saw everything in economic terms. The world, he maintained, has always operated according to economic laws; material conditions determine the character of both man and his society. It is a man's productive activity, he believed, that determines his politics, his morals, his religion, his art, and his philosophy of life. Marx had seen verification of this principle at an early age. In a showdown between religion and economic feasibility, his own father had thrown religion over. As far as Karl Marx was concerned, his father was one small example of human activity throughout time.

While he was promulgating his economic views, Marx's own finances were in a state of disaster. Exiled from Paris, he was living in the worst slums in London, his family miserably poor. One of his children died of poverty and starvation. Desperately in need of money, he went to Henrietta, whose thrift and bourgeois values had served her very nicely. But he was not as successful with his mother as he hoped to be. The best he was able to accomplish was cancellation of some of the debts he already owed her.

Two years after this visit from her son, Henrietta died. Marx was not heartbroken. His mother had always represented everything he found contemptible and distasteful in society. His philosophy advocated destruction of the bourgeois mentality she stood for. He wrote to Engels:

> *Two hours ago a telegram arrived to say that my mother is dead. Fate needed to take one member of the family. I already had one foot in the grave. In the circumstances, I am needed more than the old woman. I have to go to Trier about the inheritance. So I must ask you to send by return enough money for me to travel to Trier immediately.*[9]

Henrietta's estate was considerable. Her careful spending and wise management had resulted in a tidy sum. The largest share of the estate went to Karl. Despite everything, he was Henrietta's favorite child until the day she died. Karl went home to Trier to collect his money.

VLADIMIR LENIN

History books are peppered with references to "eras" and "epochs" and "ages." There have been the "Age of Napoleon," the "Middle Ages," the "Industrial Era," and the "Enlightenment." The list goes on. What of the twentieth century? What distinguishing characteristic will future generations pick out as the most significant of the last eight decades? From a political and historical perspective, the twentieth century may well be known as the age of totalitarianism.

Totalitarian rule is unique to this era of world wars and mass destruction. The rule of kings and czars that dominated the globe for centuries was of a different character, for such rule never professed to be rooted in the masses, as do dictatorships of both left and right. Only totalitarian governments, whether fascist or communist, label themselves as democratic while controlling every aspect of the state. Kings do not hold elections. Totalitarian governments hold elections, but only one party is allowed to run for office. Both kings and totalitarian leaders routinely destroy all organized opposition. Kings do so for the good of the king. Totalitarian leaders profess to do so for the good of "the people."

The philosophy of Karl Marx never recommended or even implied totalitarianism. When he spoke in his writings of the "dictatorship of the proletariat," he envisioned the proletariat as the vast majority of the people. He was advocating majority rule. Nothing could be further from the elite corps in totalitarian government that controls and oversees every aspect of society.

Russia was the world's first totalitarian state, and the revolution that brought it about was engineered by disciples of Karl Marx. But Marx and Engels assumed that the revolution would take place spontaneously, in a highly industrialized, western capitalist society. Russia was a peasant country used to czarist autocracy, with virtually no industrialization and a small working class. Yet it was in Russia that the revolution took place. How was this possible? How did the vision of Karl Marx end up being realized in a land so different from that of his prediction? And how did that state become the antithesis of what Marx advocated, Marxist in claim only, ruthlessly totalitarian in execution? The best way to find an answer to this question is to study the man responsible for bringing Marxism to Russian soil. The missing piece of the puzzle is contained in the character and personality of Vladimir Lenin.

Lenin's name was actually Vladimir Ilyich Ulyanov. He adopted "N. Lenin" as a pen name; the "N." stood for the Russian word for "nobody," but it led to the popular misconception that his first name was Nikolai. He was born in 1868 to one of

Russia's few middle-class families. His father was a self-made man, his mother an educated and aristocratic woman.

Maria Alexandrovna Blank was of German and Swedish ancestry, the daughter of a physician. The Blanks were landowners who owned serfs, and Maria grew up in an atmosphere of ease and refinement. She had a quick mind and was able to teach herself to read English and French, in addition to her knowledge of German and Russian. Maria loved to read, and eventually she collected a complete set of Shakespeare written in English and a history of the French Revolution written in French.

Maria married Ilya Ulyanov in 1863. Ilya's ancestors were serfs, but his father had become a tailor when the czar liberated the serfs in 1861. Ilya graduated from Kazan University with honor, and he was an industrious and able man. Together, Maria and Ilya produced six children (one died in infancy) in ten years.

The Ulyanov home was a traditional one. Ilya Ulyanov was a religious man, a man loyal to the Russian government and to the czar. Furthermore, the respective roles of husband and wife were sharply defined. Ilya was the provider and Maria the caretaker. As provincial school inspector of Simbirsk, Ilya built an undeveloped school system into a strong and efficient one. He was rewarded for his abilities, rising to an eminent position in the civil service of the czar. In fact, Ilya was admitted to the lowest level of Russian nobility. Ilya did what every good Russian subject was expected to do, and the system rewarded him.

Maria was the center of the family. Ilya's job often took him away on inspection tours, sometimes for as long as two or three months. It was more than mere circumstance, however, that made Mama Maria the ruler of the family. The family was Maria's world. She loved her husband, and she adored her children. Her children returned her feelings, for Maria was a naturally warm and affectionate woman. Even more important, she gave her family a sense of stability and contentment, making certain that each of her children had a strong sense of self and a good measure of independence.

Death intruded on the Ulyanov family when the children were reaching adolescence. Ilya died suddenly of a brain hemorrhage when the eldest child, Alexander, was eighteen and Vladimir was sixteen. With Ilya dead, the family's esteem for and emphasis on tradition also died. It had been Ilya who had fostered loyalty to the czar, Ilya who took the children to church. While Maria had concentrated on teaching each child to read and to play the piano, Ilya had seen to it that his children received their proper religious training. With Ilya's death died respect for the traditional in the Ulyanov home. Vladimir, shocked and angered by his father's unexpected death, declared himself an atheist. Alexander felt freer to voice his objections to the czar and his government. Realizing that they, especially the two older children, were now old enough to think and make their own decisions, Maria accepted their beliefs. She loved them; she did not judge them. It simply would not have occurred to her to do so.

At the time of Ilya's death, Alexander was a scholar, a biology student at the University of St. Petersburg. Just fourteen months later, he was arrested by the Russian police. The charge: attempting to assassinate the czar. When Maria received word of the arrest, she left immediately for St. Petersburg. To get there, she rode a horse for sixty miles and then boarded a train.

When she arrived, Maria petitioned the czar to spare her son's life. The czar promised clemency for Alexander on the condition that he recant and ask for mercy. Maria begged her son to do just that. But she had raised five very independent and resolute children. Alexander was convinced that his mission in life was to free Russia from the czar. He refused to ask pardon for an action he did not regret. Alexander was tried, condemned to death, and hanged. Maria walked with him to the gallows.

Alexander's death changed Maria. She was still a warm and resolute woman, but her easy laughter and spontaneous gaiety disappeared. Death made her sober. But her pride in and affection for her children was unshaken. Alexander's trial and death brought the remaining Ulyanovs even closer together. They were shunned by the townspeople, and Maria determined that her children would learn to rely only on themselves and on each other. Other people could not be trusted; they were not loyal, and they surely were not reliable.

The same year that Alexander died, Vladimir entered Kazan University, from which his father had graduated with honors. He was not there long when he became involved in a student demonstration. The demonstration itself was not serious, but the

University at Kazan knew all about Alexander Ulyanov and wanted no part of his rabble-rousing brother. Given this slight provocation, they expelled Vladimir. He applied for readmission and was refused, on the grounds that he was a troublemaker.

Vladimir did not lose heart. He began to study the law on his own. When the time came for the law examinations at the University, Maria traveled to St. Petersburg. She went directly to the Ministry of Education, and she was so persistent that they granted her son permission to take the law examinations without completing formal course work.

Vladimir passed the examinations with highest honors and was admitted to the Russian bar in 1891, four years after his brother's execution. In that same year, one of his sisters died of natural causes. Ironically, she died on the fourth anniversary of Alexander's death. Maria reacted by concentrating even more of her love and attention on the three children left to her, especially Vladimir, who was now her eldest son.

Vladimir never forgot nor forgave Alexander's execution. In fact, every one of the remaining Ulyanov children took Alexander's revolutionary cause as his or her own. Thus it was that when Vladimir read the philosophy of Karl Marx, the German struck a responsive chord. Here, Vladimir thought, was a man who had a vision of the future in which a man's value was not measured by his inherited rank, but by his ability. Czars would not be able to tread arbitrarily on anyone who displeased them in a Marxist society. Vladimir joined a group of Marxist thinkers and revolutionaries.

One year later, a medical problem sent Vladimir to western Europe for treatment. In Europe he was at the cutting edge of Marxist thought, and he welcomed the opportunity to immerse himself in revolutionary philosophy. Since he had been a small boy learning his letters from Maria, Vladimir had displayed an incisive and quick intellect. Always, he had been able to grasp the essentials of a situation or a problem, and his response to Marxist philosophy mirrored this trait.

Perfect theory, however, was not sufficient. Marx was a philosopher, Ulyanov a man of action. Marx seemed content to wait for spontaneous revolution. Ulyanov did not think such patience a virtue. He saw the world crying out for justice now, not at some theoretical future date; his brother's blood was a constant reminder of that.

When Ulyanov, now known as N. Lenin, returned to Russia, he brought Marxist literature with him. Such material was illegal in czarist Russia, and Lenin was arrested. He spent fourteen months in prison. As the Ulyanovs had done since Alexander's death, he turned to his family for help. Maria's response was immediate and quick. She brought him food regularly, sought out the books he asked for, even acted as a messenger between her son and his revolutionary associates. When Lenin was sentenced to exile in Siberia, she paid for his transportation so that he could travel in comfort.

Maria never refused her children's requests for financial help. Her financial position was fairly strong. She received a widow's pension, in addition to income from her father's estate, and she never hesitated to offer it whenever her family expressed a need. Maria never discouraged her children in their revolutionary activities. She reasoned that they were now adults, capable of making responsible decisions. As to the morality of their activities, Maria held her counsel. After all, the czar's government had killed her first-born son.

Deciding that it was better to plan revolution from afar than from prison, Lenin went abroad after having spent three years in Siberia. While in Europe, he never lost contact with Maria. He wrote to her frequently, not about revolutions, but about the things a son would write to his mother: what the bakery clerk said, how the snow looked when the sun shone on it, how often he thought of her. When she died in 1916, he missed her terribly. It especially pained him that he could not even attend her funeral or visit her grave; Russia's borders were closed to him.

During Lenin's years abroad, Russia was in turmoil. The outbreak of World War I in 1914 had initially called forth Russian patriotism, diverting the people for a while from their own country's problems. But as the war dragged on, this patriotism wore thin and was replaced first by frustration and then by fury. The war pointed out, better than any revolutionary could, the government's flaws and weaknesses.

Lenin was in Switzerland when the Russian people revolted in November of 1917, and when Lenin heard of it, he was desperate in his desire to get back to his homeland. He firmly believed that only he had the vision necessary to lead his people to their future.

It was frustrating for Lenin to be so far away from events. The provisional government that took control after the czar's abdication was, he was convinced, wrongheaded and inadequate. The Russian people wanted two things: peace and land. The provisional government offered neither. To pull out of the war, they decided, would be a dishonor. As for land, the provisional government envisioned a future that included representation and equal opportunity for everyone. Meanwhile, they gave the people only bromides and bandages.

Lenin was a man of action, and he wanted very much to seize the wheel of this revolution. He saw with clarity and precision that the time had come for Marxism's dictatorship of the proletariat. Marx, he thought, had trusted too much to the forces of history. Lenin knew that men make history, and now was his time to make it. His plan for Russia included immediate withdrawal from the war, which he viewed as a capitalist class war and nothing else. Furthermore, he wanted to oust the hesitant provisional government, confiscate all Russian land, and abolish the Russian army. He was convinced that his plan echoed the deepest desires of the Russian people.

He was right. The Germans were eager to see Russia pull out of the war, so that they could concentrate on their other enemies. Knowing that Lenin's return might abet their purposes, in March of 1917 the German government transported him in a sealed railroad car across Germany from Switzerland and over the Russian border. Once inside Russia, Lenin took his place at the helm of the Marxist agitators and at the center of twentieth-century political history. The day after his return to his homeland, Lenin—Vladimir Ilyanov—went to the cemetery where his mother was buried and knelt at her grave.

CHAPTER FIVE

"MAMA'S BOYS" AND MOTHERS OF VISION

At one time or another, everyone has heard the indictment "He's a real Mama's boy." The phrase is rich in meaning; it usually implies a man whose umbilical cord has never been cut, a good *boy* but a weak *man*. The negative overtones of the phrase, however, are not always borne out by the facts of history.

Every mother and every mother's son knows that a mother's influence can be formidable, reaching far into every corner of a man's future. A warm and supportive mother often shows up in her son's social life, his intellectual achievements, his very emotional well-being. Mom is every boy's first love, as Freud pointed out, and her influence goes far beyond the cradle.

When the cradle is tended with love and concern, a boy tends to grow in assurance as he grows in years. If Mom has faith in her son's abilities, that son naturally acquires faith in himself. When mother is her son's first and biggest fan, her son often goes on to bigger audiences and more applause.

"Mama's boy." What does it really mean? What are "Mama's boys" really like? Surely no better place exists to see a mother's influence than in the lives of those most strongly tied to her. The twentieth century offers an interesting panorama of "Mama's boys" who went from mother's arms to accomplish deeds far beyond their mothers' fondest dreams. Looking at recent American history, one can see a variety of powerful men. The men who shaped history are as different in character and personality as men can be, yet many of the outstanding political personalities who made the present day what it is share one thing: mothers who lavished them with both attention and affection.

These women are as various in personality as their sons, but each of them in her way rocked the cradle with a firm and loving hand. The results of such attention flowered in their sons. Would Franklin Delano Roosevelt have been half as tenacious and confident without Sara Delano Roosevelt in his background? One can almost picture the scene: a young Franklin, hesitant and tremulous about some task, only to be told that fear was the thing most to be feared. One can just as easily envision Martha Truman's determination to instill in her son the same backbone and iron will that she possessed. Would President Truman have been able to decide to use the atomic bomb had his mother not encouraged a careful but firm decisiveness in her son?

Similarly, would General Douglas MacArthur ever have had the sheer nerve to wade ashore to the Philippines had his mother, Mary, not pushed him relentlessly never to quit short of his goals? The best way to answer such queries is by looking at these men who helped shape our century, and at the first and most important women in their lives—their mothers.

FRANKLIN DELANO ROOSEVELT

Sara Delano was twenty-five years old when she married James Roosevelt, a widower nearly twice her age. Roosevelt's advanced years made the marriage a comparatively short one, but by all appearances it was a happy one. Both James and Sara wanted a child, and both were joyous when their union produced a ten-pound son. The child of James and Sara Roosevelt was known simply as "Baby" during his first seven weeks in the world, because his parents could not agree on a suitable name.

James favored Isaac, a traditional family name, but Sara abhorred the name and was adamant in her opposition to it, tradition or no. In Sara's mind, it lacked distinction, and above all, her son required a name that would be worthy of him. James had his first but probably by no means his last taste of the iron will of his wife: Sara named the baby. Her first choice was Warren Delano, the name of her beloved father, but Sara's brother's son, named Warren IV, had recently died. In deference to her brother's feelings, Sara instead named the baby after her Uncle Frank. It had a strong ring to it: Franklin Delano Roosevelt. A name worthy of the son of Sara Delano.

The umbilical cord was long indeed in the case of Sara Delano Roosevelt and her son. Little Franklin wore long curls and dresses until he was five years old; then he graduated to kilts and Little Lord Fauntleroy suits. His first pair of long pants had to wait until he was eight years old, and it was not until that same year that Franklin took a bath without his mother there to supervise. That first solo bath was important enough that Franklin wrote a letter just to tell his father about it.

Sara adored her son, but she neither spoiled him nor pampered him. She wanted Franklin's upbringing to be gentle but firm, resulting in a "Hyde Park gentleman" of whom she could be proud. To that end, Sara had more at her disposal than character alone. Her son had been born into a tradition of wealth and social status. Young Franklin grew up on an estate that spread well over several hundred acres. To administer to the family's needs, the Roosevelts employed a butler, a cook, a housekeeper, and a nurse, not to mention several maids, grooms, and gardeners. In addition, there was a succession of tutors and governesses hired to attend to the education of Sara's only son. It was Sara herself, however, who was ultimately in charge of Franklin's upbringing. Despite the menagerie of men and women dancing attendance on her son, Sara never relinquished her role as the most important figure in Franklin's boyhood. Sara had definite ideas on how her son was to be reared, and her employees did things her way or found themselves no longer employed by the Roosevelt family.

Sara expected a lot from her son; Franklin came later to echo Sara's expectations, expecting a lot of himself. Sara's love never wavered, and Franklin was secure, confident, and assured in that love, qualities that later expanded beyond his mother's horizons to that of the world. Franklin grew up with the sunny confidence that he could handle anything, and it was no coincidence that he would later be able to impart that assurance to a country starved for a morsel of just such a hope.

As president, Franklin Roosevelt did not often allow himself to be surprised. America's entrance into World War II was no chance event, regardless of what Pearl Harbor looked like to the average citizen. Roosevelt had carefully laid the foundation for America's joining of forces with the Allied powers through programs such as lend-lease, in which the United States supported the Allied cause with money and material. Such long-range vision was no accident; after all, Sara had the foresight to enroll her son in Groton soon after his birth, fully expecting that he would one day attend Harvard. According to plan, Franklin attended Groton when he was fourteen years old. It was his first extended stay away from home without his mother.

The separation of mother and son did not last long. While

at school, Franklin contracted scarlet fever, and Sara went immediately to be at her son's side. The injunction against visitors to patients suffering from scarlet fever did not faze Sara Delano Roosevelt. What the doctors would not allow, a simple stepladder would. Every day until he recovered, Sara climbed a ladder and sat outside his room, talking to him and reading to him. Sara's philosophy was not "If there's a way, it will be found." Rather, she believed that "There's a way and I will find it." Franklin never forgot this lesson; it enabled him to become the first and only disabled man to lead the strongest nation in the world.

Young Franklin graduated from Groton and then went to Harvard, just as Sara had planned. During Franklin's freshman year at Harvard, James Roosevelt died. The elder Roosevelt was seventy-two years old at the time and had suffered for some time from heart trouble, so the death came as no real surprise either to his son or his relatively young widow. Sara was forty-six at the time. James Roosevelt made his wishes regarding both members of his family clear in his last will and testament: Sara was appointed executor of the Roosevelt estate. As for Franklin, James stipulated, "I wish him [Franklin] to be under the supervision of his mother."[1]

Sara took her husband's wish to heart. Even more than before, Franklin became the center of her life. This affected the young man in various ways. Franklin was old enough to hunger for a world of his own, a space apart from that shared by his mother. His love for her was unflagging, but his desire for his own life was just as strong.

Franklin learned to listen carefully to his mother's advice and to disregard any that was not in accord with his own best judgment. He also learned to keep silent on areas of his life that he wished to keep private. Perhaps there was no better way for Franklin to develop the subtlety and charm necessary to a statesman than by finding ways to have both his mother's love and his own world.

Sara Delano Roosevelt was an affluent widow, having inherited $1.3 million from her husband's estate. After her financial affairs were in order, Sara moved to an apartment in Boston, to be closer to her son. Sara actually never realized, however, just how much of his life her son actually kept to himself until he announced to her (as a *fait accompli*) his upcoming marriage to his distant cousin Eleanor Roosevelt.

Franklin had carried on his courtship with Eleanor with neither his mother's knowledge nor her consent. On this score, Franklin had made up his mind on his own, bringing to bear the very assurance and confidence picked up at Sara's knee. The young Roosevelt had yet to earn an honest day's wages and had not a clue as to when or how he would do so. Yet Franklin was undaunted in asking for the hand of the homely niece of Theodore Roosevelt. Why, Sara wondered, had her only darling son chosen as his life's partner a young woman with buck teeth and no chin to speak of? Sara chalked it up to the impetuousness of youth: Eleanor was but nineteen years old, Franklin only twenty-two.

Franklin's announcement came as no small shock to his • mother. It had been just three years since James Roosevelt's death, and Sara had assumed that she and her son would only continue to get closer with the years. The last thing Sara had envisioned was being thrown over for another woman, and a plain one at that. The possibility of her own loneliness was matched by her unhappy surprise that Franklin had made such an important decision without her counsel. Her son had learned all too well from Sara how to be self-confident.

Dead set against her son's hasty and what she considered unfortuitous choice, Sara knew that time was her best ally. First, she convinced the young couple that secrecy was their best recourse for a while; she then persuaded her son to embark with her upon the time-honored distraction of a cruise to the Caribbean. Franklin accompanied Sara on the cruise but was not dissuaded from his commitment to Eleanor. One thing Sara had instilled in her son was determination. Franklin married Eleanor Roosevelt the following autumn, his first year in law school at Columbia.

The newlyweds spent their honeymoon in Europe. Sara, meanwhile, rallied from her defeat and consolidated her losses, finding a house for her son and his wife just three blocks from her own home. She rented the place immediately and kept busy in her son's absence by furnishing it and decorating it. Pity the poor bride, who faced a woman who made real all the mother-in-law myths ever conceived; Sara dominated almost every aspect of the couple's life.

Eleanor was by no means an assured and self-confident woman in those early days of her marriage to Franklin. She did not object to her mother-in-law's control; in fact, as Eleanor's son Elliot later pointed out:

> She [Eleanor] leaned on her mother-in-law for help, advice and sometimes consolation. Mother was so incredibly unaware and inexperienced in every kind of situation that she welcomed many of the things, always intended as kindnesses, which Granny insisted on doing for her.[2]

Three blocks soon became too great a distance for Sara's taste; in 1907, she had twin houses built, giving Franklin and Eleanor one as a Christmas present. Adjoining houses were not enough for Sara; the houses actually shared walls, that of the respective dining rooms and drawing rooms. Eleanor, of course, had never been consulted about the "gift," not to mention the floor plans and decorating. After all, Sara reasoned, there were two ways to do these things: her way and the wrong way. As Sara saw it, Eleanor could only be grateful for the much-needed guidance.

Franklin was unquestionably the center of Sara's life. He was not, however, the whole of her life. While Franklin moved from the world of law to discover and cultivate his interest in political life, Sara continued to enjoy the life of a wealthy society matron. Gradually, Franklin and Eleanor did begin to acquire some independence, some life of their own. In time, they were less and less under Sara's wing, both financially and emotionally. The young bridegroom slowly developed into a force to be reckoned with in the Democratic Party, while his wife grew in assurance as she increased in years.

Sara was, in fact, on one of her many trips to Europe when Franklin contracted polio. She did not learn of her son's illness until her return home. Once Sara did find out about the serious nature of Franklin's illness, she made a decision. Echoing her resolute decisiveness after the death of James, Sara decided that her son would be an invalid for the rest of his life and that she would spend the rest of her life caring for him.

As Sara saw it, Franklin could no longer hope to pursue the life in politics he had planned. He could, however, still fulfill Sara's earliest and dearest wish: He could return to Hyde Park and live the life of a gentleman. As for her son's determination to remain in politics—nonsense. There was instead his stamp collection; there were books to be written. Her son had a fine mind, Sara had made certain of that. If fate had chosen to deny him of his physical strength, why then, he would fall back on his mental strength. As for what Franklin wanted, as for Franklin's hopes, he did not know what was best for him. She, Sara, had always known what was best for her child—more than the tutors and governesses when he was a boy, more than his own father, more than his wife, more than even Franklin himself. As Sara's grandson Elliot put it: "She always thought she understood what was best, particularly where her child was concerned."[3]

Sara's sole aim and goal became Franklin's return to the sheltered safety of Hyde Park. Any vestiges of a life apart from her son's fell away, as Franklin once again became Sara's private crusade. His illness convinced her that her son needed her every bit as much as he ever had. She wanted to support him, emotionally and financially. No one, Sara was certain, could care for her son as she could.

As for Eleanor, and Franklin's friend and political advisor Louis Howe, Sara was appalled at the way they treated Franklin. It horrified her to see him struggle; she had painstakingly planned a life for Franklin that was to be without struggle, without pain. She had centered her life on that goal. Now she saw Franklin in constant pain, and Eleanor and Howe were constantly pushing him, exhorting him, piling even more agony on him.

Such were Sara's ideas and Sara's plans for her son. But Sara had wanted to raise a man with her husband's strength, her father's courage, her own decisiveness. The degree of her success came as quite a surprise to Sara. Franklin Roosevelt knew what he wanted from life, and it did not involve sitting at Hyde Park and working on his stamp collection. He had found his greatest happiness in the bustle and bravado of politics, and there he would remain.

Sara did not approve. Her reaction during the time that her son was climbing the political ladder, moving from the New

York Senate to the post of undersecretary of the Navy and then running as the vice-presidential candidate on the Democratic ticket in 1920, had been either silence or disapproval. When Sara learned that Franklin, her Hyde Park gentleman, had decided to run for the office of governor of New York as a Democrat, she knew she would have to live with her son's stubbornness, but she was not happy about it.

It was true enough that the Roosevelts had always been members of the Democratic Party, but in Sara's mind, politics was no place for a gentleman. She had wanted to raise an aristocrat. Now she was incredulous; Franklin wanted to forgo a life of social position forever and mingle with the masses of ordinary men. Sara had meant for her son's hands to be ever the perfectly manicured hands of a gentleman. Now she watched as that son willingly, even eagerly, plunged his hands into the dirt of politics.

Franklin, of course, did not look at it that way. He thought there was more to life than what he had seen—a few idle men and women served and supported by the majority of the people. Sara really should not have been surprised. She was the one who had schooled her son in the philosophy of *noblesse oblige,* the conviction that those of social position ought to behave well toward others. Their only real disagreement was what constituted "good behavior." Sara liked "the people" as well as anyone, but not at such close range.

Franklin Roosevelt's decision to run for the presidency of the United States in 1932 heaped insult upon injury, in Sara's mind. She wrote to her son:

> *One can be as democratic as one likes, but if we love our own and if we love our neighbor, we owe a great example. I deplore the trend to shirtsleeves and the tendency to be all things to all men. I cannot believe my precious Franklin really believes in what he is doing.*[4]

But when her son was elected president, Sara abruptly changed her tune. She was even heard to call that night "the greatest in my life." In fact, she took to her new role as the president's mother as a bird takes to the air. As for her Republican friends, they knew better than to say a word against Franklin in her presence.

The White House shares its walls with no other house, and Sara was not about to build any adjoining residences on *those* grounds. Franklin and Eleanor had long been out of Sara's physical reach, and they were slowly but surely moving out of her psychological reach. Sara's financial arms, however, were still long: She subsidized her son (and the presidency) to the tune of $100,000 a year.

Sara Delano Roosevelt lived until she was eighty-seven years old. She died in 1941 and viewed even her own death in terms of how it would affect her son. While in the hospital, she said:

> *I know I am getting old and will have to die sometime, but I hope it won't be while Franklin is in office. When I die, he will feel so bad. If he is in office, it will upset him for his duties and I don't want to be the cause of that.* [5]

Franklin Delano Roosevelt had his flaws, both as a president and as a man. But no one can deny that his forcefulness, his enthusiasm, and his vision did much to shape the twentieth century. It is hard, if not impossible, to imagine what America would have become without him.

Similarly, Sara Delano Roosevelt was far from a sterling character. Her determination was not always matched by her sensitivity, and more than once she refused to let the truth get in the way of her opinions. But her love for Franklin was constant, if sometimes misguided. Franklin Roosevelt shaped history, and Sara shaped Franklin. Sara did not allow much to stand between herself and her goals. Surely, she saw that same quality made manifest as she watched her polio-stricken son stand on the steps of the United States Capitol and take the oath of office as the president of the United States.

Strong characters are generally not universally loved or admired, and Sara was no exception. After her death, Eleanor wrote to a friend, "It is dreadful to have lived so close to someone for thirty-six years and feel no deep sense of loss." But Sara was loved as well as hated. Eleanor's letter went on:

Franklin wept when he cleaned out her belongings and found the cradle he had slept in as a baby, satin slippers and a lace-trimmed robe which he had been christened in fifty-nine years ago.[6]

Franklin no doubt realized what his wife did not: Sara had tended Franklin's cradle with resolute love and unflagging faith. He would not have been what he was without her.

HARRY S TRUMAN

Harry Truman was never the sort of child one expects to grow up to be president of the United States. He was not a popular child; indeed, other children made fun of him because of his glasses. Harry was unable to participate in sports, earning the label "sissy" from the other children. Because he was physically not much to behold, he was a natural target for his playground peers. They taunted him and teased him, calling him "four eyes." Harry was treated as a curiosity, sometimes a monstrosity, because at that time a child with glasses was a rare sight.

Why did such a child defy the expectations, even predictions, of psychological profiles? How did Harry avoid losing himself in fear and insecurity? How did he ever grow up to be the humorous and confident man that he was? The only answer Harry would give to such queries would be: Martha Truman. Harry's mother loved and admired her son so much that he was virtually immune to the damage that his traumatic school days might otherwise have caused him.

Martha Young Truman was never anything but "Mama" to her son. Harry Truman was always keenly aware of the debt he owed his mother, and he let the world know it at every opportunity. When Harry was President Truman, Martha's portrait hung in the Oval Office. Other presidents might have viewed the office in terms of history or of politics or even ambition. Harry Truman viewed it in terms of what his mother would have expected of him. As he said, "I grew up to be as good as my mother wanted me to be."[7]

Martha Truman's first child was stillborn. The death was a

terrible blow to the young woman, but characteristically, Martha endured it. When her second child, Harry, was born healthy and normal, she rejoiced and threw herself into the rearing of her treasured baby boy. Her marriage was not unhappy, but John Truman was an average man of average potential, less educated and less ambitious than his wife. Martha found in her son what she despaired of in her husband: hope of greatness—if not greatness in the sense of accomplishing great deeds, then at least the satisfaction of being a fine human being, a great man. She directed most of her energies toward that goal, even prodding her husband off their farm into the city of Independence, Missouri, where the schools were of better quality. Her Harry would have every advantage possible if she had anything to say about it.

Although Harry was not an only child—he had a sister, Mary Jane, and a brother, Vivian—Martha concentrated her energy and her love on Harry. She taught him to read when he was four years old; when Harry was five, Martha noticed that he was having trouble making out the letters on the page. When Martha questioned him, Harry said that the letters looked "blurry."

Martha took her son to an eye doctor immediately, who diagnosed "flat eyeballs." Thus it was that Harry had to wear eyeglasses for the rest of his life. Martha knew that the glasses made her son miserable, often left out from the neighborhood activities. She responded by finding things that Harry could do and excel at, regardless of his physical limitations.

She encouraged him to read, and Harry found in literature both escape and expansion. Reading gave him horizons beyond those of Independence, a perspective wider than that of his own world. Guided by his mother, Harry read the Bible, Plutarch, and histories, especially those of the Civil War. Harry also took music lessons at his mother's instigation, which made Harry feel less lonely while other boys played baseball. Harry Truman grew up to be not only a fairly good piano player, but a devotee of history and of the biographies of great men and women. Martha's constructive search for a solution to her son's isolation and unhappiness is what opened up to Harry the world of great deeds and great men. For example, Harry knew every mistake Andrew Johnson made upon succeeding a great president. It was lessons such as this that would later serve him well. Perhaps such acquaintance with history did more to put Harry in the White House than after-school football ever could have.

When he was nine years old, Harry contracted diptheria. Almost every illness was serious then, and diptheria was especially grave, often fatal. Martha had lost one child and she was determined not to lose another. The disease temporarily paralyzed Harry's arms, legs, and throat. Martha wheeled her nine-year-old son around in a baby carriage so that he would not be completely confined to bed. She nursed him, entertained him, and encouraged him. Harry eventually recovered physically from the disease, but there was one key psychological aftereffect that remained: Harry was even closer to his mother in both love and admiration. By no means, however, did Martha ever mollycoddle Harry or baby him. She fully expected him to pull his weight around the house and the yard. What Harry did not know how to do, Martha expected him to learn by doing. No small coincidence, perhaps, that Harry was later able to learn quickly and ably what his duties were when Franklin Delano Roosevelt died in 1945.

John Truman died when Harry was thirty years old; at the time, Harry was still unmarried and lived at home. When the United States went to war with Germany, Harry went overseas (he had for some time been a member of the National Guard) and fought in France. He was thirty-three years old. Both before and after his time overseas, Harry shouldered the financial responsibility for his mother and sister, since his brother, who was married and had a farm, had other responsibilities.

When he was thirty-five, Harry married Bess Wallace, his "sweetheart" since kindergarten days. Soon after the wedding, a friend remarked to Martha, "Well now, Mrs. Truman, you've lost Harry." Martha's reply: "Indeed I have not and never will."[8] She was right. Until the day his mother died, Harry kept in touch with her by letter or by telephone. History has portrayed Harry Truman as an earthy and sensible man, and much of this common-sense quality he attributed directly to Martha.

After marrying Bess, Harry went into the haberdashery business in Kansas City and promptly failed. Undaunted, he turned to politics, as he had once turned from sports to reading and music. Harry never pounded his fists against life's obstacles; instead, he turned and found another road to pursue. Beginning with ward politics in Kansas City, Harry discovered an aptitude for this line of work and graduated to the United States Senate in 1934.

While Truman served in the United States Senate, his mother often wrote to him, advising him how to vote on certain pieces of legislation. (The Trumans were longtime Democrats.) At one point a reporter questioned the president about the propriety of such "advice." Truman responded:

> She [Martha] reads the Congressional Record every day and knows what's going on much better than some senators. She was one of my constituents as well as my mother so she had every right to write me.[9]

The reporter then followed up: "Did you always agree [with] and follow her suggestions?" Harry responded:

> Most of the time, yes. We agreed most of the time. But when she thought I voted wrong, you can bet I heard from her in no uncertain terms. She was a woman who knew her own mind.[10]

After Franklin Roosevelt's election to the presidency for his fourth term in 1944, Vice-President Truman telephoned his mother and asked if she had listened to the inaugural ceremonies on the radio. Martha replied, "Of course I did," and then went on to say: "Now you behave yourself up there, Harry," to which Harry replied, "I will, Mama."[11]

Harry Truman became the president of the United States when he was sixty-one years old. Franklin Roosevelt's death was sudden, but Harry had learned early in life how to catch on quickly, and as president, he made few mistakes in a difficult era that required several decisions of immense proportion. Even as president, Truman wrote to "Mama" often and called her every weekend. The soothsayer at the Wallace–Truman wedding had been mistaken. Martha never lost Harry. Neither did she ever lose her perspective, nor her common sense view of the world. On one occasion, a reporter asked Martha if she was proud of her son in the White House. She replied that she was proud—but no more proud of Harry than of her son who lived down the road.

Martha's mind remained sharp all the way into her nineties. She never lost interest in world events. When her eyes had deteriorated to the point where she could no longer read, she asked that the newspapers and the Congressional Record be read to her every day.

When she was ninety-four years old, Martha broke her hip. The president promptly traveled to Independence to stay with her, explaining, "She sat up with me many times when I needed her."[12] When his mother appeared to be "on the mend," Harry returned to the White House. Two months later, his sister, Mary Jane, telephoned and advised him to return to Independence immediately. Harry was on a plane headed for home when he received word that Martha was dead. She did not live to see her son elected to the presidency in his own right, but his success would not have surprised her.

After Dwight Eisenhower's election to the presidency in 1952, Harry and Bess Truman returned to Independence and retirement. By all rights, Harry Truman was an able president, a man of courage and integrity at a crucial juncture in American history. During Truman's tenure at the White House, the Marshall Plan was enacted with unprecedented success, the Berlin Airlift preserved freedom against overpowering odds, the North Atlantic Treaty Organization was established, thus containing Soviet influence in Europe, and the Truman Doctrine pledged America to aid free peoples fighting against subjugation. It is a record that shines through the years of comparative darkness that followed his presidency.

As for Harry Truman, he once remarked that his favorite epitaph was one from America's Old West: "He did his damnedest."[13] That he did. Martha would not have asked for anything more. She would not have expected anything less.

DOUGLAS MacARTHUR

To mention the name "Douglas MacArthur" to anyone knowledgeable about twentieth-century American history is to invite either adulation or derision. General MacArthur rarely evokes a neutral reaction. He was a man of broad dimension who often took definite stands, and this gained him as many enemies as admirers. His was an iron will that bordered on stubbornness. His determination and desire to achieve his goals led him to a unique place in United States history, but it also cost him a great deal, finally including his profession.

Douglas MacArthur was everything his mother decided he would be. Mary, or Pinky, as she was sometimes called, did not make wishes about her son's future. She made plans and then set about fulfilling them. Mary Hardy, a pretty and aristocratic southern girl, married Arthur MacArthur when she was twenty-two years old. The sweet blossom of Mary's southern charm, however, covered a root of willfulness and stubbornness that made tempered steel seem weak by comparison.

The couple had three children, all of them boys: Arthur, Malcolm, and Douglas. Malcolm caught the measles and died while he was still an infant. Mary reacted to the loss by redoubling her devotion to her two remaining children. She was responsible for their early education, teaching the boys what seemed to Mary to be the rules necessary for the conduct of a good life. Above all, she forbade dishonesty. She encouraged a strong sense of obligation in her sons and cultivated in them a love of their country. Every night when she put the boys to bed, she told them they must grow up to be great men like their father and Robert E. Lee. For Mary, it was not a wish, not a prayer. As her sons, they simply *had* to grow up as she desired.

Douglas, like Franklin Delano Roosevelt, another "favorite son," wore skirts and long curls well into his childhood. Mary was in no hurry to see her son grow up. But when Douglas did begin to move from the encirclement of his mother's arms, Mary made certain he did so according to the direction she had chosen. Like his father before him, Douglas would be an army general. Therefore, Mary's first objective was to enroll her son at West Point. With that in mind, Mary secured recommendations from governors of various states and from some bishops.

Her initial efforts were to no avail. Douglas did not get into West Point in spite of the recommendations. But Mary was far from finished. Douglas had flunked the preliminary physical examination because he suffered from curvature of the spine. Mary's response to her son's rejection was immediate and decisive.

At that time, Douglas's father was stationed in St. Paul, Minnesota. Mary's father, who had been a wealthy Virginia cotton broker, had established several high connections in government during the course of his life. None of these connections were in St. Paul. Mary packed her bags and those of her son and moved to Milwaukee, Wisconsin, in order to establish residence in the congressional district of a congressman who had been close to her father and who might help Douglas get the West Point appointment. Wisconsin was also a fortuitous location for medical reasons. Mary was able to consult with Doctor Frazier Pfister, a noted doctor who specialized in curvature of the spine. Doctor Pfister was in his eighties at the time, but he took Douglas on as a patient nonetheless. Mary would not have taken "no" for an answer. Together, Mary and the doctor worked with Douglas for a year to correct the problem. The medical obstacle was thus taken care of, but as it turned out, thirteen other boys were vying for the congressman's endorsement. The only solution was to hold a competitive examination at the Milwaukee City Hall. To the winner would go the congressman's endorsement, assuring the aspirant a place in the entering class of West Point.

Douglas was doubtful of his chances to be that one boy. The odds seemed to be against him; one chance in fourteen was not reassuring. On the day of the examination, Douglas felt nauseated. When he told his mother, she was not sympathetic. She told him:

> *You'll win if you don't lose your nerve. You must believe in yourself or no one else will believe in you. Be confident and self-reliant and even if you don't make it, you'll have done your best. Now, go to it.*[14]

Douglas placed first in the examination. With the congressman's recommendations, and with a straight spine, Douglas entered West Point.

There were no teary farewells when Douglas left for West

Point, because Mary went with him, moving into the Craney Hotel, which was near the Academy. She was apparently convinced that Douglas could not survive without her—after all, who had gotten him in?—and she was not about to let him try. Every evening after classes, Douglas and Mary went for a walk together. If it rained, they spent the time in her hotel room. Mary would listen to the story of Douglas's day, down to the most minute detail.

Douglas was in classes during the day, but Mary had plenty to keep her busy. Foremost among her diversions was having tea with several young ladies. As a young man in uniform, Douglas attracted his share of female attention. Douglas enjoyed this attention immensely, even becoming serious about some of the girls. Any women who entertained thoughts about being engaged to Douglas were quickly invited to tea with Mary at the Craney Hotel. There, along with their petits fours, the girls were forced to digest some unwelcome news. Mary MacArthur did not hesitate to be clear and to the point: Douglas was already married to his future career in the United States Army. Any other commitment was simply out of the question, regardless of what Douglas may have said or promised the young lady in question. In every case, Douglas went along with his mother's decision. Had not she always known what was best for him? Mother MacArthur said Douglas's farewells to disappointed young ladies on more than one occasion.

When not turning young ladies away from her son, Mary found time to send poems to him. One such poem illustrates Mary's views of the mother–son relationship:

> Do you know that your soul is of my soul such a part
> That you seem to be fiber and core of my heart?
> None other can pain me as you, son, can do:
> None other can please me or praise me as you
> Remember the world will be quick with its blame
> If shadow or shame ever darken your name,
> Like mother like son is a saying so true
> The world will judge largely your mother by you
> Be sure it will say when its verdict you've won
> She reaps as she sowed: This man is her son. [15]

Arthur MacArthur died in 1912. Pinky fell into a state of shock, and her two sons had to make all the funeral arrangements. Mary did not recover after the funeral; in fact, she became convinced that she was desperately ill, and neither son could convince her otherwise. Indeed, Mary convinced them that one of them would have to stay with their mother at all times. Arthur Jr. was assigned to a navy ship, so Douglas got the job by default.

Douglas requested an assignment in Milwaukee, claiming that his mother was dangerously ill and in danger of death. The army was far more skeptical of Mary's illness than either of her sons. The request was denied. Douglas was to remain at his post in Leavenworth, Kansas. Mary roused herself from her sickbed long enough to travel to Leavenworth to be with her son.

When the United States entered World War I, Douglas was called up for service in Europe. He would be moving from his mother's physical reach but not before she did her best to further his career. Mary MacArthur wrote to the secretary of State requesting a promotion for her son:

> I am taking the liberty of addressing you on a matter very close to my heart, and in behalf of my son, Douglas. I am deeply anxious to have Colonel MacArthur considered for the rank of Brigadier General, and it is only through you that he can hope to get an advancement of any kind.

She continued in this vein for five paragraphs, summarizing his career. The letter then concluded: "This officer is an instrument ready at hand for larger things as you see fit to use him. He is a loyal and devoted officer . . . ."[16]

When the secretary of State did not reply, Mary refused to be put off. She merely wrote more letters, until exasperation finally compelled the secretary of State to respond that General Pershing was in charge of promotions. Mary was heartened by this piece of news, because General Pershing had been a personal friend of Arthur Sr.'s. She sent the general a letter immediately; Douglas was promoted soon thereafter.

When World War I ended in 1918, Pinky looked forward to Douglas's return after their longest separation. When she received word that Douglas would have to remain in France, she promptly "took sick" again. Douglas wired his superiors: "Mother's health critical and I fear the consequences if I don't set off as scheduled. I would greatly appreciate your help."[17] Brigadier General MacArthur apparently had more clout than Colonel MacArthur had enjoyed. Douglas was permitted to return to his mother.

In 1923 Arthur MacArthur Jr. died of appendicitis. Douglas was now an only child and the sole focus of his mother's life. She threw herself into the task of obtaining yet another promotion for him. Ten days before General Pershing was due to leave the office of army chief of staff, Mary MacArthur wrote him the following note:

> Dear Jack,
>
> It was a real joy to see you looking so young and wonderfully handsome. I think you will never grow old. I am presuming on a long and loyal friendship for you to open your heart—to appeal for my boy and ask if you can't find it convenient to give him his promotion by a stroke of your pen! You have never failed me yet—and somehow I feel you will not in this request. Won't you be real good and sweet, the "dear old Jack" of long ago and give me some assurance that you will give my boy his well-earned promotion before you leave the army?
>
> God bless you—and crown your valued life—by taking you to the White House.[18]

Douglas was promoted to the rank of major general.

In 1930 Douglas was appointed to the same post once held by his mentor—that of army chief of staff, though when Herbert Hoover asked him to accept the post, MacArthur hesitated. He later wrote:

> I knew the dreadful ordeal that would fall to the new Chief of Staff and shrank from it. But my mother sensed what was on my mind and cabled me to accept. She said my father would be ashamed if I showed timidity. That settled it.[19]

Whenever MacArthur had trouble making up his mind, Mary had no trouble making it up for him. Douglas MacArthur accepted the position.

When he was forty-two years old, Douglas fell in love with Louise Brooks, a young divorcee with two children, and despite his mother's icy disapproval, he married her. Mary refused to attend her son's wedding, instead taking once again to her sickbed. It appeared as if Douglas was ready to stand on his own; he did not cave in to his mother's wishes. The newlyweds moved to the Philippines and began to settle into their life there.

Their time together was short-lived. It was not long before Douglas received a cable from his sister-in-law telling him that his mother was critically ill and that he was to come home at once. Mary MacArthur's illnesses were as well timed as they were mysterious. Douglas flew to his mother's bedside. Her recovery was almost immediate.

The marriage did not last very long and in later years Douglas's wife commented that "it was an interfering mother-in-law who eventually succeeded in disrupting our married life."[20]

Douglas was transferred from the Philippines to Washington. Pinky was in heaven; she had her son all to herself once again. They shared an apartment in Washington but Douglas MacArthur was sharing more than one apartment in Washington. He was keeping a mistress, a Eurasian girl named Isabel Cooper. As part of his official duties, however, MacArthur had to travel quite a bit. The young woman quickly found a life of waiting in a hotel apartment to be dull. She complained, and Douglas gave her a limousine, so that she could go out into the city.

She used the car to frequent nightclubs in the vicinity, but even this became monotonous. Eventually, she rebelled against the restrictions of life as Douglas MacArthur's mistress and began to make more strident demands. Above all else, Douglas wanted to prevent his mother from discovering that her son kept a woman. At the time, MacArthur was fifty-four years old and a four-star general. Douglas bought the girl off; many years later she committed suicide.

In 1941 Douglas MacArthur was appointed to the post of first high commissioner to the Commonwealth of Manila. He accepted the position but made it contingent on whether Mary, who was eighty-four years old at the time, could accompany him. She could. He accepted. En route to the Philippines, Douglas met Jean Faircloth, a woman of whom even his mother approved. She later became his second wife.

One month after their arrival in Manila, Pinky really became ill. She died of cerebral thrombosis, after having first lapsed into a coma. Douglas was stricken. Whether for good or bad, Mary MacArthur had been part of every day, every event in his life. He did not know what to make of life without her. General MacArthur ordered that his mother's suite be locked and unoccupied for a year after her death.

General MacArthur never got over his mother, either her life or her death. At his mother's knee, he learned how to get his own way, and from her example he learned how to use power, how to influence others to carry out his wishes. Whenever he failed to achieve a goal, Mary would not allow her son to give up or settle for less. This quality often served him well in his military career. But that same stubbornness ultimately caused Mac-Arthur's downfall: Dismissing him, Harry Truman said he would not abide disobedience, even that of a four-star general.

One can only conjecture what Mary's reaction to her son's dismissal would have been. It is almost certain that there would not have been any love lost on her part for President Truman. After losing his command at age seventy-one, Mac-Arthur returned to the United States and delivered a farewell speech that rivaled Mary's silver-tongued best. In that speech, he mentioned the debt he owed to his sainted mother.

CHAPTER SIX

MOTHERS OF A WORLD DIVIDED

Only the twentieth century has the dubious honor of containing within its bounds not one but two world wars. War in any guise, and especially a world war, alters forever the society and culture of those who engage in it.

World War I was the "war to end all wars." World War II began twenty-one years later. The problems created by the First World War were in great part responsible for the Second World War. It is an old adage that all wars create more problems than they solve, and the twentieth century testifies to its truth. The world today has been shaped by the wars fought in this century; the conflict and tensions that many fear will culminate in World War III have their seed in World War II.

One cannot look at the path of human history without finding men at war with each other. In the case of the world wars fought in the twentieth century, the stakes have become not just one particular race of men, but the human race itself. The world of the late twentieth century is incomprehensible without an understanding of the context of its immediate past.

When one looks back on the Second World War, what stands out above all is the domination of history by several men of remarkably strong and vivid character. During the decades of the twenties, thirties, and forties, certain men emerged who rode the wave of history, rather than letting history ride them. Only unusual times produce such unusually strong figures. The era of World War II counts as such a time. It produced not only Franklin Roosevelt, but Winston Churchill, Joseph Stalin, Adolf Hitler, and Benito Mussolini. These men were figures in a rare and exciting drama, the kind usually seen only in the pages of fiction. They came to represent absolute good and absolute evil, and they waged war.

Who were these men who shaped the world we know today? The best way to answer is to look at the women who shaped them. In so doing, some startling similarities appear. Joseph Stalin, Benito Mussolini, and Adolf Hitler grew up under the domination of strong father figures. None of them were reared by mothers who wielded any real power. In all three cases, the mother was a loving force in the home, but not a figure of authority. The fathers of all three men were the ones who imparted values to the children, while the mothers merely indulged and pampered them.

As the chapter dealing with "Mama's Boys" has already pointed out, such was not the case for Franklin Roosevelt. Unlike Stalin, Hitler, and Mussolini, Roosevelt grew up under the firm guidance of his mother. James Roosevelt was a loved and respected figure in the Roosevelt home, but a distant one. It was Sara Delano Roosevelt who reared her son.

Stalin, Mussolini, and Hitler stand out in twentieth-century history as dark figures, menaces to human hope and decency. Franklin Roosevelt is one figure who offers strong contrast to that picture. When one looks back on those years of World War II, his confident and sunny air shines on the shadows cast by the other three. But Roosevelt was not the only such "white knight" of the World War II era; across the ocean, Winston Churchill set an example for all men by inciting the British to courage and moral fervor.

Churchill, like Roosevelt, was reared primarily by a woman. Unlike Roosevelt, however, it was not Churchill's mother who exercised the greatest influence on him. Rather, it was his nurse, Mrs. Everest, who Winston felt was his "mother" as he was growing up. Mrs. Everest cared for him, loved him, and imparted to him a value system that would order not only his life but eventually the lives of millions of men and women.

What conclusions can one draw from a study of these epic figures of the twentieth century? Any such process is tenuous at best; one cannot reach back into their past and say, "Here is where Stalin became a potential murderer of millions," or "Here is where Churchill learned the value of fortitude." But looking into the past of these men can offer deeper understanding of what they ultimately became. To understand that is the first step toward understanding that epoch of human history, which is essential so as to make sense of the present.

Let us look, then, at these men who starred in the twentieth century's most fascinating drama and at the women who were responsible for their character and their destiny. A more dissimilar group would be hard to imagine, but the best place to begin is with their one common ground: all were born of a woman.

WINSTON CHURCHILL

When Jennie Jerome and Lord Randolph Churchill fell in love and decided to marry, they were the only ones who were happy about it. No one ever seems "good enough" to the parents of beloved children, and the Jeromes and Churchills were no exception. Few people, however, are more headstrong than young lovers. Jennie and Randolph were engaged just six weeks after their first meeting and were married one year later. Jennie's family had money, and Randolph's family had a good name; however, the Randolphs were not impressed by money and the Jeromes were not impressed by names. The Jeromes were American, unlike the very British Randolphs, and American girls were considered a breed apart from the rest. In fact, at that time in England, American girls were viewed as odd creatures with character traits somewhere between those of a savage and a prostitute. The Churchills refused to attend the wedding, which took place in Paris.

The marriage appears to have been a fairly happy one at first. Winston Spencer Churchill, the couple's first son, was born in 1874. In 1875, Lord Randolph contracted syphilis, not an unusual occurrence in the Victorian era, but as a result, the couple could no longer sleep together. There was, at the time, no cure for syphilis, so celibacy was the only form of protection for Jennie. In 1879, however, Jennie gave birth to another son, whom she named John Strange Churchill. Either Lord Randolph transgressed his wife's bedroom door, or as rumor had it at the time, Jennie had gone elsewhere for comfort. Coincidentally, Jennie's favorite riding partner at the time was John Strange Joycelin. In any event, the marriage went on as before.

Randolph Churchill wanted to pursue a life in politics. Contrary to his parents' fears, Jennie was not a detriment to her husband's ambitions but was, in fact, an asset. With Jennie's help, Randolph became a member of Parliament, gaining from his wife the confidence he had lacked prior to their marriage. But even as she helped him gain social and professional prestige, Jennie was growing away from her husband. His social interests were also hers, because Jennie's own position and prestige depended upon Randolph's. As became more and more apparent through the years, however, Jennie's personal life was her own.

A number of lovers came into Jennie's life and disappeared from it. They amused and entertained her, and she welcomed the diversion. Jennie was a social woman, and her calendar was always filled; sometimes these engagements involved her husband, but more often, they did not.

Where did the children fit into all this activity? They did not. This was Victorian England, where children were to be seen and not heard—and rarely seen, at that. To be a parent was a hobby in wealthy Victorian families, pursued in one's free time when social commitments permitted. Parents were to enjoy their children, not raise them. Nannies were hired for that.

Thus it was by no means unusual that Winston Churchill remembered his nanny, rather than his mother, when he looked back on his childhood. Mrs. Everest filled the void left by his busy and self-centered parents. It was she who sang to him, told him stories, bandaged his scraped knees, and wiped away his tears. Mrs. Everest loved Winston unconditionally and guided him with a firm hand. It was she who encouraged him to dream big dreams; she believed Winston possessed intelligence and character, and she passed that faith on to her young charge. Jennie Jerome Churchill was Winston's biological mother, but Mrs. Everest was the real force in his early years. Winston himself later said that he owed his life not to his mother but to his nanny.

This is not to imply that Winston did not love Jennie. He did, but more as a boy might love a faraway movie star than as a mother. Whereas his nanny took a deep and real interest in his everyday activities, Jennie flitted in and out of his days, remote and glamorous. It was Mrs. Everest who applauded Winston's successes and consoled him when he cried. Jennie was not around, and even if she was there, she simply did not care. Young children bored her. She preferred to leave them to someone else until they matured enough to be interesting.

Winston felt sure that Jennie loved him, but his feelings regarding his father were a different story. Lord Randolph did not like his son, and Winston knew it. Jennie was remote, she was busy, but Winston could better depend on her. When he contracted double pneumonia while away at school, Jennie dropped her schedule and moved into a nearby hotel in order to be close to him. But she was not a constant source of love in his life. At one point, when Winston won a role in the school play, he wrote to his mother and begged her to come. Jennie had a social engagement that same evening. She answered her son's plaintive invitation with a note explaining that the dinner was important and could not be called off. When the curtain rose in the school's auditorium, Winston's mother was not there.

In fact, Jennie visited her son at school only once during the entire ten years he was away. She was a beautiful and intriguing mother, but a far-off one. Winston was not a major part of her life. He remembered his mother as a flash of beauty, a jangle of bracelets, a whiff of perfume, and then she was gone. When, as a young boy, he contracted measles, Jennie did not nurse him or feed him soup and juices. Far from it: She reacted in disgust and fury, because Winston managed to pass the disease on to one of her favorite lovers.[1]

When Lord Randolph finally died of syphilis, Jennie changed the focus of her energies. Without a husband to define herself, Jennie Churchill turned, at last, to her sons. Winston and John were young men by this time, and so Jennie found them to be much more interesting. As Lady Churchill, Jennie occupied a lofty position in London society, and she enjoyed the further advantage of being well liked. Jennie began to use her influence to further the careers of her children.

One needs more than character and intelligence to go far in British circles. Social contacts are essential. Winston had character and he was very intelligent. Furthermore, he had self-confidence and he had stamina, both qualities gained from Mrs. Everest. Jennie was able to elevate her son into a world where he could display the qualities he had developed. In fact, his mother was so devoted to her son's future that she was not above sleeping with several prominent Englishmen in order to gain favors for Winston. (Any pleasures Jennie received from such activities must have been considered a mere fringe benefit.)

Winston obtained his first important job as a war correspondent with his mother's help. When he attempted to sell his first book, Jennie acted as his agent. When he decided to follow his father into the world of politics, Jennie campaigned for him. Winston never downplayed the importance of what his mother did for him, and he never forgot it. Later on in his life, Winston maintained that he owed nothing to his father; whatever parental care and love he received came from Jennie.

Winston Churchill's personal history offers an interesting dilemma to those who pursue it. While Winston was growing up, his "mother" was, for all practical purposes, his nanny. It was she who changed his diapers, wiped his nose, listened to his troubles, and rejoiced in his successes. Had Mrs. Everest not been a part of Winston's childhood, he would not have developed the qualities that shaped his own life and that of the world. Yet, those same qualities might have existed in a vacuum, might never have reached the world, had Jennie Churchill not stepped into his life. Mrs. Everest may have done more than anyone to form Winston's character, but Jennie gave him the world as a stage. Both Jennie and Mrs. Everest were crucial to the life of the man who Winston Churchill later became. He was lucky to have them both, and he never forgot it.

ADOLF HITLER

Klara Potzl was seventeen years old when she moved into the household of Alois Hitler. Alois was her cousin, and his wife was very ill, so following the time-honored role of one family member helping out another one in need, Klara's family sent her to him. Alois's wife died. Klara was dismissed when Alois found and married another woman to run his household.

Alois Hitler was not lucky in his choice of wives. His second wife contracted a severe case of tuberculosis and had to be sent away to recuperate. Alois once again sent for his cousin Klara to take over the house and the care of his two children. This time, Klara also took care of Alois; she became his lover. Klara was not a beautiful woman, but she was gentle, quiet, and reserved. She brought peace and stability into the household. When Hitler's second wife died, Hitler did not send Klara away. She continued on as a mother to the children and mistress to the father.

This arrangement continued until Klara discovered that she was pregnant. Hitler married her in her fourth month, but whatever romantic dreams the simple farm girl may have cherished did not come true in her marriage to Alois. When he married her, Hitler was forty-seven years old; Klara was twenty-four. Because they were cousins and both were Catholic, they had to apply for a dispensation from the impediment of affinity from the Vatican. It was granted, for better or worse, and the two were married.

There was no honeymoon. In fact, the wedding took place at six in the morning and Alois was at work by seven o'clock. Their reception had to wait until Alois had time off from his job. Klara knew by that time that her marriage would have little in common with her hopes and dreams. She tried to be philosophical about it, deciding that no young girl's marriage ever measures up to her expectations. Klara tried not to expect too much from life—to do so led only to disappointment.

Klara concentrated on her duties as a wife and mother. She kept a spotless home and poured herself into caring for the needs of her husband and children. She left to Alois the role of disciplinarian and authority in the family; Klara was not a strong-willed woman, and she did not cross her husband. A devout Catholic, she found beauty in religion and solace through prayer. Otherwise, those qualities were absent from her life.

Klara was not only mother to Hitler's two children from his prior marriage, but she gave birth to six children of her own, four sons and two daughters. It was not unusual at that time, however, to bear many children and raise only a few. As fast as women could have children, disease carried them off; the mortality rate for children was so high that raising a family was akin to playing Russian roulette. In the case of the Hitler family, only two children lived to become adults. Those two were Adolf and Paula.

Both were difficult children, but for very different reasons. Paula was docile and easily led, but she was by no means a bright child. Adolf was more volatile, but both children loved their mother, and Klara loved them back. Adolf was her favorite; perhaps she saw more hope for a good future for her brighter child.

The Hitler family, to all outward appearances, lived a typical middle-class family life. They were known and liked well enough in the community. Although Alois drank, he was not regarded as a drunk. Like any workingman, Alois Hitler enjoyed his daily beer in the local tavern, and that was all.

Klara was regarded as a hard-working and pious woman who made a good home for her husband despite her lack of education. Her background did not suit her for her role as wife of a customs official, but she adjusted to it well. She centered her life on her children, dividing herself between her religion and their care. Klara loved her children with her whole heart, but it was Alois who enforced the rules, and everyone's will, including Klara's, was bent to his.

Alois Hitler died when his son Adolf was thirteen years old. The family was taken care of financially after Hitler's death; Klara received one half of her husband's pension and a death benefit in addition to that. With a steady source of income and a house on which Adolf's father had made the final payment, money was not a major worry for Klara and her children. Shortly after Alois's death, Klara sold the house at a profit and moved the family into a one-bedroom apartment. Klara and Paula slept in the living room, and Adolf was given the small bedroom as his own.

Klara was convinced that her son was bright, although Adolf was a poor student who received low grades in school. One of the reasons for his low grades was Adolf's poor attendance record. The boy hated school and skipped out as often as he could. He stopped attending school completely when he was sixteen, without even receiving the usual leaving certificate.

Hitler found little in his school subjects to hold his interest. His ultimate goals were fuzzy, but they always involved dazzling accomplishments and public recognition. Adolf fancied himself becoming a great artist or a famous architect. At one point he decided that his future lay in music. Klara's reaction to this boy who made no effort in school and preferred to stay home dreaming of grandeur was characteristic of her. As she had once passively submitted to Alois's desires and bent her will to his, so now she acquiesced to her son's choices. When Adolf decided to become a musician, Klara bought him an expensive piano. What Adolf wanted, Klara tried to get for him, at whatever cost to herself or her daughter. This was the only way of which she knew to show her son how much she loved him.

Klara would have liked Adolf to find a job, but she did not push him. She allowed him, instead, to stay home and fantasize about his future as a renowned architect. The boy was financially dependent on Klara and made no effort to help out, but Klara remained passive. She was not by nature disposed to giving orders, and after all the years of marriage to Alois, she probably did not even know how to do so.

During this time, Klara was silently worrying about a recurrent pain in her breast. As time went on, the pain became so severe that she could not sleep through the night. Finally, Klara went to see her doctor—Dr. Bloch, a Jew, who was known as the "doctor of the poor."[2] Dr. Bloch examined Klara and found a massive tumor. Rather than tell Klara his diagnosis, Dr. Bloch summoned Klara's sister and Adolf to the office. He informed them that Klara was critically, probably terminally ill and that an operation would prolong but not save her life. Adolf cried in the doctor's office when he heard the news.

Klara entered a Catholic hospital. True to form, she rarely complained, although her pain must have been excruciating. At the time, Klara was only forty-eight years old, but the disease had taken its toll. She lost a great deal of weight, taking on a wasted appearance. During the entire time that she was sick, Klara's major concern was for her children, especially her son. Adolf depended on her utterly for both emotional and financial support, and she did not know what would become of him without her. She had taken care of Adolf all her life, but Klara realized that she had neglected to teach Adolf to take care of himself.

The operation over, Klara went home to recuperate. Adolf

was deeply shaken by his mother's illness. He stayed close to home when she returned and nursed her to the best of his ability. Dr. Bloch made daily visits to administer morphine to help alleviate Klara's pain and later remembered Adolf hovering solicitously at his mother's bedside. He said, "I have never witnessed a closer attachment. The mother adored the son and the son adored the mother. He suffered whenever she was in pain."[3]

During the time of Klara's illness, Adolf started thinking about his own future. Hoping to reassure Klara and find his role in life, Hitler finally stopped dreaming and took the entrance examination to the Academy of Fine Arts. He anticipated his mother's joy when she learned that he was finally on his way to becoming a great painter. Hitler failed the examination; he did not tell Klara.

Adolf was devastated by his mother's death, despite the length and severity of Klara's illness. While the other mourners left the graveside after her burial, Hitler remained. Prostrate with grief, he could not bear to leave his mother, could not face life without her protective shield and passive support. Adolf left his home town and traveled to Vienna. Unable to find a steady job, the young man lived like a vagabond. He did whatever temporary menial labor he could find, sleeping in cheap rooming houses and often eating in soup kitchens.

Adolf continued to dream of greatness. He painted pictures and envisioned a future as an accomplished artist, despite his previous failure to gain admission to the Arts Academy. His paintings were commonplace, and his life was lonely and mean. Klara had sheltered him from the harsh realities of making a living, and now Adolf found himself in a world that he was ill-equipped to handle. World War I solved Adolf Hitler's job hunt; he enlisted in 1914, fought in France, won the Iron Cross, and left the army with the rank of corporal.

No one had an easy time of it in Germany after World War I. Soaring inflation, food shortages, and floods of job-hungry veterans did not help the situation. Adolf Hitler was a victim of Germany's postwar depression; he was one of many young men looking for work and finding only bitter disillusionment. But Adolf Hitler would later marshal the powerful discontent of the

German masses and use it as a weapon against the world in general and Jews in particular.

That Klara Potzl loved her son is unquestionable. Intrinsic to her love for him was her constancy and her protectiveness. Klara took the responsibility for her son's financial and personal well-being as long as she was alive. In so doing, she never forced Adolf to assume responsibility on his own. When things did not go his way, Adolf always looked for something or someone to blame; he never acquired a sense of his own faults. Klara's love allowed Hitler to remain in a fantastic world of his own making. When his dreams crashed into reality, Adolf never questioned those dreams. He looked, instead, for a scapegoat.

Anyone familiar with twentieth-century history knows the tragic result of Hitler's search for scapegoats and his outlandish dreams of glory. Twelve million slaughtered men and women are silent witnesses to the results of those character traits. Adolf Hitler was responsible for the deaths of more than six million Jews alone. Of all those murdered human beings, one Jew is known to have been granted special favors—Dr. Bloch, the man who cared for Adolf Hitler's mother before her death.

BENITO MUSSOLINI

When Rosa Maltoni, a dignified, gentle young girl, told her parents that she was in love with an uneducated blacksmith who had served time in prison, they were shocked and unhappy. The Maltonis would not give their consent to the marriage, hoping that in time they could persuade their daughter to change her mind. But Rosa remained steadfast; she was twenty-three years old and knew her own mind. Her parents relented and gave their consent for the marriage.

The wedding took place in a Catholic church, even though Rosa's future husband was an avowed atheist. He was a man in love, and he was willing to go along to please Rosa. But Rosa and Alessandro were vastly different in temperament and in the values they held. Religion and family were the center of Rosa's world; not so for Alessandro. His major interests were political; his heroes were not saints but revolutionaries. Mussolini scoffed at talk of other-worldly gods and angels, viewing such things as ways to escape the world's problems. Even the couple's bedroom mirrored their differences: On the wall above Rosa's side of the bed hung a portrait of the Virgin Mary, while a picture of Garibaldi, liberator of Sicily, hung over Mussolini's side.

When Rosa and Alessandro's first child was born, a son, he was baptized in the Catholic faith at Rosa's wish, yet named Benito Amilcare Andrea after three political revolutionaries. It was apparent from the very start of the child's life that he would be exposed to diverse and warring influences.

Mussolini was an uneducated laborer, but Rosa was a refined and gracious woman. She was qualified to be a school teacher and taught classes in her home while Benito was growing up. It was Rosa's salary that the family counted on for steady income, but even that was a meager amount. They were desperately poor, and it became progressively harder to make ends meet as Rosa bore two more children, both of them boys.

With four males in the household, and little money, food was always in short supply. The frequency of times that the boys felt hungry after their meal constantly sharpened their desire for more food. Their mother did the best she could, stretching black bread and soup as far as it could go. Only on Sundays could Rosa serve meat to her sons and her husband.

The love that enabled the atheist, Alessandro, to marry Rosa in a church did not last long into the marriage. Mussolini was a drunkard and a womanizer who beat and bullied his children. Rosa's love for her children did nothing to remove the sting of Alessandro's frequent beatings, and she could do nothing to prevent her husband's brutality. Rosa had a strong faith and a deep love for her sons, but that love could not stand up in the face of their father's harshness.

Benito Mussolini had been baptized in the Catholic church, a victory for Rosa. But Benito's father wielded more power and influence over him than either Rosa or the Church ever could. The boy learned lessons from paternal vengeance that maternal love did not teach him.

Despite his mother's religious devotion, Benito grew up to

hate the Church and the State as his father did, who called both Church and State the oppressors of the human spirit. Rosa never gave up her desire to influence her son's soul, though. She took Benito to church every Sunday morning and even dreamed that her son might one day become a priest. Rosa saw in the Church a possible escape from the drudgery of the world in which they lived, a route to a possible education.

Rosa's dreams, however, had little to do with the reality of her son's character. Benito was a difficult, at times uncontrollable child. He had learned the lessons of violence early and thoroughly from his father, and Rosa could do little to quiet him. She finally sent Benito to a Catholic boarding school, hoping that the atmosphere of order and piety would have a settling effect on her son. But nothing could ultimately mitigate the elder Mussolini's influence on Benito.

When Mussolini took his son to boarding school, he told him to learn all that he could about history and geography, but to ignore any nonsense about God and the saints. Benito took his father's advice to heart; he did not believe in God and promised his father that he never would.

The Salesian friars had no more luck handling Benito than Rosa had. The boy understood only violence; any other kind of order and discipline was lost on him. In his second year at the school, Benito got into one of many fights with another student, but this time he drew a pocketknife on the other boy. Benito Mussolini was expelled.

Benito did not have any friends; his was a restless and pugnacious nature. He was always on the lookout for a fight. Impotent in the face of his father's beatings, Benito took out his anger and frustration on other boys, boys who were younger and weaker than he was. As a result, the young boy was lonely and miserable. He would always remember his childhood as a bleak time punctuated by bursts of violence.

Mussolini's father eventually gave up his job as a blacksmith and devoted himself to running a tavern frequented by his beloved political revolutionaries. Benito visited the tavern often; it was the one place in which he felt comfortable. He would sit and listen to the men who came and talked about exciting deeds and interesting ideas, and Benito became fascinated with these men and their way of life. He found their revolutionary talks to be far more exciting than Rosa's vision of his future had ever been. Rosa did make some difference in the life of her son, insisting upon an education for him. Without that education, Benito as a young man would never have gotten the jobs that he did in teaching and journalism. But Rosa was unable to impart one morsel of her religious faith to Benito, and her quiet love was not enough to offset her husband's cruel vitality. Benito Mussolini loved his mother, but it was his father whom he respected and feared.

When Rosa died at the age of forty-seven, Benito followed her coffin throughout the funeral procession, weeping uncontrollably. He knew that Rosa was the only human being who had ever loved him completely and without reservation, who had ever thought him as capable of being good. Benito Mussolini was a man without close friends, and the loss of his mother's patient and faithful love was the loss of his only real contact with human warmth and compassion.

Rosa would have been surprised to see the power and position her son eventually achieved. But she would also have been dismayed to see in Benito so many of the qualities of her husband. Benito inherited his father's interest in revolutionary politics and his disdain for anything but brute force. Yet, interestingly enough, Rosa became almost a cult figure in Italy after Mussolini came into power. Her tomb was a national shrine, and school children intoned the *Felix Mater* in her memory.[4]

At one point, Mussolini controlled virtually all of Italy. Everything as far as he could see was in his reach; he could take whatever he desired, so great was the power he wielded. But of all the lives he controlled and all the possessions that were his for the taking, the two items that Benito Mussolini treasured above all else were a worn-out prayer book and a simple gold chain,[5] the only worldly possessions of Rosa Maltoni.

JOSEPH STALIN

Ekaterina Geladze Stalin was married at the age of seventeen. Her first three children died in infancy; when her fourth child was born, Ekaterina was not yet twenty years old. Her life was a difficult one. Vissarion Stalin was a cobbler, but Ekaterina rarely saw what little money he earned, because Stalin was a drunkard and a spendthrift. She did not dare cross him, for the man had a violent temper and did not hesitate to use his fists. Ekaterina and her children lived in fear of his outbursts; he often beat them with little or no provocation.

Ekaterina—or Keke, as she was sometimes called—lived a life of drudgery. She cowered in fear of her husband and worried constantly about money. In order to feed her children, Keke took whatever work she could get, doing laundry, baking bread, running errands, and even sewing for the wealthier families in town. She did all she could, but it was never enough. With Stalin's drinking bouts and wild spending sprees, the family was constantly in debt.

Everywhere Keke looked, she saw nothing but dead ends and desolation for people of low social status. Resigned to her own fate, Keke hoped for something better in her son Joseph's future. She saw the Orthodox Church as his deliverance, his ticket to dignity and a decent way of life. Just as Mussolini's mother had dreamt, it became Ekaterina's hope to see her son become a priest. She envisioned him as a quiet, intelligent man, perhaps in charge of a parish. As a priest he could make something good and important of his life. Keke cherished the idea of a life for her boy, whom she called Soso, that would be free of the insecurity and violence and poverty she endured.

As a young boy, Joseph lived in utter fear of his father. One of the most vivid childhood memories was of trying to protect his mother from yet another of his father's merciless beatings. In anger, the boy had thrown a knife at his father. He recalled his father lunging after him, screaming with rage. Joseph was convinced that his father would gladly have killed him had a neighbor not intervened. The boy was not always so fortunate, however. His left arm was severely injured when he was young, perhaps in yet another beating. As a result of the injury, Stalin's left arm was three inches shorter than his right arm and he could not bend that arm at the elbow. It is possible that such physical scars were more than matched by the psychological scars of Joseph Stalin's early upbringing.

The elder Stalin was stabbed to death in a drunken brawl when Joseph was eleven years old. No one in the Stalin family grieved over the quick and early demise of the head of the household. Joseph had despised his father. The repeated harsh beatings had built up in Joseph a hard and protective shell against the world. As a child, Joseph believed that to feel at all was to feel pain. He became inured to any emotion, developing a hard heart and an unyielding will in order to survive in his world. Even his mother's love was eventually unable to penetrate his shell. Any positive effect his mother's gentle love might have had was more than offset by his father's bitter cruelty.

Ekaterina Stalin believed her son's best chance for a better life lay in education. Because of the emancipation of the serfs a generation before, theological colleges in Russia had opened their doors to peasant boys of unusual talents. Ekaterina enrolled Joseph in one of the schools, giving every cent she could earn or save toward the tuition.

Joseph finished at the school and actually enrolled in the seminary. Ekaterina thought that she would live to see her son escape from their lowly and meager life to attain a rank of worth and decency. But it was not to be. Joseph was expelled from the seminary for unreliability. He did not return home to his mother. He had endured enough control and authority, and he hated anything that resembled discipline.

Stalin drifted about, unsure where his interests were. Eventually, he found himself involved in political causes, and he became an agitator for political change. He learned to channel his aggressiveness into revolutionary activity; he turned his considerable pent-up anger and frustration outward, toward society. In so doing, Joseph Stalin displayed a genius for acquiring and using power. He learned how to use fear as a formidable weapon, and that lesson changed his life and the lives of millions of Russian people.

Stalin spent the years of the 1920s rising in the communist underground and in getting in and out of prison. When the Bolshevik Revolution was successful, Joseph Stalin was in a position of solid power.

In 1930 Ekaterina Stalin was seventy-one years old. Joseph was in a position to give her an opulent home, but she refused the offer. Instead, she preferred to live in the simple rooms that had once been the servants quarters in the former palace of the Viceroy of Tiflis. Joseph went to visit her there just before she died at the age of eighty, hoping perhaps to impress and gratify his mother with the prominent position he had earned in Russia.

Ekaterina was not impressed with the achievements of her son. His accomplishments did not mirror her dreams for him. Joseph Stalin was followed and feared by all of Russia, but Ekaterina had not envisioned her son as a figure of adulation and terror. She had dreamed for him a life as a simple but worthy parish priest, a far cry from what he actually became. In her eyes, the hated and feared Joseph Stalin was simply Soso, a good boy, who studied hard and loved to read and learn.

Ekaterina Stalin was the only person Joseph Stalin ever loved unreservedly. He admired his mother and respected her, but he did not live up to her expectations for him. Ekaterina had dreamed that her son would one day escape the cruelty and violence of their life at home. She never knew that Joseph Stalin would instead build that cruelty into the very structure of the society he helped to form. Ekaterina gave her son love, but she could not give him strength, for she had none to give. In the end, it was his father from whom Joseph Stalin learned his lessons most thoroughly.

CHAPTER SEVEN

WE REMEMBER MAMA

DWIGHT DAVID EISENHOWER

In 1952 the American people were sated with crises. The previous forty years had brought them the worst depression in United States history, the world war to end all wars, and the world war after that. They had thrilled to the idealism of Woodrow Wilson, the eloquence of Winston Churchill, the energy of Franklin Roosevelt. They had battled in trenches, taken on Hitler, liberated Jews from human ovens. Communism, the antithesis of American ideals, had taken over Russia and then China and threatened to advance even further. In 1952 America was weary of crusades, tired of worrying and warring and doing without. Americans wanted a rest.

Dwight David Eisenhower offered them exactly that. With his easygoing nature and his ready grin, he embodied the serenity and optimism the nation so sorely needed. A popular and well-respected five-star general who led the successful invasion at Normandy during World War II, "Ike" was an appealing and likable presidential candidate. An avid sportsman and "team player," Ike engendered good will wherever he went. Everybody liked Ike. Americans liked him enough to elect him president in 1952 and again in 1956.

Eisenhower's charm was precisely that he *was* a "regular guy," an ordinary fellow. He became one of the twentieth century's most respected and famous men, but he never relinquished his faith in the values with which he was raised. Dwight Eisenhower was brought up with small-town values and a small-town approach to doing things. That disarming simplicity was his greatest strength. He firmly believed that his upbringing was remarkable only in its universality. The values he learned from his family were the backbone of his life. Those same values were the backbone of America. He was convinced of it, and the nation wanted to be convinced, too.

Eisenhower always remembered his childhood as an idyll of normalcy, but the family actually lived on the edge of poverty. David Eisenhower had no head for business, and his one chance for financial security ended in failure when the store he had opened with a partner went bankrupt, and the partner absconded, leaving David with a handful of unpaid bills. The elder

Eisenhower moved his pregnant wife and two sons from Abilene, Kansas, to Denison, Texas, in search of a job. Soon after they arrived, Ida gave birth to the couple's third son and named him David Dwight. She switched the names soon afterward, because two Davids in the house were one too many.

After a year of working for the railroad at a wage of $10 a week, Eisenhower decided to move the family back to Abilene, where he could work in a creamery for $50 a month. As the family continued to expand, the $50 continued to shrink. The house in which the Eisenhowers lived had seemed snug when they moved into it, but it became impossibly small as the family grew to not five but seven. David's brother was moving West and offered to rent his two-story house to the young family for a small fee if they would act as caretakers. They accepted gratefully.

Suddenly the Eisenhowers found themselves with three acres, a spacious house, and a barn, but by then the failure of his store had sapped a great deal of David's ambition. Both David and Ida had dreamed of accomplishment and success. With five sons to raise and another on the way, they channeled the energy from their own hopes into hope for their children. Ida especially focused her drive and ambition on carving out a future for the boys.

Ida was the kind of woman whom everyone liked to be around. Gregarious almost to a fault, she was known for her hearty laugh and her infectious grin. She was a religious woman, a Fundamentalist and later a Jehovah's Witness. But religion was no grim affair by Ida's lights. She loved it in the same way that she loved music: It was a source of joy and laughter.

Ida Stover Eisenhower was a woman with plenty of dreams but few illusions. She knew that her family was very poor, three acres or no. She saw to it that they made good use of those acres; they bought chickens and cows, so that they never wanted for eggs or meat. She planted vegetables and fruit and assigned a section of the garden to each one of the boys. Each was responsible for his patch of earth and sold its yield door to door. Ida reserved some of the produce for canning, so that the family had food all year long.

The Eisenhowers were well respected and well liked in Abilene. David was not a financial success, but he was a hard worker, and Ida was a good mother. The family, while poor, was self-sufficient, and David and Ida always paid their bills promptly. The long period of debt after David's store failed had made the Eisenhowers chary of ever using "credit" again.

The family lived on the brink of financial desperation without ever succumbing to it. As Eisenhower later said, "I have found out in later years we were very poor, but the glory of America is that we didn't know it then. All we knew was that our parents—of great courage—could say to us: 'Opportunity is all about you. Reach out and take it.'"[1]

Both parents offered their sons encouragement and confidence. They fostered competition among the six boys and welcomed achievement. Both David and Ida demanded a lot from the children, but it was Ida who gave as much as she asked for.

David Eisenhower was a distant and rather frightening figure to the boys. He worked hard, and they knew he loved them, but he never showed any interest in their daily concerns, their achievements, their defeats. Eisenhower later recalled that "Mother was by far the greatest personal influence in our lives."[2] Whereas David was the disciplinarian, the authority figure, Ida was the one who worried when they worried and rejoiced when they rejoiced. She cared about every facet of their lives, and they knew it. Ida smiled. She laughed. She sang songs. David never did.

Both parents expected their children to strive for success. They encouraged "toughness," cheering the boys when they participated in games and letting them fight their own battles whenever it was feasible. Ida made certain that the family chores rotated regularly, so that each of their sons would be capable of any household task. By the time he was a teen-ager, every Eisenhower boy knew how to clean, wash, plant, and cook. Ike's brother Edgar Eisenhower later recalled, "We all learned a degree of the spirit of service . . . from mother."[3]

They learned more than that. "Little Ike," as Eisenhower was called when he was young, had a violent temper. Once, when his parents would not allow him to accompany his older brothers on a trick-or-treat outing, he howled in fury, ran outside and bashed his fists repeatedly into a tree, beating his hands into a pulp. After he had cried in his room for a while, Ida came in and bandaged the aching hands. When she was finished, Ida told her son that he would never amount to anything if he did not learn to control himself. If he did not find a way to rein in his temper, she warned, he would be miserable for the rest of his life. Eisenhower never forgot his mother's counsel and spent the rest of his life living up to the advice she gave him that evening.

One point on which mother and son did not agree was war. Ida was originally from Virginia and was well schooled in the horrors of the Civil War. She was a resolute and avowed pacifist. When Eisenhower began to exhibit an inordinate enthusiasm for military history, Ida locked his history books in the closet. But Ike merely waited until his mother went to the store or out visiting and then got the key to the closet and read to his mind's delight.

Ida believed firmly in the value of education—not as an end in itself, but as a means to a better life. Ida herself had attended Lane College in Lecompton, Kansas, for two years before dropping out to marry David. She believed that college was a route to greater and more varied opportunity. David and Ida had no money to offer their sons to finance college, so the Eisenhower boys went out and earned it themselves.

With her pacifist beliefs, Ida must have been startled when Dwight announced his acceptance at West Point. But if that was to be his choice, then Ida would support him. She did not approve of war or armies, but she loved her son. On the day that Dwight left for West Point, she walked out onto the porch with him and hugged him. After she watched him amble away from the house, Ida turned and went to her room. One of the boys later recalled that day as the only time he ever heard his mother cry.

After graduating from West Point in 1915, Eisenhower served in World War I as a tank instructor. His rank was second lieutenant, and he rose through the ranks after the war ended. By June 1942, he was commander of the American forces in Europe. The days of command decisions on the battlefield were long past, and Washington made all the strategic decisions. Thus, Ike had precisely the qualities necessary to be a successful general: He was a good administrator and a talented conciliator. The press loved him, and as a result, the world loved him too.

When the war was over, Eisenhower accepted an offer to

be president of Columbia University in New York City. After only two years of academic life, however, he readily accepted an offer in 1950 to head the Western forces of the North Atlantic Treaty Organization. Eisenhower served with NATO until 1952, when the Republican party asked him to be their candidate for the presidency.

When the Republican convention drafted him on their first ballot, Eisenhower accepted the nomination—despite the fact that he had declared himself a Republican only six months earlier. His opponent was Adlai Stevenson, the witty and articulate governor of Illinois. Stevenson was a strong candidate, but Ike's personality made the 1952 election a landslide.

As president, Eisenhower never wavered from the traditional values he learned in Abilene. As his parents had taught him, so too did Ike try to lead the nation toward the values of religion, honest ambition, and plucky self-reliance. He never questioned these values, nor their applicability to an ever-changing and growing American society. Ike had learned the importance of accomplishment, but not of curiosity. He believed that achievement mattered, but not criticism. He had been raised in an unquestioning home, and his was an unquestioning presidency.

Eisenhower was a doer, but his positive actions were virtually always managerial rather than innovative. He was not a creative president; he sought after no New Frontiers, he offered no New Deals. Just as his parents had done, Ike, the avid golfer and fisherman, valued the ordinary, the commonplace. When he was a boy, the family had read the Bible together every night. But they never discussed its meaning, never questioned its content.

The Eisenhower administrations echoed this approach. Calling his policy "dynamic conservatism," Eisenhower sought to heal old divisions rather than foster new policies. He ran the United States government in the same manner that Ida had run the family; he let his charges settle their own differences and fight their own battles. He expected to be consulted concerning only the most crucial decisions.

As for the rest of government business, that was up to the men he had appointed. Each had his section of government operations and was expected to tend to it. Above it all, Ike spent a good deal of time on the golf course, especially after a series of health problems. He did not even read the newspaper except on Sunday. As president, Eisenhower engendered an enormous amount of good will. He was as well liked in America as Ida had been in Abilene. His presidency was ideal in the same sense that his boyhood was ideal: It celebrated what was good and dismissed what might be bad. Ida's good will and hard work had resulted in a strong and loving family. But that same good will was perhaps not sufficient to sustain a strong and effective presidency. The United States drifted benevolently during Eisenhower's eight years in office. There is no doubt that the nation needed a chance to catch its breath in 1952. But an eight-year rest may have been a lengthier one than the country, or the world, could afford.

MARTIN LUTHER KING JR.

Americans who lived through the 1960s share a common and painful knowledge. After the placid, almost sleepy prior decade, January 1, 1960, was embraced as the beginning of a renewed and energetic nation. John Fitzgerald Kennedy called it the "New Frontier," and the American people welcomed the challenge, the call to break from lethargy and reclaim the ideal of struggle and growth. But growth usually involves pain, and by the time 1970 closed the door on the "turbulent decade," the country had endured great loss and terrible tragedy.

The very man who had come to symbolize soaring hope at the outset of the decade, John Kennedy, was gunned down in Dallas. In 1963 Robert Kennedy took up his brother's torch only to be assassinated in the same senseless fashion in 1968. The loss of both Kennedys convulsed the nation with shock and grief. Only two months before Robert Kennedy's death they had watched in numb horror as the decade's most prominent and peaceful civil rights leader, Martin Luther King Jr., was murdered. John F. Kennedy was a man of hope and Robert F. Kennedy a man of idealism. Martin Luther King Jr. was a man of dignity and justice. The nation struggled to hold onto these ideals while hatred snuffed out the men who stood up for them.

Martin Luther King was a man who asked for peace and

love in a world that was knotted in violence. From the mid-1950s until his death in 1968, King battled racial discrimination, meeting white aggression with passive resistance. King disagreed with black spokesmen such as Stokely Carmichael and Eldridge Cleaver who proposed violent countermeasures against "whitey." Unlike them, King was convinced that the sheer righteousness of the black cause would win the nation over.

Even in a decade as memorable as the 1960s, few figures stand out as clearly and as poignantly as does King. Who was this passionate yet reasoned man, this man who called for an end to strife and hatred until the very day he was brutally gunned down? King was a winner of the Nobel Peace Prize, a slave's grandson, a minister, a doctor of philosophy. But beyond all such categories, Martin Luther King was simply a man who, when confronted with what the world *was,* tried to open other people's eyes to what it *could be.* In that sense, King was a prophet. His speeches remain as a testament to the best that the nation can achieve. His death is witness to the worst that the nation is capable of.

Martin Luther King Sr. leapt up to touch the ceiling in joy on January 15, 1929, the day that his first son and second child was born. The baby was named after his father, but was known throughout his childhood as "M.L." So quiet was he upon entering the world that everyone in Alberta King's bedroom feared that the baby was dead. When he finally opened his mouth and yelled, Alberta thanked the Lord.

M.L. was born into a family for whom religion was the center of existence. Martin Luther King Sr. was the pastor of Ebenezer Baptist Church, one of the most respected churches in Atlanta, Georgia. His predecessor at Ebenezer was Alberta's father. Services at the church were a family affair: "Mike" King preached, and Alberta played the piano. The Kings spent most of Sunday at the church, attending services.

At home during the week, the family prayed together daily. Alberta often called upon the children—Christine, M.L., Alfred Daniel ("A.D.")—to read scripture after dinner. But one of the children's favorite treats was listening to their grandmother's colorful and action-packed Bible tales. God was a vivid and living presence in the two-story brick house in Atlanta. M.L. became a religious man, because religion was in the air he breathed. He was no Paul at Damascus; there were no startling revelations on this prophet's path.

Women were a great influence on M.L.'s development. The King home was a traditional one: Mike King was the authority, and Alberta did not interfere with his decisions or question his right to rule. But the children viewed their father with a mixture of awe and trepidation. He was the disciplinarian, the lawmaker. The only figure more important than their daddy was God. But, like God, Mike King was a distant and sometimes frightening presence. The sources of the children's comfort and support were their "mother dear" and their grandmother, Jennie Williams, whom Martin called "Mama."

M.L. loved "Mama" more than anyone in the world, for she loved him without judging him, with a love so pure and accepting that it amazed him. It was Jennie who sobbed in the next room whenever Mike took the strap to Martin. It was Jennie who told him wonderful stories, Jennie who made him feel as if he were the most intelligent and interesting little boy that God ever made.

M.L.'s love for his "Mama" did not exclude Alberta. He had a great deal of affection for his mother, and her unflagging serenity made him feel secure. He actually was far more comfortable with his mother's calm than with Mike's emotional exuberance; his father's tempestuous nature often embarrassed the boy in church and frightened him at home.

M.L. resembled his mother physically as well as temperamentally. Alberta was well dressed, quiet but not shy; she knew the names of every member of Ebenezer Church. She never argued or disagreed with her husband, but neither did she cower in fear of him. She simply believed that a household should have one center of authority, and the elder King was that center. Her deference to Mike King was not the result of low self-esteem. It was a conscious choice. Alberta was well educated, a former teacher and a musically talented women, and she had grown up in a home where the father had the "final word." Her home followed that pattern, because Alberta thought it to be the healthiest environment in which to raise children.

M.L. admired and respected his father. Even when he was

very young, the boy observed that his daddy knew how to stand up for his rights. Mike King never joined a riot or instigated one; he never had to. When Atlanta's white elite mistreated blacks, King used nonviolent tools to bring about justice. At one point, an Atlanta newspaper slurred the entire black population. Mike King organized a boycott that put the paper out of business.

While his father served as a role model, M.L.'s grand-mother and mother continually strengthened his self-image. Martin was bright, and his family knew it. They made certain that he knew it too. Curious even as a baby, M.L. was gifted with a good memory. When he was six, he sang hymns, with Alberta accompanying him on the piano. He entered high school at thir-teen and enrolled in college at fifteen. But King's intelligence and curiosity had one disturbing consequence: He noticed, at a very young age, the difference between himself and his white friend across the street. When it was time for first grade, the boys went to separate schools, and M.L. began to wonder why.

Other things began to jar him as he grew up. When he traveled downtown, he had to sit in the back of the bus. If he wanted a drink, he had to find a "colored" water fountain. If he went to a movie, he had to sit in the "colored" section—the back rows of the balcony—and he heard that section referred to as "nigger heaven." If he stopped for a soft drink or a hamburger, he had to find a restaurant that did not have a "Whites Only" sign in front. He saw blacks beaten by white policemen with little or no provocation.

The disparity of his life confused King. When he had been a first grader, questioning why he could not go to the same school as his white friend, Alberta had told him, "You must never feel that you are less than anyone else. You are *somebody*."[4] But now he was insulted everywhere he turned. The white world shouted to him at every opportunity, "You are *nobody*." King's early childhood proved to be the stronger influence. He *knew* he was somebody. The white man's desire to keep him down made King feel quiet outrage rather than bitter defeat.

It was this sense of injustice that guided King along the path he followed. When he was still in high school, an essay he wrote on "The Negro and the Constitution" won first prize in a statewide contest. M.L. and his teacher traveled to the state capitol for the award. It was a day to be proud, and on the bus trip home, M.L. was still elated and excited. When some white people boarded, Martin and his teacher had to get up and move to the back. King's sense of pride and well-being crashed into the reality of the white world. He never forgot the anger and hurt he felt that night.

King passionately believed that if the United States was the country that its Constitution and Declaration claimed, then people deserved an equal chance to pursue life, liberty, and happiness. He was convinced that most Americans, black or white, believed it, too. He felt certain that violence against whites (whom he found hard not to hate) was not the solution. If reasonable people opened their eyes to the injustice around them, he believed, those people would cease condoning it. His job, as he saw it, was to open those eyes. After graduating from Morehouse College in Atlanta, King did graduate work at Crozer Seminary in Pennsylvania and then earned his doctorate in philosophy from Boston University.

Open people's eyes he did. In 1955 Martin Luther King organized a black boycott of the segregated buses in Montgomery, Alabama. In one year the boycott resulted in legal desegregation of the buses. In April of 1963 he organized a similar campaign to end discrimination in Birmingham's shops and restaurants. The white police force reacted by attacking the peaceful black demonstrators with firehoses and cattle prods.

The nation, watching these scenes on the national news, was appalled. King's crusade ceased to be exclusively a black cause and became a human one. Both blacks and whites marched to the Lincoln Memorial in Washington, D.C., to hear King speak of his "dream" of an America that lived up to the hope and promise of its founding fathers. Again, in the spring of 1965 thousands of whites joined forces with blacks in a fifty-four-mile march from Selma to Montgomery to protest treatment of blacks in Alabama: Blacks were routinely being beaten for such things as sitting in the "white" section of restaurants or for trying to vote.

King was a peacemaker with a vision of the future. His eloquence sparked the nation and the world to share in that vision. When he was shot to death on April 4, 1968, in Memphis,

Tennessee, the nation reacted with grief and horror. The violence against which King had preached during his life unleashed itself in the wake of his death. A white racist had murdered the brightest light of the black movement, and the black population was left only with fury.

Vicious, bloody riots swept the country's cities. Forty-three people were killed, over 3,500 injured. When King's voice was stilled, the voices that shouted "kill whitey" were clearer and more commanding. On that April night, while their M.L. bled to death, his parents were at Ebenezer Church. They heard the news of their son's assassination on the radio. Alberta had thanked God the day he was born. Martin Sr. had touched the ceiling for joy. While the United States and the world mourned the loss of one of its great prophets, Mike and Alberta King sat together in silence and wept.

JOHN F. KENNEDY

Rose Fitzgerald was her father's treasure. John Fitzgerald, known as "Honey Fitz," was the mayor of Boston, an Irish immigrant who wanted to use the well-worn path of politics to find his place in society. Boston "society," however, was a small and tightly knit group; as the old phrase put it, "The Lowells talk to the Cabots, and the Cabots talk only to God." These "society" people expected Irish Catholic politicians to look up to them. But the Irish usually had power, and they often had money. Honey Fitz had both and wanted to use them so that his Rose would never have to look up to anyone.

When Rose was sixteen, Fitzgerald spared no expense on her coming-out party. He wanted Rose to be the most stunning and talked-about debutante of Boston's Irish Catholic elite. There were 450 guests who saw Rose Fitzgerald dance at her first cotillion. The ball would pave the way, Fitzgerald was sure, for a marriage to one of the brightest lights on Beacon Hill. Rose did, in fact, become the belle of Irish Boston society. Its wealthy and prominent Irish Catholic families were much taken with Rose's simple beauty and quiet grace.

But Honey Fitz's plans did not include Joe Kennedy. Kennedy, at the age of 25 already president of a Boston bank, seemed to be an industrious and able young man, but he was the son of a saloon-keeper. Fitzgerald was convinced that his daughter could make a far better marriage. He erected every possible roadblock in the couple's path, but Rose and Joe were in love, and Fitz's resistance only strengthened their determination to be together. When he discovered that his daughter was arranging to meet Kennedy in secret, Honey Fitz capitulated. He gave his consent, but it was with mixed feelings that he stood in the Archbishop's chapel among seventy-five guests to give his Rose away.

Rose and Joe had nine children. The belief in family as the most important thing in life was their greatest shared value. Her family was the center of Rose's existence; it was her deepest love and her greatest commitment. Joe broke his marriage vows to Rose early and often, and she was aware of his infidelities. She never confronted Joe, never threatened him, never lamented her fate to anyone. Commitment was more important to her than love, because commitment endured. Love, Rose realized, was like the leaves on the trees at Hyannis Port; it changed, it faded, it sometimes died. But commitment was the rock, the soil from which the trees grew—always there, ever present. Joe was committed to their children, and so was Rose. When the first stirring of love was long dead, this foundation remained. For Rose, it was enough.

Joe Kennedy is often credited with shaping the Kennedy children to his own mold. From Joe they learned that nothing in life is more important than winning, that competition is never for its own sake. It was Joe who wanted his eldest son to be president of the United States, Joe who earned the millions that would pave the way to social acceptance. But Rose Kennedy was not merely dancing to the music Joe piped. The children were very much *her* children, and her mark on them is indelible.

Small children bored Joe Kennedy. They cried but could not talk. They responded to smiles but not to orders. Like Jennie Churchill, Kennedy paid attention to his children only when they became old enough to be interesting. Until then, they were Rose's exclusive task, and she welcomed it.

The children were her world. Unlike most mothers, she

never had to worry about wet diapers, sticky high-chair trays, or formula. Joe's money, which provided nurses, maids, and governesses, allowed Rose the freedom to enjoy all nine children. Rather than concentrate on satisfying their physical needs, she spent a great deal of time with each of them. It was Rose who disciplined them when they deserved it.

Joe was often away from home. In fact, he often went weeks without seeing either his wife or his children. At one point, he lived in Hollywood and carried on an affair with actress Gloria Swanson. For three and a half years, his family saw very little of Joe. But eventually he always came home, and Rose was always there. As one of the children said later, "She was the glue that held the family together."[5] Joe wanted a close family, but it was Rose who made certain that he had one.

Family was the focus of Rose's life, but it was her Catholic faith that gave it direction. The Catholic Church was a source of strength that Rose sorely needed. She relied on the mystery and beauty of Catholic ritual and turned to the wisdom of the Church when she was hurt and confused. Joe Kennedy wanted to amass a fortune so that he could ensure lifetime financial comfort and security for his children. Rose, too, wanted the children to be comfortable and secure, but not merely financially. She wanted to share with them the comfort and security of faith.

Without fail, Rose attended daily Mass. Her mother had been a devout Catholic, and Rose wanted to impress religion upon her children as her mother had impressed it on her. While her religion was of great help to Rose throughout her life, personal comfort was not the sole reason for her devotion. The Church, she believed, was the greatest source of moral truth in the world. To teach her family the tenets of her religion was to teach them to be moral, to instill in them the "rules" for living well and happily. As she put it, "You must tend the roots as well as the stems and slowly and carefully plant ideas and concepts of right and wrong."[6]

The Kennedy children responded to their mother with respect and with love. In fact, some of her friends referred to her in jest as "Pope Rose."[7] This respect did not arise from anything Rose did or said. It arose simply because of what she was. As they grew up, the Kennedy children saw their mother face incredible loss and debilitating tragedy. She never lost control of herself. She never fell apart. And she never hung her head.

Joe's flagrant and chronic unfaithfulness marred the early years of Rose Kennedy's marriage. Gone was the naive young debutante who had walked down the aisle convinced that love was inviolable. In her place was a much wiser and stronger woman. She turned her hopes from her husband to her children, and her children rewarded her with their successes. Three of her boys—Jack, Bobby, and Ted—were elected to the United States Senate. Jack went on to the presidency and appointed Bobby his attorney general.

Joe had orchestrated the political success of his sons, but it was Rose who was an indefatigable campaigner. The public adored her, for she was not only intelligent and articulate, but she still possessed the charm and understated elegance with which she had won the hearts of Irish Bostonians in her years as a debutante. The Kennedy children were all so bright and so attractive that many Americans viewed them as examples of an American family at its best. Rose, then, as the mother of this smiling and energetic clan, was hailed as a mother to be emulated.

When Jack decided to run for the Senate, Rose poured herself into the campaign effort. Joe had always been the one with the political plans, but Rose was the daughter of a mayor and a congressman. Politics was dear and familiar ground for her. She covered the city of Boston to speak in behalf of her son.

Essential to victory in any campaign is a sense of what the people want to see. Rose was a woman of simple taste, but she knew that women wanted to see her in all her finery. When she campaigned in the suburbs, she dressed herself to the hilt in her jewels and furs. The public loved it. She hosted teas on behalf of Jack, and those teas were packed with people. A Kennedy always drew crowds. Kennedy's opponent, Henry Cabot Lodge Jr., later complained that "it was those damn tea parties"[8] that defeated him.

Rose called the day that Jack was elected president the most thrilling moment of her life. Joe had targeted Joe Jr. for the presidency, but that dream had died when Joe was killed in

World War II. Jack was second choice for Joe Sr. but not for Rose. She had always loved history and had tried to inspire the same love and interest in her children. Jack had responded to her encouragement, and she felt certain that his respect for and knowledge of history would make him a good, even a great, president. When he was elected president, Rose commented with pride that she had been like every American mother in dreaming of the day her son might become president. Brahms' "Lullaby" was rarely heard in the Kennedy nursery; Rose tended to hum "Hail to the Chief."

There is an old belief that dates back to ancient Greece. You must never be too happy or too successful, the story goes, because if you are, the gods will become jealous and strike you down. Jack's election to the United States presidency was a happy moment for Rose, but it was a single gold thread in an ever-darkening cloth.

She had lost her eldest son, Joe Jr., in World War II, but that was, at least, a heroic death. But her eldest daughter, Kathleen, had hurt Rose deeply when she left the Catholic Church in 1944 to marry William Cavendish, a non-Catholic. Cavendish's status as a member of British royalty did nothing to allay Rose's grief and anger at Kathleen's act. She did not attend her daughter's wedding, and hurt deepened into tragedy when Kathleen was killed in a plane crash in 1948. Two of her children were dead accidentally, but one of them, much to Rose's grief, had been lost to her before she died.

Another child, Rosemary, had been born mentally retarded. Rose struggled hard to keep Rosemary at home, to teach her as much as possible and surround her with love. But as the child grew older, she became harder to control. Rose had to give in and give her up. It was a very painful day for Rose when the family brought Rosemary to an institution and left her there.

As President Kennedy's mother, Rose was admired and loved, not because tragedy had touched her life, but because she had withstood it. She had suffered the loss of three of her children, and she had survived. Then the unthinkable happened. An assassin's bullet ripped through the head of her son Jack, bringing an entire nation to its knees in anguish. The world mourned John

Kennedy, but only Rose mourned as a mother. Only Rose remembered rocking him, telling him stories, feeling his hand reach up to hold hers.

How did she bear it? The world watched her, wondering whether a mother could withstand such pain. Rose endured it. How? "Will power," she said later. "Will power keeps you going."[9] That is what she did—she kept going. She kept busy, stayed active, concentrated on the children left to her. And she relied on her faith for the rest. Her religion taught, and Rose believed it, that God never made a cross for a back that was not strong enough to carry it. She had been given many crosses. She would bear them.

But there were more crosses ahead. Rose had barely recovered from losing Jack when Bobby was killed. Whereas the two older boys had always taken after their father, Bobby Kennedy had been most like Rose. He, more than any other of her children, had taken his mother's moral teachings to heart. Bobby had always been a strong Catholic; even though he was shy and often inarticulate, he had shared Rose's quiet but passionate commitment to moral ideals. Bobby's compassion and idealism had always been a source of joy and satisfaction for his mother. She saw all of that potential, all of that liveliness senselessly destroyed when Bobby was killed.

After Bobby's death, Rose put his picture on her dresser beside Jack's. Next to the pictures was a copy of one of her favorite poems, written by Padraic Pearse in 1916, the year before John Kennedy was born. The poem spoke of a mother's sorrow but celebrated a mother's joy. The last line thanks God for this: "My sons were faithful and they fought."[10]

Rose Kennedy gave birth to nine children and stood at the graves of four of them. Joe Kennedy was never the same after the death of Joe Jr. and could not even speak of him. "Ask Rose," he would tell people who tried to talk to him about Joe Jr. "She can talk about him. I can't."[11] Joe himself was felled by a stroke, and for eight years—until his death—he was mute and paralyzed. Rose had not even the comfort of sharing her grief with her husband.

There are some people, the Irish used to believe, who seem to be "born to sorrow." Certainly Rose Kennedy seems to be such a person. Her life was laced with death. Her greatest love—her family—was felled before her eyes. Many people have admired Rose, but not many have pitied her. Why not? Certainly she has had sorrow enough. Her innocence, her husband, so many of her children—all gone. But Rose Kennedy never wanted to be an object of pity. Pity is for those who cannot survive their burdens. Rose wanted to be strong enough to survive.

Jack Kennedy was fond of saying, "I know not age nor weariness nor defeat."[12] In that sentence, he unwittingly spoke the theme of his mother's life. Rose was not defeated, because she realized that death does not merely stand at the end of life, but that every moment is permeated with its possibility. Her knowledge of loss sharpened the value of what she had had. She had always maintained that the little things were the important things; she treasured them, and death could not take them away. The world remembered Joe Jr.'s reckless intelligence, Jack's sunny optimism, Kathleen's stubborn willfulness, Rosemary's smile, Bobby's earnest idealism, and the world cried. But Rose remembered, instead, Kathleen's first prom dress, the light in Bobby's eyes when he laughed, Jack's little-boy face when it was covered with ice cream and mud, Joe's glee when he won at football. Rose remembered those things instead, and she went on.

LYNDON BAINES JOHNSON

Tragedy catapulted Lyndon Baines Johnson into the office of the United States presidency. The photographs that preserve those days in memory bear this out: a solemn Johnson standing next to his own wife and the stunned widow of John F. Kennedy, taking the oath of office in the airplane that held the body of the slain president. A hideous accident, a bizarre chain of events led up to that scene, which is seared into the national memory.

Not even Lyndon Johnson would deny the role that fate played in his ascension to the presidency. But apart from the circumstances under which he took office, Johnson himself was neither surprised nor dismayed to find himself suddenly the leader of the world's most powerful nation. It was a role for which he had been preparing as long as he could remember. Beyond the power of his own memory, it was the kind of role for which his mother had reared him.

Rebekah Baines Johnson was a woman of illusion in a world of disillusionment. In an environment that starved her of the beauty and refinement she craved, she placed her hopes in a future apart from that environment. She dreamed her dreams through her firstborn son, Lyndon.

Rebekah had been born to a world of culture and social status; her father was an attorney, and the family was wealthy and well respected within their community. As the only daughter of such parents, Rebekah was certain that she was born to live a refined and cultured life. Toward that end, she attended college and eventually became a teacher of elocution. Insulated by privilege and protected by the naiveté of youth, Rebekah saw the world in terms of romance and excitement.

Sam Johnson was a farmer of small means and less culture, but that did not stop Rebekah Baines from falling in love with him. When Johnson proposed, Rebekah accepted, but she soon found that life as the wife of a farmer was a far cry from her previous life as the daughter of a professional man. Her fine education had prepared her for cultural evenings of intimate talk, but Sam Johnson had neither the interest nor the ability to discuss much beyond the weather and crops.

Rebekah found herself married to a man she found to be both vulgar and ignorant, with no thoughts of the intimate exchange of ideas. Indeed, Sam Johnson's version of a good time was to drink beer with the boys, telling bawdy stories and playing dominoes, leaving no room for Rebekah in such scenes. She was utterly alone. All her visions of love and marriage crumbled, and the reality of her life seemed harsh and ugly. The first year of her marriage was the saddest of Rebekah's life.

Then everything changed. Rebekah discovered that she was pregnant. Her misery vanished in the face of new hope; her ideals for her own life had been shattered, but she could fulfill them instead through her child. Her baby would grow up to live the life Rebekah had somehow missed, a life apart from dreary days punctuated by the drunken sprees of Sam, the foul language, the mean and paltry living standard. Her husband was a coarse drunkard and a fool who squandered what little money he had, but her child would be different. He would have the nice things she could never have. Rebekah would raise her child to abide by the Protestant ethic, as she herself had been raised.

The self-discipline and self-control that Rebekah's parents had embraced was only a far-off memory for her now, living in a cabin on a muddy stream with a loud and boorish husband. But Rebekah was determined to re-create her parents' values, their taste for fine things, in her son Lyndon. She considered her baby son the "greatest marvel in the world";[13] he was certainly the greatest marvel in Rebekah's bleak world.

With renewed interest in the future, Rebekah set about concerning herself with the education of her son. By using alphabet blocks, she taught Lyndon his letters before he was two years old, and he could read and spell by the time he was four. Lyndon's power of recall was strengthened through frequent stimulation; he could recite lengthy passages from Tennyson and Longfellow when he was only three years old. Rebekah lavished her son with attention, and he thrived. When the toddler recited a poem, his mother would impulsively hug and kiss him until, as he later put it, "I sometimes thought I'd be strangled to death."[14]

Rebekah educated all her children, but not with the enthusiasm she devoted to Lyndon. However, she often neglected their tangible needs. Rebekah had grown up in an environment where a lady learned to speak well and act in a refined manner. She was trained neither as a laundress nor a cook. The basic physical requirements of motherhood were out of her area of expertise.

A neighbor of the family noticed that Rebekah Johnson was not like the other mothers in the community. She did not get up in the morning to get the children ready for school. She did not cook a substantial breakfast. She did not clean her house. Rebekah simply was not prepared for the tasks that were routine for other women of the community.

Lyndon was always dressed in fine little suits, but his clothes were seldom washed and rarely ironed. Rebekah sent her wash out and when it was returned, she simply dumped it in the bathtub. When the children dressed themselves for school they chose their outfits from the tub. If they wanted ironed clothes, the children ironed them.[15]

Rebekah did not see her role as mother to be the maintenance of her children's physical needs, at least beyond the bare necessities. She was a lady; her responsibility was for the children's intellectual and spiritual development. Lyndon may not have had ironed clothes, but he had violin lessons. He may not have had an immaculate house, but Lyndon could recite poetry by the time he entered grade school. In fact, when Lyndon was in first grade, he recited a poem of his own choosing for the school production. The poem? "I'd Rather Be a Mama's Boy."[16]

Rebekah's world revolved around her first-born son, and as Lyndon matured, he realized how much his mother needed him. Many children would have rebelled or worried about measuring up, but not Lyndon. He knew how important he was to his mother's happiness, and he cherished that feeling of being needed. As he later said, it made him feel "big and important." From the day he was born, Rebekah believed that her son could do or be anything he desired. She communicated that confidence to her son, and he reveled in it.

Rebekah's lofty dreams for her son ran headfirst into reality when Lyndon graduated from high school. He announced to his mother that he had no intention of entering college. Rebekah would not even look at her son, much less speak to him, for weeks. None of the disappointment and disillusionment her marriage had brought her was as great as this. Lyndon wanted to try his hand at living, to get out of the classroom and into the world. But Rebekah had wanted her son to be more than a common workingman without an education. Now she could not see how he could ever be more than that.

Lyndon left home in search of the "real world" he was so eager to find. What he discovered did not measure up to his expectations, and Lyndon was back home in two years. Ironically, the important lesson the "real world" taught him was that successful people were educated people. Lyndon decided to enter college after all. There was just one problem; it had been two years since he had studied or read in the disciplined environment of a classroom. The entrance examination loomed before him as a major obstacle.

Characteristically, Lyndon turned to his mother for help, and characteristically Rebekah helped him. Joyous that her son had returned and wanted to continue his studies, Rebekah gladly helped Lyndon. The night before the test was a sleepless one for both mother and son. Rebekah drilled Lyndon again and again on the areas to be covered in the test. By the time dawn greeted them, Lyndon felt fairly confident.

Southwestern Texas State Teacher's College in San Marcos accepted Lyndon Johnson into its freshman class. This time Rebekah was only too happy to wave goodbye to her son; he was going on to a better world. While he was at school, Lyndon wrote to his mother regularly. She wrote back, and Lyndon attributed his success at school to the encouragement Rebekah offered him in those letters:

> *The end of another busy day brought me a letter from you. Your letters always give me strength, renewed courage and that bulldog tenacity so essential to the success of any man. There is no force that exerts the power over me that your letters do. . . .* [17]

Rebekah missed her son, but she was not unhappy. She felt that she had rescued Lyndon from enduring her own fate. Away from Sam Johnson and his environment, he could escape a vulgar and mean life as a small-time trader or farmer. For his own part, Lyndon was lonely for his mother. In December 1929 he wrote to her:

> *I have been thinking of you all afternoon. As I passed through downtown on my way home to supper, I could see mothers doing their Christmas shopping and it made me wish for my mother so much.* [18]

After he was graduated from college, Lyndon followed in his mother's footsteps: He became a teacher. Teaching did not offer the kind of life he wanted, however. He had fled the academic walls once for the excitement and challenge of the world. History repeated itself, with one crucial difference: This time, Lyndon went out into the world armed with a college degree.

Lyndon was Rebekah's son, but half the blood in his veins

was Sam Johnson's. Rebekah had prevented him from seeking pleasure in a life punctuated by barrooms and coarse humor. But the bawdiness and vulgarity of his father was an undeniable facet of the son's character. For Lyndon, the outlet was politics. Indeed, politics often resembles nothing so much as a barroom brawl.

As Johnson rose through the ranks, from the House of Representatives through the Senate, he remained close to Rebekah. While he served in the Senate, it was not unusual for him to break off a conference so that he could call his mother to get her perspective. Rebekah was only too happy to offer it. Her own life had not been especially happy or exciting, but her hopes had been fulfilled in her son. She once wrote to him:

> *You have always justified my expectations, my hopes and my dreams. Always remember that I love you and am behind you in everything that comes to you.* [19]

Rebekah died in 1958. She never saw Lyndon become the vice-president or later the president of the United States. But Lyndon fervently believed that her love, her faith, is what made his accomplishments possible. Moreover, with her help, Lyndon found a world where his father's qualities were acceptable, even useful. After his mother's funeral, Lyndon Johnson put it this way:

> *She was the greatest female I ever knew without any exception. She was quiet and shy but she was the strongest person I ever knew.* [20]

Rebekah Johnson did as much as any mother in history to prove that children are more than what their heredity gives them.

RICHARD M. NIXON

The twentieth century is peopled with heroes and villains. There are the champions of justice and sanity—great men like Churchill and Roosevelt. But there are also men such as Stalin and Hitler, who represent just as clearly the dark side of human character. In the history of the last hundred years, men and women can see figures who embody hope for what heights of strength and purpose human beings can achieve and figures who inspire fear and horror at what terrible evils human beings can bring upon their world. In the midst of this panorama of recent history stands an enigma, a paradox named Richard Nixon. Historians will be puzzling for a long while over this man of so many contradictions.

Will the men and women of the future regard Richard Milhous Nixon as a great party leader and statesman, or as a ruthless opportunist brought down by his own lack of character? Was he a talented and qualified president who was severely punished for a small transgression? Or was he a dangerously vindictive politician, a man of small, mean devices and petty deceptions who came all too close to bringing his country down about him when he fell?

The paradox only deepens when one studies the man's six years in the presidency. Nixon "made his name" investigating Alger Hiss on charges of spying for Russia, and as Eisenhower's vice-president, he regularly denounced Democrats and "left-wingers" for their communist sympathies. Yet, during his own presidency, this same man actively pursued détente with the Soviet Union and "opened the door" to Red China.

When Nixon campaigned for the presidency in 1968, he promised to bring "law and order" back to American life. Yet he had illegally evaded paying his own taxes while he was vice-president. As president, Nixon painted himself as a knight who fought daily against crime and corruption. But it was he who besmirched the presidency as no man had before or since. A long trail of evidence attests to this: extensive wiretapping of political opposition, burglaries, acceptance of illegal campaign contributions, kickbacks, and illegal political use of the Federal Bureau of Investigation and the Central Intelligence Agency.

How is one to understand such a figure? How is one to come to terms with his impact on history? It is impossible to assess Nixon's impact on the presidency and upon the American people without some insight into the man himself. One cannot begin to explain *how* the Nixon story happened without first asking *why* it happened. At the center of all the questions stands the man himself, and all questions both begin and end in the person of Richard M. Nixon.

It was always cold in the Nixon house, but all the stoves were burning on January 9, 1913, for Hannah Milhous Nixon was in labor. When the midwife delivered the baby, Hannah's second child and another boy, she named him Richard. Not Dick, or Richie, or Rick—Hannah meant for her boy to be called Richard. It was a nice strong name, and Hannah liked strong names and strong people.

When Richard Nixon was born, the family lived in Yorba Linda, a small farming village about thirty miles inland from Los Angeles. Richard's father was an uneducated "black" Irishman. (When the Spanish Armada was defeated by England in 1588, legend says, some of the sailors from capsized Spanish ships washed up on Ireland's shores. As sailors do, the Spanish seamen dallied with the Irish girls, and some even fell in love and remained in Ireland. As a result of this Spanish "visit," there are Irish men and women who are not fair but dark; instead of the light eyes and fair skin of a Celtic race, the "black" Irish are known for their snapping eyes and dark curling hair. Frank Nixon was known for more than that. His Irish good looks graced a man whose only consistent character trait was failure.)

Hannah's Quaker family objected when their college-educated daughter announced her intention to marry the crude and tyrannical Methodist, but they tried to help Frank out once he was their son-in-law, to no avail. Frank failed in one enterprise after another. A motorman when Hannah met him, Frank worked as a conductor on a trolley car, as a carpenter, and as the operator of a citrus grove. Finally, he settled down enough to buy land and build a gas station and general store in Whittier, California. But even that modest success had overtones of failure. There were two possible sites for sale, about two miles apart. After long deliberation, Frank chose one of the sites. One year later, oil began to gush out of the site that Frank had rejected. The Nixons were two miles and one unlucky decision away from being millionaires.

The Nixons lived very close to the poverty level. Frank worked long hours and expected his wife and children to work alongside him. Work they did. Hannah awoke before dawn every morning so that she could bake pies to sell in the store, using the unsold and overripe fruit from the day before. While the pies were in the oven, she prepared a complete breakfast for her husband and sons, who now numbered four—Harold, Richard, Donald, and Arthur. At Hannah's insistence, the Nixons breakfasted together each morning, after prayers and Bible verses.

Frank had converted to Hannah's Quaker faith when they married. Hannah treated her religion as seriously as she treated all of life. The family regularly attended services, and Hannah was gratified that Richard taught Sunday School. The Quaker creed preaches that success and salvation result from work and prayer. There was no mention of laughter, or spontaneity, or fun in that philosophy, and no evidence of those qualities in the Nixon home.

The Nixon household was never joyful or carefree. Life was serious, and survival was hard work. There was no time for smiling, for fairy tales, for silliness. Hannah's religion accounted for some of her sternness, and her life accounted for the rest. Frank had turned out to be as crude and tight-fisted as her parents had predicted. He was given to black moods and sudden outbursts of temper. The boys cowered in fear of his unprovoked spankings, and Richard especially kept his distance from this tyrannical intimidator.

Nixon began working as a bean-picker when he was ten and then began helping in the family store. Richard resembled Hannah physically more than did Harold, his older brother, or Donald and Arthur, his younger brothers. It was from her that he inherited the jutting jaw, thick eyebrows, heavy jowls, and the upswept nose so often caricatured later on. It was also from Hannah that Richard derived his fatalistic approach to life. For the entire Nixon family, life was often disappointing rather than humorous, tragic rather than meaningful.

When Richard was just entering his teens, his older brother, Harold, came down with tuberculosis. Hannah took the boy to Arizona, hoping that the dry air would cure him. Once there, she rented a house and took in three other tubercular boys. She collected a fee from each, cooking and cleaning for all of them. Hannah and Harold stayed in Arizona for two years, during which time Frank and the other boys had to make do for themselves. Hannah was a wonderful cook, but her substantial meals were a memory in Whittier as Frank, Richard, Donald, and Arthur fed themselves hot dogs, canned spaghetti, and baked beans. No one watched what Richard ate anymore. No one cared. He often ate candy bars for breakfast. No one stopped him.

Harold was dangerously ill, but that fact did not alleviate Richard's pain at the absence of his mother. He had never been close to his father, and he missed her terribly. Like many second children, Richard suspected that Harold was his parents' favorite, and the Arizona rest-cure only aggravated his feeling of isolation and loneliness. Later, Nixon himself admitted to these sentiments: "And my brother . . . kept saying, 'Oh, I want this pony more than anything in the world.' Now being the oldest son, he was kind of a favorite, as you can imagine. . . ."[21] Rationally, Richard knew that Hannah's departure was necessary. But he was still a relatively young boy, and he felt deserted.

The Arizona air did not cure Harold. Dispirited, Hannah brought him home to Whittier. They were home only a short while when seven-year-old Arthur became ill with tubercular meningitis. While Harold and Richard were out buying their mother a hand mixer for her birthday, they received a message to come home immediately. Little Arthur had died. Hannah had been preparing for Harold's inevitable death, and the sudden loss of Arthur was a cruel blow. But Hannah never broke down. She relied more than ever on her faith in God, telling a friend that "we know there is a plan and the best happens for each individual."[22] She did not waver, even when Harold, too, died a few years later.

After the deaths of his brothers and his father's failures as a provider, Richard burned with the desire to be successful. He loved his mother intensely, and he wanted to make up to her for the cruelty and drudgery of her life. Harold had been Hannah's favorite and Arthur the pampered baby, but Richard was determined to be so great a man that Hannah would be compensated for her losses.

Richard felt very close to his mother. They thought alike, in addition to resembling each other physically. They both viewed life as a contest in which only the strongest survived. Mother and son worked together in the store, and Richard often helped with the housework in the evenings. When he washed the dishes for his mother, however, Richard always lowered the shade. He was afraid that the other boys in the neighborhood might see him and think him a sissy.

In addition to his hours in the store, Richard worked during the summers as a lifeguard, a janitor, a handyman—anything to earn money for college. He was a very bright student, often earning straight As, and he impressed his high school classmates and teachers as a serious and determined young man. Once enrolled at Whittier College, Nixon was active in his fraternity and a renowned debate-team captain.

After college, Nixon earned a scholarship to Duke Law School. He did well there, and after graduation he traveled to New York with two of his friends in the hope of finding employment with one of the country's prestigious law firms. Both of his friends found positions. Nixon did not. He returned to Whittier and worked in a law office. Nixon had wanted very badly to be a Wall Street corporate lawyer, and his failure ate at him. He feared a life of repeating Frank's near-misses and failures.

It was in Whittier, at an amateur theater tryout, that Nixon met Thelma (Pat) Ryan, a quiet and reserved schoolteacher. In the sole impulsive gesture of his life, Nixon proposed to her that very night. Pat's first response was "No." A few years later it changed to "Yes." Nixon was a struggling lawyer living with his wife above a garage when the Japanese attacked Pearl Harbor on December 7, 1941. He traveled to Washington, D.C., and applied for a job in the Office of Price Administration. He was hired but left soon afterward to enlist in the navy as a lieutenant.

When the war ended, Nixon returned to Whittier. The district in which he lived was staunchly Republican, but a Democrat, Jerry Voorhis, was holding the seat in the House of Representatives. The Republican hierarchy in Whittier needed a solid, dependable young man to run against Voorhis. They found him in Richard Nixon, the solemn lawyer and accomplished debater. Nixon accepted the offer of the Republican nomination, and he won the election. The Nixons left Whittier for Washington.

It was during his years as a congressman that Nixon earned his reputation as a pugnacious fighter against "reds" and "left-wingers." His role in the trial and conviction of Alger Hiss on charges of espionage impressed a nation in the throes of a "red scare." Vaulted into the limelight, Nixon decided, after two terms in the House, that he would run for the United States Senate. His opponent was Helen Gahagan Douglas.

Nixon saw the Senate as the beginning of his drive for real success. He feared failure as much as he ever had. He longed for greatness as much as he ever had. The juxtaposition of his fear of failing and his desire to be great made Nixon a driven and often ruthless campaigner. The Nixon–Douglas contest was one of the most hateful and vicious in California history. On the first day of the campaign, Nixon accused Mrs. Douglas (without solid evidence) of being "soft on communism," at one point going so far as to proclaim that the lady was "pink right down to her underwear."[23] Nixon won the election.

When Dwight D. Eisenhower, a World War II hero, was nominated by the Republican Party for president in 1952, he chose Senator Richard Nixon as his running mate. Eisenhower was not close to Nixon nor was he fond of him, but he knew that Nixon was young and earnest, a hard campaigner who complemented Ike's easygoing, relaxed approach. The Eisenhower–Nixon ticket won in 1952, and again in 1956. The country liked Ike, but many people did not like Nixon. Harry Truman termed him an "S.O.B."; Adlai Stevenson proclaimed him "dangerous." Nikita Kruschev labeled him a "bumbler and a grocery clerk."[24]

Even within the Republican Party, opinion on Nixon was divided. In fact, a small delegation at the 1956 Republican Convention even went so far as to nominate a mythical "Joe Smith" for vice-president—anyone to replace Nixon. Even Eisenhower had grave doubts about his vice-president's character and had nearly dropped Nixon from the ticket in 1952 when he was accused of having an $18,000 campaign slush fund.

All of this had its effect on Nixon. He had always resented being wronged, even as a boy. His brother Donald later recalled that Nixon's ability to hold a grudge always amazed him. As Eisenhower's vice-president, he felt that other people's distrust and dislike of him (both in and out of the Republican Party) was unwarranted, and it hurt him. Political life invariably involves degrees of pressure, pain, and even ridicule. Nixon received plenty, and he could never forget it. He especially hated the ridicule in political cartoons and caricatures, in phrases such as "Tricky Dick." Deep down, he was still the boy who pulled the shades down for fear of being made fun of for helping his mother wash dishes. One of his goals as a politician was to ensure that one day no one would have the power to hurt or humiliate him again.

As Eisenhower's second term came to a close in 1960, the Republicans nominated Nixon as their presidential candidate. His opponent was a charismatic and engaging young senator named John F. Kennedy. In one of the closest elections in American history, Kennedy won. One of Nixon's greatest fears had again come to pass—he had tried for something, and failed. The Nixons returned to California.

In 1962 Nixon ran for governor of his home state. He lost. Two important defeats in a row firmly affixed the "loser" label on the forty-nine-year-old politician, and most political soothsayers proclaimed that Richard Nixon had gone down for the count. Stung and bitter, Nixon tearfully told the press that it wouldn't "have Dick Nixon to kick around anymore," and it looked as if Nixon's political life had ended.

The Nixons left California for New York, where Nixon was snubbed by the members of his own party as a "has-been." He practiced law and kept a low profile. He had changed his mind, however, about leaving political life. Nixon still burned with the desire to be accepted, to be acclaimed great in the present and remembered in the future as a great man. But he knew that he had to bide his time until the right moment presented itself.

That moment came in 1968. The Democrats had virtually self-destructed at their violent and divisive convention in Chicago, and the time was right for a Republican to win back the White House. Nixon wanted the Republican nomination, and he got it, followed by an election that was nearly as close as that of 1960, but in which he defeated Hubert Humphrey. Richard Nixon became the thirty-seventh president of the United States. Hannah, who had died in 1967, would have been gratified.

Nixon was a minority president in 1968—only 43 percent of the people had voted for him, and if George Wallace's independent campaign had not drained Southern votes from the Democratic Party, Nixon might well have lost. He knew that, and he knew that he was the first Republican president who failed to deliver a G.O.P. majority in either house of the Congress. As the 1972 election neared, much of his time was spent in preparation for his next campaign.

The Democratic party nominated George McGovern, after yet another fractious convention. This time, Nixon won handily. But a minor incident five months prior to the election refused to die quietly, as two Washington *Post* reporters named Bob Woodward and Carl Bernstein pursued what looked like a second-rate burglary attempt at the Democratic headquarters in Washington's Watergate complex.

At first, Nixon ignored the hubbub. But Woodward and Bernstein were dogged, and as their persistence began to pay off, Nixon became increasingly defensive. Investigations revealed that the Watergate burglars had been employed by the Committee to Re-Elect the President. Furthermore, there had also been an attempt to burglarize the office of Daniel Ellsberg's psychiatrist. Ellsberg was on trial for "leaking" the "Pentagon papers" (the secret official study of the decisions that led the United States into the Vietnam War) to *The New York Times*, and the Nixon administration wanted to see him convicted.

Revelations about covert activity in the Nixon administration multiplied. John Dean, Nixon's White House counsel, publicly accused Nixon and his two top aides, H. R. Haldeman and John Ehrlichman, of ordering a cover-up of the Watergate affair. But the Watergate scandal exploded when a minor official named Alexander Butterfield revealed, in an appearance before a Senate investigating committee, that the Oval Office was monitored by an extensive taping system. Nixon had stoutly denied any involvement in the sordid activities surrounding his presidency. The tapes would give the country a chance to verify his story.

A long battle over the tapes ensued, until Federal Judge John J. Sirica and an Appeals Court ruled against Nixon. Ordered to release the tapes, he instead offered doctored transcripts. Haldeman and Ehrlichman had resigned months earlier.

Both Republicans and Democrats were appalled at what they read in the White House transcripts—and at what they did not read: A crucial tape had an eighteen-minute blank spot, for which Nixon's secretary offered an excuse that left almost everyone incredulous. The transcripts that were available revealed a president who conversed in gutter-type language and referred to minorities in degrading terms. Important tapes were still "missing" because the system had allegedly been "on the blink" on crucial days.

The House of Representatives began taking the first steps toward impeachment. Nixon's vice-president, Spiro Agnew, had already, under unrelated circumstances, been forced to resign under a cloud of evidence that he had been accepting kickbacks and evading his income taxes. The tumult multiplied in the face of information about Nixon's own tax evasion while he was vice-president in the 1950s. The United States was in a furor, as even Nixon loyalists seriously doubted their man's integrity. Impeachment was inevitable. The suggestion that Nixon resign his office became a nearly universal clamor.

On August 5, 1974, after the Supreme Court unanimously ordered him to release the tapes and the House Judiciary Committee had approved three articles of impeachment, Nixon admitted what was already a foregone conclusion: that he had known of the Watergate cover-up and had, in fact, ordered it. He resigned the presidency on August 9, the first man in history to do so, and turned the reins over to Gerald Ford, the man whom he had appointed to replace the departed Agnew.

It was an ignominious end for a man who had wanted to be remembered as great. But Watergate was not an aberration. It was the culmination of many acts, and when one looks at Richard Nixon's career, a pattern emerges that leads straight to Watergate's door.

Nixon wanted to succeed. Those who had hurt him, ridiculed him in the past, called him a loser—they were his enemies. He carried those wounds forever, and he desperately wanted to retaliate at anyone who might hurt him again. Much of the Nixon administration's sleaziest doings were aimed at eliminating political "enemies."

Furthermore, Nixon failed to understand that the ability to compromise is necessary in politics, that a good politician welcomes debate and listens to dissent. The Nixon administration was closed to consultation. Nixon surrounded himself with his friends rather than with seasoned former officeholders. He did not rely on his cabinet, nor did he forge any relationships with congressmen. Instead, he appointed a vast White House staff, the largest one up to that point in history. Nixon appointed only men who shared his viewpoint and whose loyalties were not to any electorate or partisan philosophy but to him.

As a result of the barriers that Nixon erected between himself and the American people, the White House was an island of isolation in a sea of ever-increasing hostility. His relationship with the Congress was abysmal, his relationship with the press even worse. His administration was a homogeneous unit that eventually lost touch with the rest of the country.

Why was Nixon compelled to surround himself with men of loyalty, even adulation? Why did he come to equate dissent with betrayal? Nixon answered the puzzle himself when he commented in reference to his drive to win a campaign early in his career, that he never in his life wanted to be left behind.

"Left behind." Nixon never really recovered from the deaths of his two brothers, deaths that had, in fact, left him behind. He never forgot that his mother had been forced to leave him to take Harold to Arizona. Though it was not Hannah's choice, and Nixon knew that, he had always been convinced that Harold had been his mother's favorite boy. Harold died, and Nixon burned with the need to prove that he, the survivor, was worthwhile, too. He was driven throughout his career by the need to be accepted.

In 1960, someone asked Hannah whether her son had changed since his early years. "No," she replied, "he has always been exactly the same. I never knew a person to change so little. From the time he was first able to understand the world around him until now, he has reacted the same way to the same situations."[25] Hannah was right. In his final speech to the American people, Nixon's voice trembled for the first time when he said,

> No one will ever write a book about my mother. Well, I guess all of you would say this about your mother. My mother was a saint.[26]

Buried in the Nixon who surrounded himself with loyal "yes men" was the boy who wanted to justify to Hannah his survival in the face of his brothers' deaths. Somewhere within the Nixon who stooped to the lowest levels to defeat his opposition was the man who explained his own ambition as a desire to never be left behind. Inside the middle-aged man whose voice shook as he resigned the United States presidency was the young boy who had worked so hard to be worthy of the love of the woman he thought of as a saint.

RONALD REAGAN

Ronald Reagan is not a crusader against laws in the United States that discriminate against women. He has come out firmly against ratification of the Equal Rights Amendment. Feminists do not stage rallies for Reagan; indeed, most of them despise him, because his policies on national defense, education, and social welfare do nothing to endear him to them, young and old. This is a man who looks the other way as single mothers become the largest group of Americans at the nation's poverty level.

Yet, this is, at the same time, a man who has appointed women to several important government posts: Jeane Kirkpatrick as ambassador to the United Nations, Sandra Day O'Connor as the first woman on the United States Supreme Court, Elizabeth Dole as secretary of Transportation, and Margaret Heckler as secretary of Health and Human Services. What stands out in these appointments is the strength and independence of the women. Few, if any, of these Reagan appointees inspire neutral reaction from informed voters. Some have inspired serious controversy.

Ronald Reagan never seems to mind the fierce independence of the female members of his administration; he even seems, at times, to welcome it. He does not appear to be threatened by forthright—even feisty—women in politics. Nor does the presence of such women in his own family seem to hold much terror for him. Both of his daughters, Maureen and Patti, are vocal and highly independent people. Reagan seems able to live with their views that differ from his own and accept his children for what they are.

What does one make of this paradox? Is Ronald Reagan

an incorrigible sexist, a dinosaur in the world women are faced with today? If so (and many would give him just such a label), it is hard to make sense of his obvious respect and admiration for strong, creative women *and* for his popularity with a vast majority of American women. The answer to the puzzle is in Ronald Reagan's childhood: In Nelle Reagan, the paradox is uncovered, the mystery unlocked. As is true with so many sons and mothers, to have known Nelle Reagan is to go a great distance toward understanding her son Ronald.

Nelle Reagan's words on February 6, 1911, when she saw her son for the first time, summed up her feeling for him until the day she died: "I think he's perfectly wonderful."[27] Nelle's opinion of her second son never changed, and Ronald Wilson Reagan grew up with the security of his mother's affection and complete devotion. Her children, Neil and Ronald, were the center of Nelle's life, the focus of her dreams. Her life had not turned out exactly as she hoped it would when she was young, but her boys were a beam of life and joy.

Nelle Wilson—a dainty girl with rich auburn hair and blue eyes—had been brought up to be a proper Protestant by her Scottish-English parents. But she did not marry a proper Protestant boy. Ronald's father, like Richard Nixon's, was a Catholic "black" Irishman. John Edward Reagan, nicknamed Jack, typified the image of unpredictability and wild daring; his roguish good looks, along with his considerable Irish charm, appealed to Nelle, and she fell in love with him.

Jack had the charm and good looks often identified with the Irish. Unfortunately for Nelle, he also had a weakness—alcoholism. Alcohol was an anchor that continually dragged Jack down, a leech that sucked away his ambition and his hope. Eventually, it destroyed him.

Nelle Reagan would not let it destroy her, nor her sons. She had not anticipated Jack's alcoholism, but once it was a fact of her life, she coped with it. Nelle believed that she had to play with the hand that life dealt her; it would do none of them any good were she to moan about the injustice of the cards in her hand.

Her actions as the wife of an alcoholic were ahead of her era. At that time, alcoholism was condemned as a weakness, a sign of a flawed moral character. Nelle never considered her husband to be a morally evil man. She continued to love him and expected Neil and Ronald to love him too. Nelle sensed that the drinking was not entirely Jack's fault, and she explained this conviction to the two boys. When they were old enough to realize that something was very much awry in their home, Nelle told them that their father was a sick man, a man with a problem; he deserved not their condemnation, but their support.

Both Neil and Ronald understood their mother's advice, but even more important, both saw how Nelle herself treated their father. She did not blame him. She did not show the fury and frustration she must have felt at times. She continued to love her husband. From the example of Nelle, her two sons learned never to treat their father with resentment or contempt.

Yet, life for the family of an alcoholic is hard. When Ronald was eleven years old, he came home one evening to find that his father had passed out on the porch. Eleven is the age when a boy most needs to rely on the strength and example of his father, most needs the security of an adult male role model. Instead, Ronald was faced with a father who had drunk himself into a stupor. He later recalled:

> I stood over him for a minute or two. I wanted to let myself into the house and go to bed and pretend he wasn't there. I bent over him smelling the sharp odor of whiskey from the speakeasy. I got a fistful of his overcoat. Opening the door, I managed to drag him inside and get him to bed.[28]

That, he knew, was what his mother would have wanted him to do. If she could be strong, Ronald wanted to be strong too.

Nelle provided the only stability in Neil's and Ronald's lives. Jack had a variety of jobs, none of them very successful, and the entire family was often uprooted as he searched for a venture that would enable him to support his family. When Ronald was born, the family was living in Tampico, Illinois, in a five-room apartment over the general store where Jack worked as a clerk. They were not there for long.

When Ronald, nicknamed "Dutch" by his father, was two years old, the Reagans moved to the South Side of Chicago. Jack found another job, this one at Marshall Field and Company. The pay was so low that the family could not subsist on it, but few businesses would even hire a man with Jack's work record. He was glad to be employed at all. Nelle augmented their meager income in any way she could, but she would not take charity. She felt that as long as she had two hands and a mind, her family could survive without depending on outside assistance.

The University of Chicago was nearby, and the football games always drew a crowd of students and spectators. Nelle figured that many of those football fans were hungry before and after the game and that she would capitalize on that hunger. She popped corn on Saturday mornings and sent the boys over to the stadium to sell it. Ronald was only four years old, but the memory stayed with him: the brisk air, the busy crowd, the smell of popcorn. It was a worthwhile idea, but it did not bring much money. The family was still earning barely enough to survive.

Once a week, the Reagans had liver. It was their Sunday treat. Every Saturday, Nelle sent seven-year-old Neil to the butcher shop to buy a soup bone for ten cents. On Nelle's instructions, Neil always asked the butcher for some liver for the cat. There was no cat. Nelle wanted no one's pity, and they needed the liver. When Neil brought the provisions home, Nelle saved the liver and cooked it for Sunday dinner. With the soup bone, she made soup that served as dinner for the rest of the week. As the soup diminished with each day, Nelle added carrots, potatoes, and water to stretch it until Saturday. Monday's soup was always a good deal tastier than Friday's.

When he worked, Jack Reagan was a shoe salesman and he was a very good one when he was not drunk. His charm sold a lot of shoes but he had trouble holding jobs. Though employers like charming employees, they demand reliability as well. Jack was hard working when he was sober, but that was rare. Everytime he lost a job, the family was uprooted and moved someplace where Jack could find work. The Reagans moved throughout Illinois, from Chicago to Galesburg and then to Monmouth. They even went back to Tampico, but life there was no better than it had been the first time.

Jack was tired of working for other people, tired of

punching in and of being ordered around, tired of earning so little for what he considered so much labor. He dreamed of being his own man, of owning his own business. He felt certain that his own shoe store would enable him to hold his head high, to stay away from alcohol. The Reagans moved yet again, from Tampico to Dixon, Illinois, where Jack Reagan decided to make his dream come true.

He found a partner who was willing to invest his capital in Jack's charm and skill as a salesman. Reagan's Fashion Boot Shop opened in 1920. Jack was trying hard to stay sober, for the store meant a great deal to him. He was working hard, and the future was starting to look brighter than the past had been.

The Great Depression wiped out the Fashion Boot Shop. Nelle knew that the shop's failure was not Jack's fault, even less so than alcoholism was. He had tried so hard, but that knowledge did not ease the difficulty in making ends meet. Nelle's heart ached for her husband as she watched him set off to sell shoes as a traveling salesman. When that was unsuccessful, Jack moved yet again, this time to Springfield, Illinois, where he found a job in a second-rate shoe store. He was back working for someone else, and his failure weighed heavily on his shoulders.

Jack made the move to Springfield without his family. Nelle stayed in Dixon because she had a job there that she could not leave. She worked in a dress shop, selling clothes and altering them for the customers. She needed every cent of the $14-a-week pay because Nelle was the only source of financial stability in the family.

She was the source of emotional stability as well. Ronald was horrified at his father's alcoholism; it made the man he so wanted to admire weak and unreliable. Nelle depended on no one, and Ronald wanted to emulate her independence and strength, her industriousness and ability to cope. He wanted to stay away from people who could not help themselves.

Nelle remained a Protestant throughout her marriage to Jack. Neil was Catholic like his father, but Ronald was Protestant like his mother. Nelle's religion was important to her, and not just on Sunday. Her faith was an integral part of her life, and she took the message very seriously. Christ had commanded his followers to love one another, and Nelle took that to mean that an hour's worship once a week was not enough.

Throughout her life, even when she had to work long hours during the day, Nelle visited prisoners in jail cells and volunteered to read to them. When prisoners were released from jail, she helped them to find housing and employment. When the family lived near a sanitarium for indigent tuberculosis patients, she visited them. The Reagan boys saw in their mother's example that religion was not a creed but a way of living.

Nelle had only an eighth-grade education, but she had the kind of knowledge that does not come from any amount of schooling: In any situation, she knew what had to be done. What is more, she did it. She never allowed life to make her its victim. But she wanted her sons to be educated, to have a life that would be more than a struggle for simple survival, and she saw education as the route to that life.

Both Ronald and Neil learned to read on Nelle's lap before they were of school age, and she was intensely proud of that. When Ronald was only five years old, she would call their neighbors in to hear him read the newspaper. As the boys grew up, she took them to plays, recitals, and lectures, hoping to expose them to a side of life that was cultured and refined. There was more than a touch of the actress in Nelle, and she loved to give dramatic readings. The boys always accompanied her, for such occasions were yet another chance for Neil and Ronald to see that life involved more than the mean fight for food and shelter.

These dramatic evenings made a lasting impression on Ronald. He enjoyed the world of make-believe; it was much nicer than reality, which could be harsh. He had inherited Jack's charm, but he was determined to emulate Nelle's perseverance. Summer stints as a lifeguard helped him to pay for college. The money he earned over the summer, however, was not sufficient. He had to borrow money to meet tuition costs, but he paid it back as soon as he could.

Armed with a college degree, Ronald tried the world of broadcasting and then moved on to acting. He had his mother's good looks—his auburn hair and blue eyes echoed hers—and her dramatic talent. Though Reagan was a modest success in Hollywood, he eventually became a wealthy man. One of the first things he did with his money was to buy a house for Nelle and Jack. Jack was by this time a weak and sick man who could not work, but Ronald kept his father busy and happy by having him answer his fan mail. It was a good life, and Ronald could have remained in Hollywood forever. But the country had slowly but surely begun to follow a policy of social welfare that he could not endorse, and eventually he decided to fight it actively.

The leadership of the United States in the 1960s focused its attention on the poor and the helpless citizens of the United States. Reagan, too, felt compassion for such people, but he did not think that money would help them. He believed with all his heart that the country's problems could be solved only by its people learning to help themselves, as his mother had done. As Ronald Reagan saw it, Nelle, who died in 1962, had endured a life nearly as hard as any life could be, and she had triumphed. Not because of charity, not because of government help, but because of personal initiative and derring-do. Ronald saw America's strength in terms of the greatest source of strength he knew: Nelle.

As a politician, Ronald Reagan has held onto his conviction that the individual can survive without governmental interference in the guise of various laws and programs. He saw in Nelle Reagan a woman who coped with life through love and strength and values, and decided that it was people like her who made the nation strong and the future bright.

As president of the United States, Ronald Reagan has not been an advocate of legislation to grant equal opportunities to women. Yet he is not anti-woman. Reagan opposes such legislation because he opposes the very attempt to legislate matters that he believes only gumption and morality can solve. His love and admiration for independent, aggressive women and his deep-seated belief in individual initiative are the result of the love Nelle Reagan kindled in him.

Ronald Reagan may not be a beloved figure to a great many American women, but even the most hostile of them will admit that he is not only not threatened by women of strong character, he values them highly. Such fortitude is something he understands and cherishes, to the curious exclusion of all else. Seared into his consciousness is the smell of popcorn on those Saturday mornings when Nelle sent him out to earn some pennies. She was the backbone of his childhood; small wonder that her example should be the backbone of his presidency.

EPILOGUE:
MOTHERS TODAY

This book has reflected on some mothers of men who changed the course of recent history. It is woefully incomplete. Many great mothers lived and died without any books, statues, or award ceremonies dedicated to their influence; every reader probably knows at least one such mother. Many women who did not have children became world leaders, great geniuses, or brilliant artists. Most children just grow up to become reasonably happy, moral, healthy human beings. That alone is a small miracle, and it is really all that most mothers seem to want.

> *I want to raise (though I have no guarantees)* happy, *emotionally strong, motivated human beings.*
>
> Sue Wollack,
> 38-year-old mother of two

My goal as a mother is to have psychologically self-sufficient, healthy children with decent values.

Marbeth Foley,
38-year-old mother of four

My goal, aside from success in toilet-training Matthew this year, is to guide my child to develop and strengthen a sense of family commitment and self-esteem.

Ellen Croke,
31-year-old mother of one

This book has told the stories of mothers whose power and influence indirectly changed the world we live in, for good or ill. In telling their stories, we have tried to give these women the attention they have always deserved. For the most part, the mothers described in these pages lived in a world of many closed doors. In the past, women were not equal in the eyes of their government or its male citizens. And yet, despite being deprived of many forms of power, women since the beginning of time have possessed the most awesome power of all: the power to give and help shape human life. This ability puts women in touch with mystery and with eternity. It leads many men to view them with awe and even a touch of fear.

Women today, unlike women of the last two hundred years, have more options available to them: They can choose to be creative without being fertile; they can choose to influence their own world at the same time that they influence their children. But the enigmatic power of motherhood remains, and women are as aware of it as ever.

It's almost scary to think of how much I influence my child's life. From basic needs such as what I give him to eat, to how I respond when he exerts his independence, I know my decisions will affect his growth and emotional development.

Ellen Croke

No one does or can prepare us for "mothering." It's often joked mothers are chauffeurs, laundresses, guidance counselors, cooks, housekeepers, and babysitters. All those jobs are easy in comparison to dealing with a person. It's easier to do what we have to than what we want to. We have to change diapers, launder clothes, and feed. We want to teach our children, talk to them, be with them.

Susan Celentani,
30-year-old mother of two

I do believe that every experience that a child has affects them, even if they don't remember it. This belief means everything is important.

Marbeth Foley

The incredible power a mother wields over her child's development is balanced against the indignity of her role. Women experience this paradox daily; it can be difficult to feel important and powerful when one is washing cereal bowls, changing diapers, and wiping noses. This contradiction lies at the heart of the experience of being a mother.

Motherhood is an endurance test. It's trying to stay one step ahead while everyone assumes you're three steps behind. It's not having time to read the newspaper because you've been asked to reread the Bear's Bedtime *just once more. It's baking cookies at midnight so that special treat is ready to take to school the next day. It's going to the zoo for the seventh time when you'd rather be doing anything else.*

Connie Maloney,
35-year-old mother of three

Although motherhood is one of the most crucial and least appreciated roles a woman can play, it is the only role that she must relinquish in order to succeed. After pouring so much heart and energy into raising a child, mothers must know how and when to let go, to watch and even applaud as their children stop turning to them, looking up to them, needing them. It is not easy.

My children all live far away from home, all lead independent, interesting lives, and all seem to need no help, no guidance, or advice from me, so I do not offer any. My two daughters were divorced in the '80s but my role through these difficult times was one of support and caring rather than active influence. We are a very close family in many ways and we love each other very much, but we still manage to maintain great independence and diversity among ourselves.

Peggy Rastetter,
63-year-old mother of three

I feel that I am still an influence. Not so much by what I say but the fact that I listen. I feel I am perhaps my children's best friend and often I hear confidences I would rather not hear— but I listen. I think it does them good to talk to me. I think that although I may not comment or answer, they know me—my sense of values and morals well enough that even by my silence, I am an influence.

Betty,
mother of three in her early sixties

Women who choose to be mothers today are faced with the most wrenching, exhausting, creative, and terrifying task they will ever take on. The option to forgo motherhood is more open in the 1980s, with contraception and abortion readily available. Yet most women are still choosing motherhood. Many of these women attempt to juggle their business roles with that of mother, having children without giving up their careers. It is a struggle.

I work part-time. The more I'm away from my kids the less I am able to cope with them. If I've been through the day with them, I know what kind of day they're having. I can cope better with a crabby, whiny two-year-old if I've been home with him all day and know why he's crabby. When I work, I get home and want time for me. I don't want to come in all dressed up after working hard all day to have a kid cry on my skirt about how he needs some soda.

Susan Celentani

To be a mother in the 1980s is a bittersweet experience. It means leaving your infant-turned-toddler to go to the office where infant-turned-toddlers often have little meaning or im-

portance. It means proving that women–mothers have a place in the working world and are capable and valuable employees. It is a lonely experience; it is a pioneering experience. It is an experience that our mothers have pushed us toward yet have not provided models for us to emulate. We are the models for our daughters and nieces. I hope that my child may one day remember the Mother Love involved in my decision to work and to bear her; to have passed up promotions and trips to be with her for a few extra minutes each day; and to know the joy that her very being has brought me, even at the end of long, weary days.

Maggie Menard-Mueller,
32-year-old mother of one

Mothers have always had a deep and lasting influence on their children. But in the contemporary world, other influences interfere sooner and more often as the child matures. This can be worrisome. It has always been true that a woman can be a good mother but have bad children. Today it seems more possible than ever, as children are subject to many loud voices other than their mother's—television, motion pictures, and music, for example, constantly have an influence that a mother may not view as beneficial.

I was going to raise nonviolent children. No play guns—no aggression. Instead my son played using his finger as a gun!

Marbeth Foley

As they get older, I'm afraid I won't have any influence. I don't expect to be their sole authority figure forever, but I'm afraid they'll fall prey to the temptations of the loose morals of the world today.

Connie Maloney

Are there any conclusions at which we can arrive about the role of mother? The value of history is that it teaches the human race about itself the best way possible—by example. What are the lessons to be learned from the mothers in these pages? Their stories are diverse. And in many ways, these mothers of the past are very different from mothers today. But some common threads run through the experience of motherhood, and despite the fast and furious changes in women's lives today, they still face motherhood with many of the same feelings as their historical counterparts. Motherhood was, is, and may well always be a curious mixture of hope and poignancy, doubt and confidence, strength and fear. Every woman who becomes a mother gives a gift to her children that no one can ever take away: a piece of herself. Whether her children grow up and become famous or not, a gift so great does more than rock cradles. It does, indeed, rock the world.

NOTES

INTRODUCTION

1. Ralph L. Woods (ed.), *A Treasury of the Familiar* (New York: Macmillan, 1942), p. 326.

2. Excerpt from *Times to Remember* by Rose Fitzgerald Kennedy, copyright © 1974 by the Joseph P. Kennedy Jr. Foundation. Reprinted by permission of Doubleday & Co., Garden City, N.Y.

3. Bernard Mayo (ed.), *Jefferson Himself* (Charlottesville, Va.: University Press of Virginia, 1974), p. 43.

4. Saul K. Padover, *Jefferson* (New York: New American Library of World Literature, 1952), p. 33.

5. Page Smith, *John Adams, Vol. II* (Garden City, N.Y.: Doubleday & Co., 1962), p. 928.

CHAPTER 1 ————————————————

1. Hendrik Ruitenbeck (ed.), *Freud As We Knew Him* (Detroit: Wayne State University Press, 1973), p. 140.

2. Ibid.

3. Ronald Clark, *Freud: The Man and the Cause* (New York: Random House, 1980), p. 9.

4. Ibid., p. 12.

5. Ibid.

6. Lucy Freeman and Herb S. Strean, *Freud and Women* (New York: Frederick Ungar Publishing Co., 1981), p. xii.

7. Ibid., p. 15.

8. Ernest Jones, *The Life and Work of Sigmund Freud, Vol. I* (New York: Basic Books, 1953), p. 8.

9. Freeman and Strean, *Freud and Women*, p. 9.

CHAPTER 2 ————————————————

1. Thomas J. Fleming (ed.), *Affectionately Yours, George Washington* (New York: W. W. Norton Co., 1967), p. 168.

2. John C. Fitzpatrick, *George Washington, Himself* (Indianapolis: The Bobbs-Merrill Co., 1933), p. 460.

3. Douglas Southall Freeman, *Washington* (New York: Charles Scribner's Sons, 1968), p. 574.

4. Charles W. Akers, *Abigail Adams, An American Woman* (Boston: Little, Brown & Co., 1980), p. 189.

5. Paul C. Nagel, *Descent from Glory: Four Generations of the Adams Family* (New York: Oxford University Press, 1983), p. 29.

6. Akers, *Abigail Adams*, p. 170.

7. Ibid., p. 165.

8. Nagel, *Descent from Glory*, p. 193.

9. John F. Kennedy, *Profiles in Courage* (New York: Harper & Brothers, 1955), pp. 32, 36.

10. Jack Shepherd, *The Adams Chronicles* (Boston: Little, Brown & Co., 1975), p. 228.

11. W. H. Auden, "The Unknown Citizen," *Collected Poems,* ed. Edward Mendelson (New York: Random House, 1966), p. 147. Copyright © 1976 by Edward Mendelson, William Meredith, and Monroe K. Spears, executors of the estate of W. H. Auden.

12. James C. Curtis, *Andrew Jackson and the Search for Vindication* (Boston: Little, Brown & Co., 1976), p. 11.

13. Ibid., p. 60.

14. Robert V. Remini, *Andrew Jackson* (New York: Twayne Publishers, 1966), p. 13.

CHAPTER 3

1. Richard Nelson Current, *The Lincoln Nobody Knows* (New York: McGraw-Hill Book Co., 1958), p. 27.

2. Stephen B. Oates, *With Malice Towards None: The Life of Abraham Lincoln* (New York: Harper & Row, Publishers, 1977), p. 96.

3. Richard Goldhurst, *Many Are the Hearts: The Agony and the Triumph of U. S. Grant* (New York: Thomas Y. Crowell Co., 1975), p. 31.

4. Samuel Eliot Morison, *The Oxford History of the American People* (New York: Oxford University Press, 1965), p. 703.

5. J. William Jones, D.D., *Personal Reminiscences of General Robert E. Lee* (New York: Appleton and Co., 1875), p. 363.

6. Morison, *The Oxford History of the American People,* p. 705.

7. Bruce Catton, *The Civil War* (New York: The Fairfax Press, 1980), p. 286.

8. Izola Forrester, *This One Mad Act* (Boston: Hale, Cushman and Flint, 1937), p. 269.

9. Philip Van Doren Stern, *The Man Who Killed Lincoln* (New York: The Literary Guild of America, 1939), p. 361.

10. William G. Shepherd, "They Tried to Stop Booth," *Collier's Weekly,* December 27, 1924.

CHAPTER 4 _____

1. Peter Collier and David Horowitz, *The Rockefellers: An American Dynasty* (New York: Holt, Rinehart & Winston, 1976), p. 10.

2. Andrew Carnegie, *Autobiography of Andrew Carnegie* (Boston: Houghton Mifflin Company, 1920), p. 12.

3. Burton J. Hendrick, *The Life of Andrew Carnegie*, Vol. II (Garden City, N.Y.: Doubleday, Doran & Co., 1932), p. 1050.

4. John K. Winkler, *Incredible Carnegie: The Life of Andrew Carnegie, 1835–1919* (New York: The Vanguard Press, 1931), p. 4.

5. Joseph Frazier Wall, *Andrew Carnegie* (New York: Oxford University Press, 1970), p. 112.

6. Hendrick, *The Life of Andrew Carnegie*, p. 19.

7. Carnegie, *Autobiography*, p. 6.

8. Werner Blumenberg, *Portrait of Marx*, trans. Douglas Scott (New York: Herder & Herder, 1972), p. 16.

9. Ibid., p. 120.

CHAPTER 5 _____

1. Nathan Miller, *F.D.R.: An Intimate History* (Garden City, N.Y.: Doubleday & Co., 1983), p. 36.

2. Elliot Roosevelt and James Brough, *The Roosevelts of Hyde Park: An Untold Story* (New York: G. P. Putnam's Sons, 1975), p. 17. Copyright © 1975 by Elliot Roosevelt and James Brough. Reprinted by the permission of the Putnam Publishing Group.

3. Roosevelt and Brough, *The Roosevelts of Hyde Park*, p. 166. Copyright © 1975 by Elliot Roosevelt and James Brough. Reprinted by the permission of the Putnam Publishing Group.

4. James MacGregor Burns, *The Lion and the Fox* (New York: Harcourt Brace & World, 1956), p. 77.

5. Roosevelt and Brough, *The Roosevelts of Hyde Park*, p. 304. Copyright © 1975 by Elliot Roosevelt and James Brough. Reprinted by the permission of the Putnam Publishing Group.

6. Elliot Roosevelt and James Brough, *The Roosevelts of the White House: A Rendezvous with Destiny* (New York: G. P. Putnam's Sons, 1975), p. 299. Copyright © 1975 by Elliot Roosevelt and James Brough. Reprinted by the permission of the Putnam Publishing Group.

7. Doris Faber, *The Presidents' Mothers* (New York: St. Martin's Press, 1968), p. 96.

8. Charles Robbins, *The Last of His Kind: An Informal Portrait of Harry S Truman* (New York: William Morrow and Co., 1979), p. 56.

9. Merle Miller, *Plain Speaking: An Oral Biography of Harry S Truman* (New York: Berkley Publishing Corp., 1973), pp. 143–44.

10. Miller, *Plain Speaking*, p. 144.

11. Alfred Steinberg, *The Man from Missouri: The Life and Times of Harry S Truman* (New York: G. P. Putnam Publishing Group, 1962), pp. 228–29.

12. Faber, *The Presidents' Mothers*, p. 62.

13. Samuel Eliot Morison, *Oxford History of the American People* (New York: Oxford University Press, 1965), p. 1078.

14. William Raymond Manchester, *American Caesar: Douglas MacArthur, 1880–1964* (Boston: Little, Brown & Co., 1978), p. 47.

15. *Reminiscences*, by General of the Army Douglas MacArthur, McGraw-Hill Book Co., © 1964 by Time, Inc. All rights reserved.

16. Manchester, *American Caesar*, p. 93.

17. James D. Clayton, *The Years of MacArthur, Vol. I* (Boston: Houghton Mifflin Co., 1970), p. 256.

18. *Pershing Papers*, Library of Congress, letter from Mrs. MacArthur to General Pershing, n.d. (c. August, 1924).

19. *Reminiscences*, by General of the Army Douglas MacArthur, McGraw-Hill Book Co., © 1964 by Time Inc. All rights reserved.

20. Manchester, *American Caesar*, p. 141.

CHAPTER 6

1. William Raymond Manchester, *The Last Lion, Winston Spencer Churchill: Visions of Glory, 1874–1932* (Boston: Little, Brown & Co., 1983), p. 131.

2. Robert Payne, *Life and Death of Adolf Hitler* (New York: Praeger Publishers, 1973), p. 56.

3. Ibid., p. 57.

4. Dennis Mack Smith, *Mussolini: A Biography* (New York: Alfred A. Knopf, 1982), p. 203.

5. Richard Collier, *Duce!: The Life and Death of a Dictator* (New York: Popular Library, 1971), p. 96.

CHAPTER 7_____

1. Stephen E. Ambrose, *Eisenhower: 1890–1952, Vol. I* (New York: Simon & Schuster, 1983), p. 19. Copyright © 1983 by Stephen E. Ambrose. Reprinted by permission of Simon & Schuster, Inc.

2. Kornitzer, Bela, *The Story of the Five Eisenhower Brothers* (New York: Farrar, Straus and Cudahy, 1955), p. 23.

3. Ambrose, *Eisenhower*, p. 21. Copyright © 1983 by Stephen E. Ambrose. Reprinted by permission of Simon & Schuster, Inc.

4. Stephen B. Oates, *Let The Trumpet Sound: The Life of Martin Luther King* (New York: Harper & Row, Publishers, 1983), p. 10.

5. Richard J. Whalen, *The Founding Father: The Story of Joseph P. Kennedy* (New York: New American Library, 1964), p. 89.

6. Doris Faber, *The Presidents' Mothers* (New York: St. Martin's Press, 1968), p. 22.

7. Gail Cameron, *Rose* (New York: G. P. Putnam's Sons, 1971), p. 20.

8. S. P. Friedman, *The Kennedy Family Scrapbook* (New York: Grossett & Dunlap, 1978), p. 71.

9. Cameron, *Rose*, p. 208.

10. Padraic Pearce (1879–1916), "The Mother," *1000 Years of Irish Poetry*, Devin-Adair Publishers, Greenwich, Connecticut, p. 647.

11. David E. Koskoff, *Joseph P. Kennedy: A Life and Times* (Englewood Cliffs, N.J.: Prentice-Hall, 1974), p. 375.

12. Cameron, *Rose*, p. 20.

13. Ronnie Dugger, *The Politician: The Life and Times of Lyndon Johnson* (New York: W. W. Norton & Co., 1982), p. 60.

14. Dugger, *The Politician*, p. 74.

15. Robert A. Caro, *The Years of Lyndon Johnson: The Path to Power* (New York: Alfred A. Knopf, 1982), p. 95. Copyright © 1982 by Robert A. Caro, Inc.

16. Dugger, *The Politician*, p. 74.

17. Merle Miller, *Lyndon: An Oral Biography* (New York: G. P. Putnam's Sons, 1980), p. 13. Reprinted by the permission of the Putnam Publishing Group.

18. Caro, *The Years of Lyndon Johnson*, p. 197. Copyright © 1982 by Robert A. Caro, Inc.

19. Hugh Sidey, *A Very Personal Presidency: Lyndon Johnson in the White House* (New York: Atheneum Publishers, 1968), p. 13. Copyright © 1968 by Hugh Sidey. Reprinted with the permission of Atheneum Publishers.

20. I. Shelton, "Lyndon Johnson's Mother," *Saturday Evening Post*, May 8, 1965.

21. Bruce Mazlish, *In Search of Nixon: A Psychohistorical Inquiry* (New York: Basic Books, 1972), p. 23. Copyright © 1972 by Basic Books, Inc.

22. Earl Mazo, *Richard Nixon: A Political and Personal Portrait* (New York: Harper and Brothers, 1959), p. 20.

23. Dan Rather and Gary Paul Gates, *The Palace Guard* (New York: Harper & Row, Publishers, 1974), p. 114.

24. Thomas A. Bailey, *The American Pageant: A History of the Republic, Vol. II* (Lexington, Mass.: D. C. Heath & Co., 1971), p. 998.

25. Quoted in *The Joint Appearances of Senator John F. Kennedy and Vice President Richard M. Nixon, Presidential Campaign of 1960* (Washington, D.C.: U.S. Government Printing Office, 1961), p. 21.

26. Public Papers of the Presidents of the United States (Aug. 9, 1974), p. 631. Cited in Fawn M. Brodie, *Richard Nixon: The Shaping of His Character* (New York: W. W. Norton & Co., 1981).

27. Ronald Reagan with Richard G. Hubler, *"Where's the Rest of Me?": The Ronald Reagan Story* (New York: Duell, Sloan and Pearce, 1965), p. 3.

28. Reagan with Hubler, *"Where's the Rest of Me?"*, p. 8.

BIBLIOGRAPHY

INTRODUCTION

Benger, Carl, *Thomas Jefferson*. New York: W. W. Norton & Co., 1970.

Bowen, Catherine Drinker, *John Adams and the American Revolution*. Boston: Little, Brown & Co., 1950.

Bowers, Claude G., *The Young Jefferson*. Boston: Houghton Mifflin Co., 1945.

Brodie, Fawn M., *Thomas Jefferson: An Intimate History*. New York: W. W. Norton & Co., 1974.

Brown, Stuart Gerry, *Thomas Jefferson*. New York: Washington Square Press, Inc., 1966.

Donovan, Frank (ed.), *Autobiography and Other Writings of Benjamin Franklin*. New York: Dodd, Mead & Co., 1963.

Friedlander, Marc, and Mary Jo Kline, *Selected Letters of the Adams Family*. Cambridge, Mass.: Harvard University Press, 1975.

Hawke, David Freeman, *Franklin*. New York: Harper & Row, Publishers, 1976.

Herbert, Eugenia W., and Claude Anne Lopez, *The Private Franklin*. New York: W. W. Norton & Co., 1975.

Kennedy, Rose Fitzgerald, *Times to Remember*. Garden City, N.Y.: Doubleday & Co., 1974.

Mayo, Bernard (ed.), *Jefferson Himself: The Personal Narrative of a Many-Sided American*. Charlottesville, Va.: University of Virginia Press, 1970.

Nagel, Paul C., *Descent from Glory: Four Generations of the Adams Family*. New York: Oxford University Press, 1983.

Nock, Albert J., *Jefferson*. New York: Blue Ribbon Books, 1926.

Olsen, Paul, *Sons and Mothers: Why Men Behave the Way They Do*. New York: Evans & Co., 1981.

Padover, Saul K., *Jefferson*. New York: New American Library of World Literature, 1952.

Rue, Dr. James J., and Louise Shanahan, *Daddy's Girl—Mama's Boy*. New York: Bobbs-Merrill Co., 1978.

Russell, Francis, *The Adamses: An American Dynasty*. New York: American Heritage Publishing Co., 1976.

Shepherd, Jack, *The Adams Chronicles*. Boston: Little, Brown & Co., 1975.

Smith, Page, *John Adams*, 2 vols. New York: Doubleday & Co., 1962.

Woods, Ralph L. (ed.), *A Treasury of the Familiar*. New York: The Macmillan Publishing Co., 1942.

CHAPTER 1

Bernays, Anna Freud, "My Brother, Sigmund Freud," *American Mercury* 51, 1940, pp. 335–52.

Clark, Ronald, *Freud: The Man and the Cause*. New York: Random House, 1980.

Freeman, Lucy, and Herb S. Strean, *Freud and Women*. New York: Frederick Ungar Publishing Co., 1980.

Jones, Ernest, *The Life and Work of Sigmund Freud, Vol. I*. New York: Basic Books, 1953.

Puner, Helen Walker, *Freud: His Life and Mind*. New York: Howell-Soskin, 1947.

Ruitenbeck, Hendrick (ed.), *Freud As We Knew Him*. Detroit: Wayne State University Press, 1973.

CHAPTER 2

Adams, James Truslow, *The Adams Family*. New York: Hillary House, 1957.

Akers, Charles W., *Abigail Adams, An American Woman*. Boston: Little, Brown & Co., 1980.

Auden, W. H., "The Unknown Citizen," *Collected Poems*, ed. Edward Mendelson. New York: Random House, 1966.

Bassett, John Spencer, *The Life of Andrew Jackson, Vol. I*. New York: The Macmillan Company, 1916.

Curtis, James C., *Andrew Jackson and the Search for Vindication*. New York: Little, Brown & Co., 1976.

Davis, Burke, *Old Hickory*. New York: The Dial Press, 1977.

Donovan, Frank (ed.), *The George Washington Papers*. New York: Dodd, Mead & Co., 1964.

Fitzpatrick, John C., *George Washington, Himself*. Indianapolis: The Bobbs-Merrill Co., 1933.

Fleming, Thomas J. (ed.), *Affectionately Yours, George Washington*. New York: W. W. Norton & Co., 1967.

Flexner, James Thomas, *Washington: The Indispensable Man*. Boston: Little, Brown & Co., 1969.

————, *George Washington*, 2 vols. Boston: Little, Brown & Co., 1967.

————, *The Young Hamilton*. Boston: Little, Brown & Co., 1978.

Freeman, Douglas Southall, *Washington*. New York: Charles Scribner's Sons, 1968.

Hecht, Marie B., *Odd Destiny*. New York: Macmillan Publishing Co., 1982.

————, *John Quincy Adams*. New York: Macmillan Publishing Co., 1972.

Hendrickson, Robert, *Hamilton, Vol. I*. New York: Mason/Charter, 1976.

James, Marquis, *Andrew Jackson*. Indianapolis: The Bobbs-Merrill Co., 1938.

Kennedy, John F., *Profiles in Courage*. New York: Harper & Brothers, 1955.

Kline, Mary Jo (ed.), *Alexander Hamilton: A Biography in His Own Words*. New York: Newsweek, 1973.

McDonald, Forrest, *Alexander Hamilton*. New York: W. W. Norton & Co., 1979.

Miller, John C., *Alexander Hamilton: A Portrait in Paradox*. New York: Harper & Brothers, 1959.

Mitchell, Broadus, *Alexander Hamilton*. New York: Thomas Y. Crowell Publishing Co., 1970.

————, *Alexander Hamilton—Youth to Maturity*. Macmillan Publishing Co., 1957.

Morgan, Helen L., *Liberty Maid*. Philadelphia: Westminster Press, 1950.

Nagel, Paul C., *Descent from Glory: Four Generations of the Adams Family*. New York: Oxford University Press, 1983.

Padover, Saul K. (ed.), *The Washington Papers*. New York: Harper & Brothers, 1955.

Remini, Robert V., *Andrew Jackson*. New York: Harper & Row, Publishers, 1977.

————, *Andrew Jackson*. New York: Twayne Publishers, 1966.

Russell, Francis, *The Adamses: An American Dynasty*. New York: American Heritage Publishing Co., 1976.

Schnachner, Nathan, *Alexander Hamilton*. New York: A. S. Barnes & Co., 1946.

Shaw, Ronald E. (ed.), *Andrew Jackson, 1767–1845*. Dobbs Ferry, N.Y.: Oceania Publications, 1969.

Shepherd, Jack, *The Adams Chronicles*. Boston: Little, Brown & Co., 1975.

Tebbel, John William, *George Washington's America*. New York: E. P. Dutton & Co., 1954.

Whitney, Janet, *Abigail Adams*. New York: Little, Brown & Co., 1947.

Withey, Lynne, *Dearest Friend: A Life of Abigail Adams*. New York: The Free Press, a division of Macmillan Publishing Co., 1981.

CHAPTER 3

Barton, William E., *The Life of Abraham Lincoln*. Indianapolis: The Bobbs-Merrill Co., 1925.

Bishop, James Alonzo, *The Day Lincoln Was Shot*. New York: Harper & Brothers, 1955.

Catton, Bruce, *The Civil War*. New York: The Fairfax Press, 1980.

Current, Richard Nelson, *The Lincoln Nobody Knows*. New York: McGraw-Hill Book Co., 1958.

Dowdy, Clifford, *Lee*. Boston: Little, Brown & Co., 1965.

Forrester, Izola, *This One Mad Act*. Boston: Hale, Cushman & Flint, 1937.

Freeman, Douglas Southall, *Lee of Virginia*. New York: Charles Scribner's Sons, 1958.

————, *Lee*, an abridgment in one volume by Richard Harwell of the 4-volume *R. E. Lee*. New York: Charles Scribner's Sons, 1961.

Goldhurst, Richard, *Many Are the Hearts: The Agony and the Triumph of U. S. Grant*. New York: Thomas Y. Crowell Co., 1975.

Grant, Ulysses S., 3rd, *Ulysses S. Grant: Warrior and Statesman*. New York: William Morrow & Co., 1969.

Hanchett, William, *The Lincoln Murder Conspiracies*. Urbana and Chicago: University of Illinois Press, 1983.

Hendrick, Burton J., *The Lees of Virginia*. Boston: Little, Brown & Co., 1935.

Hesseltine, William B., *Ulysses S. Grant, Politician*. New York: Dodd, Mead & Company, 1935.

Jones, Rev. J. William, *Personal Reminiscences of General Robert E. Lee*. New York: D. Appleton & Co., 1875.

Kimmel, Stanley, *The Mad Booths of Maryland*. Indianapolis: The Bobbs-Merrill Co., 1940.

Long, E. B. (ed.), *The Personal Memoirs of U. S. Grant*. New York: The World Publishing Co., 1952.

McFeeley, William S., *Grant: A Biography*. New York: W. W. Norton & Co., 1981.

Morison, Samuel E. *The Oxford History of the American People*. New York: Oxford University Press, 1965.

Oates, Stephen B., *With Malice Toward None*. New York: Harper & Row, Publishers, 1977.

Ruggles, Eleanor, *The Prince of Players, Edwin Booth*. New York: W. W. Norton & Co., 1953.

Sandborn, Margaret, *Robert E. Lee: A Portrait*. Philadelphia: J. B. Lippincott Co., 1966.

Sandburg, Carl, *Abraham Lincoln: The Prairie Years and the War Years*. New York: Harcourt Brace & World, 1954.

Shepherd, William G., "They Tried to Stop Booth," *Collier's Weekly*. December 27, 1924.

Stern, Philip Van Doren, *The Man Who Killed Lincoln*. New York: The Literary Guild of America, 1939.

Thomas, Benjamin P., *Portrait for Posterity*. Freeport, N.Y.: Books for Libraries Press, 1947.

————, *Abraham Lincoln*. New York: Alfred A. Knopf, 1952.

Warren, Louis A., *Lincoln's Youth: The Indiana Years*. New York: Appleton-Century-Crofts, 1959.

————, *Lincoln's Parentage and Childhood*. New York: The Century Company, 1926.

Wilson, Francis, *John Wilkes Booth: Fact and Fiction of Lincoln's Assassination*. Boston: Houghton Mifflin Co., 1929.

Woodward, W. E., *Meet General Grant*. New York: Liveright Publishing Corp., 1928.

CHAPTER 4

Abels, Jules, *The Rockefeller Billions*. New York: The Macmillan Co., 1965.

Alderson, Barnard, *Andrew Carnegie*. New York: Doubleday, Page & Co., 1902.

Berlin, Isaiah, *Karl Marx: His Life and Environment*. New York: Oxford University Press, 1963.

Blumenberg, Werner, *Portrait of Marx*, translated by Douglas Scott. New York: Herder & Herder, 1972.

Carnegie, Andrew, *Autobiography of Andrew Carnegie*. Boston: Houghton Mifflin Co., 1920.

Collier, Peter, and David Horowitz, *The Rockefellers: An American Dynasty*. New York: Holt, Rinehart & Winston, 1976.

Fischer, Louis, *The Life of Lenin*. New York: Harper & Row, Publishers, 1964.

Gourfinkel, Nina, *Portrait of Lenin*, translated by Maurice Thornton. New York: Harper & Row, Publishers, 1964.

Hacker, Louis M., *The World of Andrew Carnegie, 1865–1901*. New York: J. B. Lippincott Co., 1968.

Hendrick, Burton J., *The Life of Andrew Carnegie,* 2 vols. Garden City, N.Y.: Doubleday, Doran & Co., 1932.

Kochan, Lionel, *Russia in Revolution, 1890–1918.* New York: The New American Library, 1966.

Kurland, Gerald, *John D. Rockefeller: 19th Century Industrialist and Oil Baron.* New York: Samhar Press, 1972.

Livesay, Harold C., and Oscar Handlin (ed.), *Andrew Carnegie and the Rise of Big Business.* Boston: Little, Brown & Co., 1975.

Nevin, Allen, *Study in Power: John D. Rockefeller, Industrialist and Philanthropist,* Vol. I. New York: Charles Scribner's Sons, 1953.

Payne, Robert, *The Life and Death of Lenin.* New York: Simon & Schuster, 1964.

———, *Marx.* London: W. H. Allen & Co., 1968.

Possony, Stefan, *Lenin, The Compulsive Revolutionary.* Chicago: Henry Regnery Co., 1964.

Rubel, Maximilien, *Marx: Life and Works* (translated by Mary Bottomore). New York: Facts of File, 1980.

Shub, David, *Lenin.* Garden City, N.Y.: Doubleday & Co., 1948.

Silverman, Saul N. (ed.), *Lenin.* Englewood Cliffs, N.J.: Prentice-Hall, 1972.

Smith, Page, *The Rise of Industrial America: A People's History of the Post-Reconstruction Era, Vol. VI.* New York: McGraw-Hill Book Co., 1984.

Trotsky, Leon, *The Young Lenin,* translated by Max Eastman, edited by Maurice Friedman. Garden City, N.Y.: Doubleday & Co., 1972.

Wall, Joseph Frazier, *Andrew Carnegie.* New York: Oxford University Press, 1970.

Weber, Gerda, and Hermann Weber, *Lenin: Life and Works.* New York: Facts on File, 1974.

Winkler, John K., *The Life of Andrew Carnegie.* New York: The Vanguard Press, 1931.

Worth, Robert D., *Lenin.* New York: Twayne Publishers, 1973.

CHAPTER 5

Asbell, Bernard, *The F.D.R. Memoirs: A Speculation on History.* Garden City, New York: Doubleday & Co., 1973.

Burns, James McGregor, *Roosevelt: The Lion and the Fox*. New York: Harcourt Brace & World, 1956.

Daniels, Jonathan, *The Man of Independence*. New York: J. B. Lippincott Co., 1950.

Davis, Kenneth S., *F.D.R.: The Beckoning of Destiny: 1882–1928*. New York: G. P. Putnam's Sons, 1971.

Faber, Doris, *The Presidents' Mothers*. New York: St. Martin's Press, 1968.

Ferrell, Robert H. (ed.), *Autobiography of Harry S Truman*. Boulder, Colo.: Colorado Associated University Press, 1980.

Hunt, Frazier, *The Untold Story of Douglas MacArthur*. New York: The Devin-Adair Co., 1954.

James, D. Clayton, *The Years of MacArthur, Vol. I*. Boston: Houghton Mifflin Co., 1970.

Kleeman, Rita Halle, *Gracious Lady: The Life of Sara Delano Roosevelt*. New York: D. Appleton-Century Company, Inc., 1935.

MacArthur, Douglas, *Reminiscences*. New York: McGraw-Hill Book Co., 1964.

Manchester, William Raymond, *American Caesar: Douglas MacArthur, 1880–1964*. Boston: Little, Brown & Co., 1978.

Miller, Merle, *Plain Speaking: An Oral Biography of Harry S Truman*. New York: Berkley Publishing Corp., 1973.

Miller, Nathan, *F.D.R.: An Intimate History*. Garden City, N.Y.: Doubleday & Co., 1983.

Morison, Samuel Eliot, *Oxford History of the American People*. New York: Oxford University Press, 1965.

Pershing Papers. Washington, D.C.: Library of Congress, Manuscript Division, n.d. (c. August 1924).

Robbins, Charles, *Last of His Kind: An Informal Portrait of Harry S Truman*. New York: William Morrow & Co., 1979.

Roosevelt, Elliot, and James Brough, *The Roosevelts of Hyde Park: An Untold Story*. New York: G. P. Putnam's Sons, 1975.

———, *The Roosevelts of the White House: A Rendezvous with Destiny*. New York: G. P. Putnam's Sons, 1975.

Roosevelt, Elliot (ed.), *The Roosevelt Letters*. New York: Duell, Sloan & Pearce, 1947.

Steinberg, Alfred, *The Man from Missouri: The Life and Times of Harry S Truman*. New York: G. P. Putnam's Sons, 1962.

Truman, Harry S, *Memoirs by Harry S Truman: Year of Decision, Vol. I*. Garden City, N.Y.: Doubleday & Co., 1955.

Truman, Margaret, *Harry S Truman*. New York: William Morrow & Co., 1973.

CHAPTER 6

Broad, Charlie Lewis, *Winston Churchill: The Years of Preparation: A Biography, Vol. I*. New York: Hawthorn Books, 1958.

Bullock, Alan, *Hitler: A Study in Tyranny*. New York: Harper & Row, Publishers, 1962.

Carter, Violet Bonham, *Winston Churchill: An Intimate Portrait*. New York: Harcourt Brace & World, 1965.

Churchill, Randolph S., *Winston S. Churchill: Youth, 1874–1900*. Boston: Houghton Mifflin Co., 1966.

Collier, Richard, *Duce!: The Life and Death of a Dictator*. New York: Popular Library, 1971.

Cowles, Virginia, *Winston Churchill: The Era and the Man*. New York: Harper & Brothers, 1953.

Fermi, Laura, *Mussolini*. Chicago: University of Chicago Press, 1961.

Fest, Joachim C., *Hitler* (translated by Richard and Clara Winston). New York: Harcourt Brace Jovanovich, 1973.

Foster, Robert Fitzroy, *Lord Randolph Churchill*. Oxford, England: Clarendon Press, 1981.

Grey, Ian, *Stalin, Man of History*. Garden City, N.Y.: Doubleday & Co., 1979.

Herdin, Konrad, *Der Fuehrer: Hitler's Rise to Power* (translated by Ralph Manheim). Boston: Houghton Mifflin Co., 1944.

Langer, Walter C., *The Secret Wartime Report: The Mind of Adolf Hitler*. New York: Basic Books, 1972.

Manchester, William Raymond, *The Last Lion, Winston Spencer Churchill: Visions of Glory, 1874–1932*. Boston: Little, Brown & Co., 1983.

Martin, Ralph H., *Jennie*, 2 vols. Englewood Cliffs, N.J.: Prentice-Hall, 1969.

Megaro, Gaudens, *Mussolini in the Making*. Boston: Houghton Mifflin Co., 1938.

Morgan, Ted, *Churchill: Young Man in a Hurry*. New York: Simon & Schuster, 1982.

Mussolini, Benito, *My Autobiography*. London: Hutchison & Co., 1928.

Payne, Robert, *The Rise and Fall of Stalin*. New York: Simon & Schuster, 1965.

Rowse, A. L., *The Churchills: The Story of a Family*. New York: Harper & Row, Publishers, 1966.

Seldes, George, *Sawdust Caesar: The Untold Story of Mussolini and Fascism*. New York: Harper & Brothers, 1935.

Smith, Denis Mack, *Mussolini: A Biography*. New York: Alfred A. Knopf, 1982.

Toland, John, *Adolf Hitler*. Garden City, N.Y.: Doubleday & Co., 1976.

Trotsky, Leon, *Stalin: An Appraisal of the Man and His Influence*. New York: Stein & Day Publishers, 1967.

Ulam, Adam B., *Stalin: The Man and His Era*. New York: The Viking Press, 1973.

CHAPTER 7

Abrahamson, David, *Nixon vs. Nixon*. New York: Farrar, Straus & Giroux, 1977.

Ambrose, Stephen E., *Eisenhower: Soldier, General of the Army, President-Elect, 1890–1952, Vol. I*. New York: Simon & Schuster, 1983.

Bailey, Thomas A., *The American Pageant: A History of the American Republic, Vol. II*. Lexington, Mass.: D. C. Heath & Co., 1971.

Bennett, Lerone Jr., *What Manner of Man: A Biography of Martin Luther King, Jr.* Chicago: Johnson Publishing Co., 1968.

Boyarsky, Bill, *The Rise of Ronald Reagan*. New York: Random House, 1968.

Brodie, Fawn M., *Richard Nixon: The Shaping of His Character*. New York: W. W. Norton & Co., 1981.

Cameron, Gail, *Rose*. New York: St. Martin's Press, 1968.

Cannon, Lou, *Reagan*. New York: G. P. Putnam's Sons, 1982.

Caro, Robert A., *The Years of Lyndon Johnson: The Path to Power*. New York: Alfred A. Knopf, 1982.

Collier, Peter, and David Horowitz, *The Kennedys: An American Drama*. New York: Summit Books, 1984.

Costello, William, *The Facts About Nixon*. New York: The Viking Press, 1960.

Damore, Leo, *The Cape Cod Years of John Fitzgerald Kennedy*. Englewood Cliffs, N.J.: Prentice-Hall, 1967.

Davis, John H., *The Kennedys: Dynasty and Disaster, 1848–1983*. New York: McGraw-Hill Book Co., 1984.

Davis, Kenneth S., *Eisenhower, American Hero: The Historical Record of His Life*. New York: American Heritage Publishing Co., 1964.

———, *Soldier of Democracy: A Biography of Dwight Eisenhower*. Garden City, N.Y.: Doubleday, Doran & Co., 1945.

De Toledano, Ralph, *One Man Alone: Richard Nixon*. New York: Funk & Wagnalls, 1969.

Dugger, Ronnie, *The Politician: The Life and Times of Lyndon Johnson*. New York: W. W. Norton & Co., 1982.

Eisenhower, Dwight D., *At Ease: Stories I Tell to Friends*. Garden City, N.Y.: Doubleday & Co., 1964.

Faber, Doris, *The Presidents' Mothers*. New York: St. Martin's Press, 1968.

Friedman, S. P., *The Kennedy Family Scrapbook*. New York: Grosset & Dunlap, 1978.

Goldman, Eric F., *The Tragedy of Lyndon Johnson*. New York: Alfred A. Knopf, 1969.

Hoaglund, Kathleen (ed.), *1000 Years of Irish Poetry*. New York: Grossett & Dunlap, 1962.

Hoyt, Edwin P., *The Nixons: An American Family*. New York: Random House, 1972.

Kearns, Doris, *Johnson and the American Dream*. New York: Harper & Row, Publishers, 1976.

Kennedy, Rose Fitzgerald, *Times to Remember*. Garden City, N.Y.: Doubleday & Co., 1974.

King, Coretta Scott, *My Life with Martin Luther King Jr.* New York: Holt, Rinehart & Winston, 1969.

Kornitzer, Bela, *The Real Nixon: An Intimate Biography*. New York: Rand, McNally & Co., 1960.

———, *The Story of the Five Eisenhower Brothers*. New York: Farrar, Straus & Cudahy, 1955.

Koskoff, David E., *Joseph P. Kennedy: A Life and Times*. Englewood Cliffs, N.J.: Prentice-Hall, 1967.

Johnson, Rebekah Baines, *A Family Album*. New York: McGraw-Hill Book Co., 1965.

Leamer, Laurence, *Make-Believe: The Story of Nancy and Ronald Reagan*. New York: Harper & Row, Publishers, 1983.

Lincoln, C. Eric (ed.), *Margin Luther King Jr.* New York: Hill & Wang, 1970.

Lyon, Peter, *Portrait of the Hero*. Boston: Little, Brown & Co., 1974.

McCarthy, Joe, *The Remarkable Kennedys*. New York: The Dial Press, 1960.

Manchester, William Raymond, *The Death of a President*. New York: Harper & Row, Publishers, 1967.

Martin, Ralph G., *A Hero of Our Time: An Intimate Story of the Kennedy Years*. New York: Macmillan Publishing Co., 1983.

Mazlish, Bruce, *In Search of Nixon*. New York: Basic Books, 1972.

Mazo, Earl, *Richard Nixon: A Political and Personal Portrait*. New York: Harper & Brothers, 1959.

Miller, Merle, *Lyndon: An Oral Biography*. New York: G. P. Putnam's Sons, 1980.

Miller, William Robert, *Martin Luther King Jr.* New York: Weybright & Tally, 1968.

Morin, Relman, *Dwight D. Eisenhower: A Gauge of Greatness*. New York: Simon & Schuster, 1969.

Morison, Samuel Eliot, *The Oxford History of the American People*. New York: Oxford University Press, 1965.

Oates, Stephen B., *Let the Trumpet Sound: The Life of Martin Luther King Jr.* New York: Harper & Row, Publishers, 1982.

Rather, Dan, and Gary Paul Gates, *The Palace Guard*. New York: Harper & Row, Publishers, 1974.

Reagan, Ronald, with Richard G. Hubler, *"Where's the Rest of Me?": The Ronald Reagan Story*. New York: Duell, Sloan & Pearce, 1965.

Reddick, L. D., *Crusader without Violence: A Biography of Martin Luther King Jr.* New York: Harper & Brothers, 1959.

Rulon, Phillip Reed, *The Compassionate Samaritan: The Life of Lyndon Baines Johnson*. Chicago: Nelson Hall Publishers, 1981.

Schulte, Renee K. (ed.), *The Young Nixon: An Oral Inquiry*. Fullerton, Calif.: California State University, 1978.

Shelton, I., "Lyndon Johnson's Mother," *Saturday Evening Post*, May 8, 1965.

Sidey, Hugh, *A Very Personal Presidency: Lyndon Johnson in the White House*. New York: Atheneum Publishers, 1968.

Sorenson, Theodore C., *Kennedy*. New York: Harper & Row, Publishers, 1965.

Whalen, Richard J., *The Founding Father: The Story of Joseph P. Kennedy*. New York: New American Library, 1964.

INDEX